"A forceful, evidence-I
for the role of agile witl

Andrew Bragg, CEO,
Association for Project Management (APM)

"An enlightening insight into grand
failures and successes in government projects."

Neil Coutts, Director,
Project Management Institute (PMI)

"A wonderful collection of real case studies.
A stream of practical advice. As broad a scope
as one could hope for. A view sorely needed in a
field long dominated by dogmatic developers and
code-centric softcrafters. I found myself 'hooked' on
this and read it cover to cover in a weekend."

Tom Gilb, the 'grandfather'
of evolutionary project management.

"A unique, insightful, and
readable guide to agile government
from a leadership perspective"

Dot Tudor, Winner of
Best Agile Coach Award 2011

Agile Project Management for Government

Brian Wernham

Maitland & Strong   *London – New York – Sydney*

Agile Project Management for Government
First Edition, Paperback – published 2012
Maitland and Strong
ISBN: 978-0-957-22340-0

Maitland and Strong
21 Berridge Mews
West Hampstead
London

Contents

Part II: The 9 Agile Leadership Behaviors 59

Guest Foreword – Tom Gilb

The 'Grandfather' of Incremental Project Management

This book is a large collection of real worldwide case studies of recent government IT project successes and failures. You get independent (academic studies, government audit bodies) assessment of *why*, as well as Brian's own analysis. The strong conclusion is that agile project management works much better in government IT projects than traditional methods.

The main reason for case study successes is in the implied definition of 'Agile'. The success is primarily due to the fact that prioritized results are delivered earlier, and in much smaller increments than for traditional projects using the waterfall approach where each step of a project must be completely finished before proceeding to the next. Secondarily there is an element of *learning*, and *proving* the system, at every delivery cycle. All other agile tactics are optional details.

You should read this book because:

♦ It is a wonderful collection of real case studies from the US, the UK, and elsewhere

♦ It provides a stream of practical advice and commentary

♦ It will be useful for you – you can quote these experiences and conclusions to others

I am impatient with most IT books, but I found myself 'hooked' on Brian's, and I read it cover to cover in a weekend. I felt it continued to give me a fresh stream of useful facts and analysis. Reading it was helping me build up, and update, my knowledge capital, as a consultant, teacher, and writer. It was well worth the time invested. It takes far less time to read this book, than the time you will waste personally if you don't. Prioritize it!

This book has as broad a scope as one could hope for, covering a management view as well as essential technical aspects. This view is sorely needed in a field long dominated by dogmatic developers and code-centric softcrafters. One of many repeated hard lessons noted in this book was failure to convert old files early. Agile is not just about writing software, it is about getting the implementation right!

I have my own practical view of agile IT projects, and this book reinforces and argues that view. And since I also have a platform here, let me share with the reader my own conclusions.

My practice for decades (it works!), and my advice to management regarding 'agile' I call 'Evo' (Evolutionary value optimization) Method:

♦ Start the first day of any IT project by deciding (as well as you can in a day) on the top ten most critical improvements that justify the project in the sponsors' eyes.

♦ Quantify the critical objectives, each in terms of the Goal and its Scale on a single page. It can always be done, but many have yet to learn the art. Clarity is the basis for real agreement. No management BS allowed!

♦ Let those quantified and agreed Top Level Critical Project Objectives be the basis for all other action in the project (architecture, management, contracts, and progress reports). Of course they can be adjusted as experience and circumstance dictate, but *start* with crystal clear, agreed, project intentions! This is where projects start to fail, if they *don't* clarify.

♦ Start frequent (weekly to monthly) cycles of measurable delivery of increments to these objectives (Value Increments). Start 'next week'. Use the old system as initial critical mass, and as a real playground. Don't accept any excuses for procrastination.

- Pay contractors, and reward teams, for measured value delivery to real stakeholders, on the 'Top Ten' agenda (No Cure, No Pay). Give them the freedom to figure out how to deliver real value to the quantified objectives. If they can't, then replace, retrain, or get coaches.

- Don't *ever* spend a single million, without getting much more than that in value, each time. A fool and his money are soon parted.

Brian's book emphasizes lessons such as the necessity of an *envelope (like Evo)* to manage the Scrum/XP agile process. It shows how to delegate power to get results, rather than prescribing too much 'best practice'. It includes the main idea of *do it quickly, do it frequently, do high value early*, all thoroughly validated in the cases in this book.

An in-depth view of my agile ideas will be found at Agilerecord.com.

Tom Gilb, Norway   July 2012
www.gilb.com
(where more detail on Evo is offered free)

Who is Tom Gilb?

Tom has been practicing 'agile' in real projects intuitively, using common sense, since 1960 (at least 20 incremental useful result deliveries were the norm). Studies[1] have shown that he was the first to evangelize for evolutionary IT project management in writing in the 70s, though many, including him, practiced it successfully long before that. Most of the Agile Manifesto signatories and other agile method creators have publicly recognized him as a sort of 'grandfather' of incremental software project management, with special reference to his depth treatment of it in his 1988 book, Principles of Software Engineering Management (which includes a foreword by Barry Boehm).[2]

Guest Foreword – Dot Tudor

Agile Coach of the Year 2011

When Brian asked me to review this book and write a foreword, I approached the task with some trepidation. So much has already been said about agile approaches. How is this book going to add to the already-burgeoning body of knowledge? However, I need not have worried. This book takes a fresh approach and is really useful to anyone wanting to introduce agile into any large organization. It is a must-read for anyone engaged in large-scale projects and trying to change the organizational culture to nurture and not stifle agility.

The book is evidence-based and I appreciated the presentation of the case studies early in the book with sufficient detail for me to understand why and how they worked. The book then reassesses the 2001 Agile Manifesto from a completely new angle, taking a leadership perspective, which will help to support leaders in establishing the agile culture from the top down, the middle out as well as the bottom up. It does not give precedence to any one particular source of agile best practice guidance: agile is a family of approaches, which came together after the signing of the Agile Manifesto, primarily because they had so much in common. In the years since that challenge to the world of tight, directive project management and over-zealous focus on process maturity, there have been many successes and failures.

In some organizations the pendulum has swung from the very bureaucratic and process-focused approaches to almost total anarchy – and often back again. This book argues that management control and

Agile are not incompatible, and gives practical guidance on how to generate a culture of management and leadership in which Agile teams can work effectively. A culture is needed that fosters creativity and a sustainable pace of collaborative work, while keeping sufficient governance and the strategic focus on the business need and deadlines.

Brian's book is the first of its kind, to my knowledge, that looks at the application of the agile approach specifically within Government projects. It recognizes the constraints and restrictions, which are an integral part of the large, controlled, transparent, and necessarily auditable world of government. These case studies show that agile government does work. It also argues that for governments to succeed in their quest to gain advantages from an agile approach to projects, the focus must be on adopting nine specific Agile Leadership Behaviors.

The book considers government, in the UK and the US and elsewhere. However, I believe that its conclusions and advice are equally applicable to any large organization. Multi-national corporations managing multi-cultural teams across the world face many of the same problems and will find this book useful and practical. The nine Agile Leadership Behaviors are equally applicable as a focus for their levels of management and facilitation. The concept of "light-tight" control is a simple but effective reminder that Agile does not mean chaotic and loose, but requires empowerment at the solution development team level and a responsible approach to governance at senior levels.

It is about time that Governments around the world adopted the agile approach as a default for projects. Agile delivers value early and regularly. It reduces risk by providing early feedback of progress, by involving the right people at all levels and by embracing change.

This book adds to the body of knowledge on agile approaches by considering its use on large-scale projects in big organizations. It gives practical, experience-based advice for its effective integration into the complex cultures of such organizations.

Dorothy J Tudor, Technical Director, TCC Ltd   July 2012
Agile Coach, Sandbach, UK, and the World

Foreword

The US Department of Defense canceled a Human Resources project after 12 years of wasted effort: $1bn was written off, costing every US taxpayer $100. The UK government terminated an emergency fire services project, and £469m was written off in a single year.

Large government technical development projects self-destruct on a regular basis despite intense political scrutiny and detailed audit. These failures must not continue....

This book explains how agile leadership reduces the risks of failure in Government. The agile approach is all about focusing on what is really important: meeting deadlines and getting feedback on what works and what doesn't before too much money is spent.

I give reasons why many large change projects have failed and how to ensure yours doesn't. I identify 9 Agile Leadership Behaviors for success, provide the low-down on US and UK government rules, regulations, and I describe agile best practice frameworks and methods.

My two main arguments are that the agile approach provides you with the best way of running technology projects, and that by exhibiting specific leadership behaviors you will facilitate and enable success in those projects.

Executive Summary

Top officials on both sides of the Atlantic have too often failed to provide agile leadership. The seductive siren call of huge fixed price contracts to deliver technology usually ends up in disaster. In one case a supplier is fired. In another there is simply a resigned acceptance by a government of a flawed solution. Government customers and their suppliers can end up in death-embraces – where neither party can admit that a project is undeliverable. As one newspaper commentator succinctly stated:

> "Yet another outsourcing company collects profits when all goes well and the state picks up the pieces if the company fails. Soon much of the state may be too atrophied to step in."[3]

Governments must stop pretending that the business risks of large project failure can be managed by suppliers. Governments must manage these risks. They must stop trying to outsource mission critical work to be built in large, indigestible deliveries.

There are agile success stories out there: US Veteran Affairs, the FBI, the UK Ministry of Defense, the UK Government Digital Service, Housing Benefits in Australia – all over the world these pockets of excellence demonstrate that governments can be agile. For example, the New Zealand government instituted a disaster compensation system within three days of the Christchurch earthquake. The team responsible for the software used an agile approach to visually track their work on a continual basis. Releases of working software were scheduled on a half daily and sometimes even hourly basis. The system paid out more than AU$200m, and ensured economic continuity in the face of a natural disaster.[4]

I present cases of projects that governments around the world have implemented successfully using agile approaches, such as a safety critical defense project, a benefits payment project, and a federal criminal and homeland security project among many others.

I am proposing that the spread of **agile thinking in governments will be accelerated by the adoption of 9 specific Agile Leadership Behaviors that I identify in this book**. These 9 Agile Leadership Behaviors are a necessary foundation that will pave the way for agile success. If the concept behind a project is bad, then the approach should change. Cancelation of the project early with little harm done may be the best decision. The ability to change direction when facts are uncovered that upset prior ideas is a fundamental characteristic of an agile approach.

Also identified here are 6 Barriers to Agile Success. Agile thinking addresses the current *addiction to process* and mega-project mania to reduce risk and deliver on time. By thinking differently about how they agree their objectives up front on projects, go about procurement, and carry out project audits, governments around the world will overcome these 6 Barriers to Agile Success.

This is the first large scale research that has been published on agile project management for government, and I have been helped enormously by Chief Information Officers in governments around the world. They have seen how agile can deliver, and they want the call for change to be loud and clear.

There are many sources for best practice guidance on the agile approach. I have chosen to describe three in this book because they have different perspectives and strengths: the Dynamic Systems Development Method framework from the not-for-profit DSDM Consortium; the Scrum method described in the writings of Schwaber and Sutherland; and the eXtreme Programming (XP) techniques developed by Kent Beck.

I give examples of how these have been combined to get the rounded approach to agile that government needs. By reading this book you will be exposed to just enough jargon to enable you to sit down and talk to agile experts and ensure that your team processes will work under your leadership.

But although best practice guidance can help project processes, it is no substitute for leadership!

Notes on References

To allow you to proceed with minimal interruption I have provided references in numbered endnotes rather than having lots of footnotes cluttering up the bottom of each page. Where a particular publication is exceptionally significant, I have occasionally included the author's name in-line with my text.

Most of the works referenced in this book can be accessed over the Internet where you will be able to read the vast majority of the references without having to leave your desk – I have provided links to web addresses where available in the bibliography. I recommend that you buy the companion "Click-Through Endnotes" eBook. This will allow you to click on an endnote web address and open up the corresponding reference immediately.

Each part of the book will also be published as a separate eBook. And each eBook license will allow you to switch between a PC, MAC, tablet, iPAD, or Kindle as you wish. The technology also can allow you to legally 'lend' your eBook license to a colleague to read at no extra cost. Various e-library subscriptions, such as Amazon Prime, Kindle Select, and Safari may allow you to borrow the eBooks online.

From my long involvement with assurance and audit bodies, both as auditor and auditee, I know the importance of only drawing conclusions when a firm base of evidence is available. As you step through the (hopefully) interesting in-depth and real life case studies, I will highlight the essential features of agile to you using the context of the case study as an explanatory vehicle.

I have decided not to provide a glossary because I introduce and explain jargon and acronyms as we go along in the natural context of each case study. If you decide to dip in and out of the book taking what you will from it then simply use the Index at the back of the book to look up the first mention of any terms you are unfamiliar with. The first mention of any new piece of terminology is marked by *italics*. Thereafter italics are not used.

Join the conversation? Perhaps a hackneyed phrase, but the Internet provides a way for authors and readers to discuss and debate. Post messages to my blog at brianwernham.wordpress.com or Twitter your thoughts to me. My Twitter name is @BrianUkulele, a handle I adopted years ago to communicate thoughts on many aspects of my life from playing ukuleles to my professional experiences. Just include the *hashtag* #APMFG in your *tweets* and everybody else interested in this book will be able to find your comments.

Despite much expert checking and endless proofreading, some errors may still exist in the text for which I accept full responsibility. Some Internet links in the references will become stale in time. Please let me know at brian@maitland-and-strong.com and I will attempt to find an alternative link for you. If you have purchased the eBook editions then any errata will update directly to your Amazon eReader software.

So read on, and spread the word about agile project management and the 9 Agile Leadership Behaviors to your colleagues and friends and the political leaders!

Acknowledgements

This book has been greatly improved by the comments and suggestions sent to me by the expert reviewers of my manuscript. Susan Atkinson, Stephan Gehring, Tom Gilb, and Dot Tudor in particular provided much needed help, commenting on facts and pointing out numerous references that I would have otherwise missed.

Staff at many of the organizations mentioned herein also helped me understand why their agile approaches were succeeding. Special mention for going above and beyond the call of duty to help me goes to Nina Hartley and Paul Rowe at the Met Office, Rick Murphy of the US CIO Council's Management Best Practices Committee, David Habershon at the NZ Ministry of Social Development, Mary Henson at the DSDM Consortium, Scott Suhy of Greenline Systems, and Merv Wyeth at Alliantist.

I would also like to thank Dean Craven, Andrew Spiers, Brian Irwin, Nic Hodgetts, Obiora Ozonzeadi, Peter Deary, Joan Dobbiej, Roger Garrini, Bernard Marshall, Adrian Royce, Martin Samphire, Sarika Kharbanda, James Findlay, Steve Ash, Roger Wooley, Jackie Gagne, Sivaram Athmakuri, Mike Burrows and Susan Atkinson. Apologies to anybody that I have left out – there were so many!

The members of staff at Maitland and Strong and its associates were wonderful to work with. Mim K. Strong played an important part in encouraging me to start the project and was a great help throughout with the proofing and typesetting of the book with Jack Dunigan. Phil Godsell of Soundcheck Books helped enormously with his advice and support. Thanks too to David Roberts for his splendid cover design, to Andy Bowles and Shireen Mohandes for their Internet work, and to Debbie and Dave at Color Division for their reprographic wizardry.

Introduction

The agile approach is best summed up as being a way of incrementally delivering change so as to get the earliest possible benefit, get feedback early on what works, and change direction accordingly. I argue in this book that governments around the world have for many years been doing the exact opposite with their technology developments. They have commissioned large projects that progress in a predetermined and unfaltering course, deliver late (if at all) and provide little or no benefit.

I have decided to lay out these arguments in the first part of this book using the Harvard MBA case study approach to compare and contrast the agile and non-agile approach. I avoided the classic book structure of 'history, theory, examples' because the first question people have been asking me when I told them about this book was "Can agile be used in governments?" Therefore I have turned that classic sequence of explanation on its head.

I start with fully attributed examples of government success stories. These are from around the world, including the USA (where the Federal Government is in the vanguard of demonstrating success with use of agile on some huge projects) and also the UK and Australia. These are real stories and are fully referenced. The case studies in this book actually happened and are fully attributed.

The central tenet of the agile approach is that we must be scientists. When we start a project we have a hypothesis that the outcome will be beneficial. We must test that hypothesis as the project progresses. Regular delivery of testable product provides the basis for ensuring that our projects are on the right track.

Much is made of the word "agile" in government today. "Government

IT needs to be more agile, more responsive and more accountable to the citizens" says the US Government. [5]

In the UK the government has vowed "to be more agile, more fleet of foot".[6] So, is agility anything more than a nebulous concept? If a government wants to be more agile what must it do?

Tom Gilb was one of the first to propose an incremental, agile approach to developing software. Rather than have large, clumsy, slow and ultimately risky projects that took years to complete, he proposed an *evolutionary approach* he termed "Evo":

> "Evo is a technique for producing the appearance of stability. A complex system will be most successful if it is implemented in small steps and if each step has a clear measure of successful achievement as well as a 'retreat' possibility to a previous successful step upon failure. You have the opportunity of receiving some feedback from the real world before throwing in all resources intended for a system, and you can correct possible design errors" [7]

In a 1985 paper, "Evolutionary Delivery versus the 'Waterfall model", Gilb introduced the EVO method as an alternative of the waterfall which he considered as "unrealistic and dangerous to the primary objectives of any software project". Gilb based EVO on three simple principles:

♦ Deliver something to the real end-user

♦ Measure the added-value to the user in all critical dimensions

♦ Adjust both design and objectives based on observed realities. [8]

Figure 1 shows a simple conceptual model that helps put this book into the context of government strategy. The outside bubble represents the desire by politicians and top management to be both *lean* and *agile*.

Lean Government has all unnecessary and wasteful 'fat' trimmed off. This is a process that not only boosts efficiency but also increases quality of output. Lean initiatives are generally internally initiated and maintained.

Agile Government is able to change direction quickly due to unforeseen or unforeseeable circumstances. This reduces risks of failure. Just as an athlete may fall attempting to jump over a hurdle that is set too high, in an agile world we set the hurdles at a comfortable height and at regular intervals. *Agility*, then, corresponds to setting short, realistic targets and reacting fast to changing circumstances.

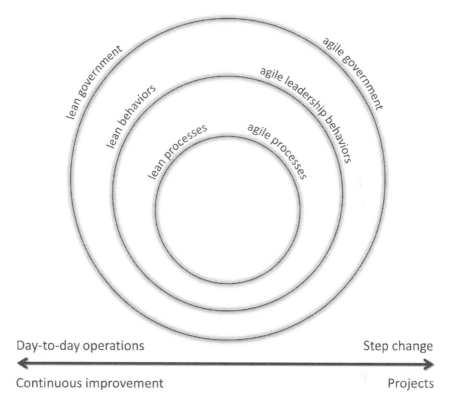

Day-to-day operations　　　　　　　　　　　　　　　　Step change

←——————————————————————————————→

Continuous improvement　　　　　　　　　　　　　　　Projects

Figure 1: What does *agile* mean?

For example, the White House 25 Point Plan to increase quality and efficiency in US Government Information Technology (IT). [9] The UK Cabinet Office has published an IT Strategy that has similar objectives, with five out of the 14 points specifically relating to the adoption of agile approaches in development. [10]

When Vivak Kundra was sworn in as Chief Information Officer (CIO) for the US Government in 2009 he inherited $27bn (and that is billion not million!) in IT projects that were behind schedule and over budget. His

$1bn cancellation of the Military Human Resources System was just one of several actions he took to try to take control of a spiraling, out of control IT project budget. From 2001 to 2009, IT spending nearly doubled, growing at an annual rate of 7 per cent. But from 2010 onwards Kundra capped the IT Budget. Spend was forecast to rise to $104bn by 2013, the new forecast was just $79bn – a saving of $25bn per year.[11]

His 25-Point Plan called for a "modular approach to development using an iterative development process". It intensified previous attempts to move to an agile approach.[12]

Agile behaviors reduce the reliance on premature agreement of detail before development work commences. The proponents of this approach (often called *Agilists*) argue that as development gets underway new requirements appear that were not considered previously. Conversely the development teams discover problems (and opportunities) that can inform strategic decisions. They say that one should not imagine that a detailed specification for a system can be written years in advance of the development taking place and being implemented for use.

On the face of it, adopting an agile approach appears to be at odds with typical government bureaucratic approaches. I argue that although the turnaround to a new way of thinking will be a challenge, there is already evidence of success.

This book is about the adoption of agile in government and how to overcome the barriers to its introduction. The application of this book is relevant at local levels, not just central government. Some geographically local projects are of a staggering size. The Mayor of London, for example, spent £161.7m in setting up a congestion charge plan for the city.[13] Public bodies have planned significant technology projects. The US National Digital Information Infrastructure and Preservation Program were allocated $100m in funding from Congress in 2000.

The trans-Atlantic interaction between technology developers and project managers in the US and the UK is a central theme of the book. There has been a continual and fruitful interaction between the Governments of the US and the UK in the development of computers. The US Navy played a pivotal role in the British development of the first large-scale vacuum tube driven computer at Bletchley Park in England, which broke encoded Nazi war messages.[14]

Other authors have argued that agile processes can be scaled up to large projects.[15] But I propose here that a bottom-up push by *agilists* will take time and will run into organizational inhibitors. What is needed is leadership, especially at the strategic level. Although many agile concepts are complementary to existing approaches, and there has been more continuity in the development of project management approaches than many recognize, a change in leadership thinking is needed. It is the emphasis and strategic philosophy of management that needs to evolve to encourage agile and allow it to thrive in a government environment.

In delivering large projects in both public bodies and large corporations, I have had to work hard to make large, inflexible procurements more incremental and customer focused. Leadership of others, such as lawyers and procurement executives, played a crucial role in steering these projects to success.

My experiences in leading large teams in the USA (in North Carolina and New York) and in Canada mirrored those in the UK and Europe. I led projects that would now be termed agile that delivered the first automatic code generators for Windows-based computers. These projects revolutionized user-friendliness, decreased training requirements, and reduced error rates by replacing mainframe terminals at large public and private sector organizations. The key was flexibility in setting the team goals, and agreeing what the business was going to realize by delivering working solutions incrementally from an early stage.

Any practical project manager will know that it is better to deliver an imperfect solution early than wait forever for perfection. The banker J.P. Morgan is reputed to have said "I want it Thursday, not perfect!" The trick is to know what level of imperfection can be handled by the business and traded off against the early realization of the benefits of the solution that the project is going to deliver. Bill Gates knew this when deciding on the right moment to release the replacement for Windows 3.1. He called it Windows 95. It was officially named for the year of its release (1995), but my sources at the time told me that it was named after an internal slogan "95% ready, not 100% perfect".

Part I then, does not start with theory – it contains proof of success.

It tells stories of effective use of agile in the face of huge challenges. These stories are provided to give you the incentive to say "Yes – we can also be agile! Tell me how I can lead my colleagues so that they can also have agile successes!" In these cases, I see how projects around the world have used popular agile best practice guidance to achieve agile success. As previously stated, I focus on three sets of best practice: the DSDM framework, the Scrum method and eXtreme Programming techniques.[16] I have chosen to examine these three in this book because they have different perspectives and strengths, and, as we shall see later, they have been used together to great effect:

♦ DSDM provides an agile framework that can be applied to any type of project. It can be used to run IT or non-technology projects such as incremental construction or engineering. The DSDM framework provides practical guidance on agile governance processes, operational implementation, and project management together with team-level structures and techniques.

♦ Scrum is a method which provides guidance on technology development via a set of processes and practices at the team level. The Scrum method takes an unpretentious, empirical approach to the development of products which is easy to follow.

♦ eXtreme Programming (XP) techniques help IT developers work together, become more productive, and create high quality computer software.

There is a growing body of opinion that these three can be used to contribute to success on large government projects. Recently Craddock, Richards, Tudor, Roberts, and Godwin have proposed a promising approach for using the DSDM framework with the Scrum method:

"One or more aspects of the DSDM Agile Project Framework may be used to supplement Scrum ... where they make the use of the Scrum (method) easier (or) more effective."

As we shall see, where management has in mind a time and budget limited project to deliver change into operations, the DSDM framework may be successfully used as a wrapper around the Scrum method to create a hybrid of the best of both sets of guidance. This ensures that all those who may be impacted by the new system (the *stakeholders*) are engaged with appropriately. In the same way, when using the DSDM framework and the Scrum method together on a project involving IT development, it can be useful to include some XP techniques because the Scrum Method does not give guidance on specific software development techniques.

Many organizations embarking on agile projects for the first time feel that they have to make an exclusive choice, and adopt one set of best practice guidance only. This can lead to a very limited set of processes and some blind spots. I suggest here that you should consider using the best of all three of these sets of Best Practice, and Incorporate Good Agile Thinking from Elsewhere Whenever Possible. **Keeping an Open Mind to New Ideas and Fresh Evidence Is a Great Agile Leadership Quality.**

Part II then proceeds to give guidance on the leadership dimension. It explains the genesis of the Agile Manifesto and the related 12 Agile Manifesto Principles which define what agile is, and what it is not. I make the argument that it is the leadership perspective, not the process perspective that is most critical, and I propose 9 Agile Leadership Behaviors that you should follow.

Your adoption of these behaviors will reduce risk and encourage the use of the agile approach in your organization. Each of the nine chapters that follow examines one of these leadership behaviors in the context of government regulations, rules, unhelpful and inconsistent 'best practice' guidance, and organizational inertia.

More evidence of agile project successes around the world is provided and contrasted with the problems of the traditional *waterfall* approach on past government projects. The waterfall approach to project management requires each step of a project to be completely finished before proceeding to the next. For example, design then developrnent then testing before use can start.

I put forward two main arguments. First, that agile project management provides a much better way of running most technology projects than waterfall approaches. Second, that without agile leadership, governments cannot become agile. Some practical advice is given in these chapters on specific improvements to make in the use of the DSDM framework and the Scrum method in your organization. At the end of each chapter I provide a list of agile leadership exercises you can do right now – even if you are working in a waterfall environment!

Part III of this book identifies 6 Barriers to Agile Success. These are the potential blockers to the adoption and spread of the agile project management approach. The 1990s was dominated by a desire to use large complicated design methods. The last decade was dominated by huge prime supplier outsourced contracts which crushed any incipient agility in many government offices. And procurement, regulations, and outdated approaches to project audit still remain the main inhibitors of agile adoption in government.

One interesting piece of news I discovered while carrying out the research for this book is that agile is being introduced into high-schools in New Zealand. Final year students are required to understand and practically use an iterative development lifecycle and the concepts of test-driven development of technology. Students will be required to demonstrate agile teamwork.

The new syllabus is very broad – ranging from how mp3 players work to e-commerce and the impact of technology on society. Although traditional technical skills are being taught, the stress is on getting a "taste of the discipline to find out if it suits them or not." The syllabus is now implemented, and researchers are tracking the students through the system to assess the results.[17]

The output of the first agile graduates into work and higher education is expected shortly not just in New Zealand, but from schools around the world. Governments need to be ready to make use of their knowledge, energy and enthusiasm....

Part I

Stories of Agile Success in Government

When I discuss the concept of the agile approach with leaders in governments in different countries, I get a lot of interest. These people understand the scale of culture change that is needed if the agile approach is to spread throughout government, and they want to know how to convince their colleagues. That is why I wrote this book.

The best way for me to convince you to adopt the 9 Agile Leadership Behaviors in the middle part of this book is to start with some real-life agile success stories. Whether you are a trainee or a senior director or politician, these case studies will provide you with the evidence that you need to lead your teams to agile success.

These events actually happened. I present a *warts and all* account of each one. Each is fully attributed – no anonymous case-studies appear in this book. I haven't selected small, experimental projects. These are all large, hairy beasts. As we progress though each case, I will introduce agile concepts and some jargon.

I start with a straightforward success story where the agile approach was adopted by the UK Ministry of Defense to develop a battlefield system to reduce the risk of friendly-fire in the wake of a series of friendly-fire incidents involving US and UK servicemen. After that we delve into an ultra-fast agile implementation at the US Department of Veterans Affairs which was on time and was a success, despite teething problems. I then tell the tale of the recovery of the failing Sentinel project at the FBI which was saved by a switch to an agile approach. Then a case from 'Down Under' where the State of Queensland in Australia has proved the worth of agile in parts of its organization, in stark contrast to its recent $1.2bn failure of the new Health payroll system.[18] Finally, I give an overview of how the UK Met Office has taken the best from agile and non-agile best practice to implement what they call "Just Enough Project Management", and how it has led to project successes.

Chapter 1

Case Study at the UK Ministry of Defense

There can be no substitute for the clear, positive ID of targets linked to unambiguous confirmation of precise location. The passage of positional data relating to both the target and the nearest friendly forces should be mandatory.

Board of Inquiry Report,
Ministry of Defence, 2004

We shall see proof in this chapter that an agile approach can incrementally deliver large mission and safety critical technology solutions. In this case, it did so quickly and is now on its way to protect the lives of coalition service personnel. It shows how the UK Ministry of Defense (MoD) successfully developed a new, improved battlefield system in the space of 18 months by using the DSDM framework.

In relating the case, I will give some concrete examples of the concepts behind agile.

We will see how the DSDM framework was used to provide governance and a project management approach to ensure that things got done on time and within budget. This is because it is important for you to be exposed, at least at an overview level, to some of the essential jargon that *agilists* use, and to get a gist of the processes they are advocating. In later chapters, I will describe the Scrum method and XP techniques which are also popular methods and are complimentary to each other and the DSDM framework. As mentioned in the introduction, each of these three sets of best practice addresses development project issues at different levels. But always bear in mind that one of the arguments of this book is that although best practice materials such as these are helpful, it is the leadership of management and those inside the teams that really make projects like the one in this chapter a success.

At the end of the case study I ask some probing questions that should prompt you to refer back to the text and provoke you into thinking more deeply about how you can adopt the agile leadership lessons therein.

Case Study Background

On January 14, 2009, Captain Tom Sawyer, 26, of the Royal Artillery, and Corporal Danny Winter, 28, of the Royal Marines, tragically died in a 'friendly fire' incident in Helmand province. A subsequent investigation revealed that they were killed by a heat-seeking missile fired by coalition forces in bad visibility while they were providing mortar ground support.

Many such incidents have occurred during combat operations in Afghanistan. This incident increased the number of British troops killed by friendly fire in Afghanistan operations to six. Incidents of friendly-fire are usually due to a lack of *situational awareness* of the combatants, not due to a lack of precision in the weaponry. Responsibility for command and control of fire is dispersed to individual units in the heat of battle, and the knowledge of who friendly units are and where they are situated is vital to those responsible for fire control in modern, fast-moving battlefield situations.

Poor situational awareness in combat is a key risk factor, often leading to friendly fire deaths. The board of inquiry into the killing of Lance Corporal Matthew Hull in Iraq 2003 found that the co-ordination between battlefield units and air units was lacking due to poor situational awareness.

The CIDS Project

The US, UK and other NATO forces have been developing and improving Combat Identification Systems (CIDS) over many years. In 2009 the UK Ministry of Defense (MoD) initiated a project to create a Combat Identification Server (CIDS). The CIDS was needed to tightly integrate close air support with shared situational position information.

A contract was awarded to General Dynamics to develop the CIDS to be in place by July 2010.[19] It needed to provide autonomous, accurate near real-time force tracking and location information to direct fire away from coalition troops. General Dynamics had only 18 months to integrate their "Net-Link tactical gateway" with specialist technology supplied by its subcontractors, Rockwell Collins and QinetiQ. Every few seconds, CIDS would integrate data from all the friendly forces in a battlefield and distribute it back to all the nearby unit commanders.[20]

Project Kick-Off and the Foundations Phase

To meet their objective of an 18 month implementation of this lifesaving software, the MoD chose an agile approach. They believed that complex military technologies could be better delivered without delay or unexpected cost overruns using agile.

A decision was made to use the DSDM framework because it gives guidance on the process for agile supplier delivery to a customer. The customer does not need to be a third-party – it could be the technology department within an organization. The important point with DSDM is that because it uses a *product centric approach* (see page 227) it has the potential to be used to formalize payment milestones with suppliers based on product deliveries.

The first phase of a DSDM project is called the *Foundations* phase. On the CIDS project the team analyzed the theoretical payment plan in the contract during their Foundations phase and found that it did not match reality. Both the MoD and General Dynamics recognized that a *win/win* situation was needed, and that traditional contract renegotiation would take time, and could lead to a deterioration of relationships before the development had even begun. They agreed to start work, and use evidence of progress to amend the scope of the required solution to fit with the planned timescales.[21]

How DSDM Avoided the Pit-Falls of Waterfall Projects

DSDM requires *just enough design up front* (EDUF), and the Foundations phase should be as short as possible, while still ensuring an essential understanding and clarity of structure of the overall solution and to create an Agile plan for delivery. This initial Foundation phase created an architecture that gave both the MoD and General Dynamics an assurance that minimum acceptable performance levels could be achieved.[22] For example, tracking information on the position of friendly forces needed to be collated from a minimum of 15 different units in any battlefield. The architecture also had to be flexible enough to allow near-real time position information to not only artillery units, but also to nearby aircraft.[23]

The approach ensured that test and evaluation of the solution was a "constant and regular activity", and allowed the development team and the stakeholders to gain more confidence with each iteration.

The project would run from February 2009 to July 2010. Overall plans were agreed at the end of the Foundations phase, which took three months. Then the Exploration and Engineering phase started with three iterations, each about 3–6 months long:

♦ Iteration 1: Create a simple version of the software that could deal with one friendly force position

♦ Iteration 2: Extend the software to process multiple position information

♦ Iteration 3: Make the solution robust and fast enough to deal with the operational number of request responses and to interface with systems from other coalition partners.[24]

The MOD planned practical demonstrations for June 2010, before final deployment took place in July 2010.

DSDM stresses the need for scalability from the smallest project to the very largest. It concentrates on governance and structures around incremental project outputs. It was first published in the UK in 1994 as an alternative rapid development method, which would avoid the pitfalls of the traditional waterfall approach.

Waterfall projects are segmented into discrete phases, each dependent on the completion of the previous phase, but without feedback or iteration. When using a waterfall approach, one cannot start a phase until the previous Has Been Completed. This Leads to a Series of One-Way 'Gates' (see Figure 2). Once One Has Committed to Swimming Downstream, It is impossible to return to an earlier stage without a lot of effort –similarly difficult to attempting to swim up a waterfall. In contrast to doing just enough design, a waterfall approach requires a grand design in detail before any solution building commences. A waterfall approach is appropriate for some civil engineering projects that are monolithic in nature, such as building a skyscraper, but in technology projects a waterfall approach will tend towards what Kent Beck called 'Big Design Up Front' (BDUF) when describing a fundamental problem of the waterfall lifecycle – that it relies upon pinpoint accuracy and perfect logic at every step if it is to produce a workable solution.[25] Kent's argument, and one that I emphasize in this book, is that we should aim for Enough Design Up-Front (EDUF), not BDUF.

Although DSDM started as a proprietary method closely controlled by a small consortium, in 2007 the decision was taken to make the method more openly available. The manual is now available to all for free on the Internet at www.dsdm.org and training may be bought from many suppliers (subject to training body certification requirements of the DSDM consortium). [26]

At 202 pages, the DSDM handbook may not at first glance appear to reflect the ideal of a 'light-weight' method. However, it supplies the role and process definitions often required for large projects by government regulations, and thus provides a useful template for a project management framework. It is process and output orientated, and gives seven main steps for every DSDM project, creating 43 products – each described in the handbook with some detail. Prior to the Foundations step, the customer (perhaps with the help of expert suppliers) should carry out the Feasibility step.

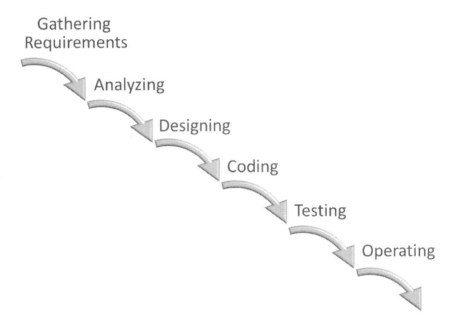

Figure 2: An example of a waterfall lifecycle

The method gives guidance as to the level and approach needed to produce an outline business case containing enough information to make a decision, but no more. If the project is given the go-ahead, then in the Foundations phase of the project this business case is expanded just enough for internal needs and government regulations. After the project is finished, DSDM gives advice on collecting lessons learned, evaluating the project performance against expectations, and monitoring the business performance of the solution against the business case.

One of the strengths and flexibilities of DSDM is that it gives guidance on how the iterative development work of Exploration and Engineering should be carried out alongside Deployment. It encourages flexibility in how these could be combined together, or omitted. Some projects initially need to iterate Exploration and Engineering many times, building models of different solution options, before proceeding with the iterative Engineering of a solution and its deployment. For example, if one month iterations are being followed, but updates to end-users are restricted by a wider organizational policy to once every three months, then only every third iteration will include a Deployment step.

Iteration and feedback is the core of DSDM, and it makes it very different from waterfall approaches. Its strength is that it presents agile concepts from a management point of view, using terms that traditional project managers understand while avoiding a waterfall approach. Like many methods, though, it has little to say about leadership behaviors. Processes and outputs are defined that are amenable to 'traditional' project management techniques, but have an agile approach. For example:

♦ Quality planning is used to define the necessary levels of acceptance for project outputs – this provides a description for each output that can be objectively tested and audited (see *definition of done* later)

♦ Requirements planning is used to maintain a Prioritized Requirements List (PRL), with mandatory release dates defined for all mandatory requirements, and tentative release dates for others

♦ Earned Value Analysis (EVA) can be carried out to compare the actual versus estimated development effort originally expected for each product feature in the PRL, thus providing feedback on the accuracy of the original estimates and the productivity of the team. (EVA is a technique that is controversial with agilists, as discussed further in Part III).

Thus a high level of compatibility with traditional formal management techniques can be achieved, but coming from the direction of flexibility and iteration, rather than upfront, detailed plans that become set in stone as *baselines* to be measured against.

The DSDM framework is an agile approach and guards against cost and time overruns by turning the *baselining* model on its head. In a waterfall project, a detailed *baseline* for the scope of a project needs to be agreed upon – supported by detailed design assumptions and theoretical estimates. Hence the phrase Big Design Up-Front (BDUF). If the estimates are inaccurate (and of course they often are because they are made before work begins and actual progress starts to be measured) the only variables left in the equation are cost and/or timescales.

Stakeholders flex their muscles and ask for additional *nice to have* features which cause the required amount of work to increase: a situation known as scope creep. This is why so many waterfall projects go over time and cost. Since the baseline is fixed, these mutually dependent parameters are allowed to run out of control. And what is more, waterfall projects usually implement one risky, disruptive, large change to operations: the *big-bang* approach which we will encounter again and again in the stories of large project failure in this book.

DSDM is an agile method and therefore has a different philosophy from the waterfall approach. When it is used as the project management framework to guide the team, only the central core of solution features is identified at the outset. The scope is allowed to change, in a controlled manner, as the inevitable mis-estimation of time and cost becomes clear. The opposite of scope creep takes place – scope is reduced if difficulties are encountered, rather than time and budget being increased. The project comes in on time and cost because DSDM fixes these variables, and in-stead re-scopes the Features to Be Delivered. in Effect, There Is Zero Time or Cost Contingency, but There Is Contingency in the Scope of Require-ments (see Figure 3).

At its Simplest, Features left out of one iteration are simply deferred to the next iteration. This can work both ways: if better than expected pro-gress is made, then features that were only on a wish list for an iteration may be included – some delight and surprise for the stakeholders!

DSDM suggests that no more than 60% of the work expected for each iteration of development should be on features classified as *Must Haves*. About 40% of the remaining work is split between *Should Haves* and *Could Haves*. The *Should Haves* are features that would be painful to leave out, but a workaround could be found for them otherwise a Must Have would be compromised.[27] *Could Haves* are features that bring additional value-add and business benefits, but can be delayed for future work without any immediate downside. To complete the picture, and to ensure that limitations to scope are understood, some requirements are classified as *Won't Haves*.

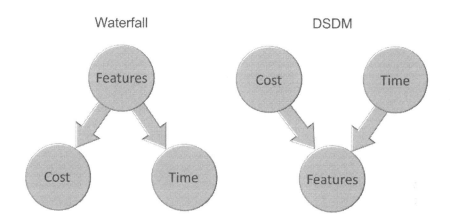

Figure 3: Waterfall: Features are the driver — DSDM: Cost and time are the drivers

Of course, 60% is a rough rule of thumb. As the project progresses, the team's *velocity* will be *calibrated* against the PRL. Each PRL item can be sized using the idea of *story points* rather than notional person-days. These story points are a relative measure of the size of each item. This concept cuts away the idea that plans can be accurately estimated in detail up-front. Progress is measured as the number of story points per day per team member, not the number of person-days notionally assigned to a set of detailed tasks at the start of a project.

It is only when the team gets going that the actual rate of progress of that particular set of people, technology and problem domain can be determined – by feedback from actual experience, rather than conjecture and theory.

The actual percentages should be reviewed with regard to the predictability of the overall scope of the project and the calibration of the velocity of the team. If the scope is well understood, in a stable business environment, and the target technology has been previously used, then perhaps a lower percentage of requirements could be in the tentative category of 'Could Have's'. However, it is tempting to make simplifying assumptions and start to move back towards traditional fixed-scope estimating. The risk is that the assumptions may be false, and development will then be more problematical than expected. It is better to achieve an over-delivery of output features than promise too many mandatory features and not deliver.

Requirements Planning in DSDM

A key control in DSDM is the list of requirements or Prioritized Requirements List (PRL). It lists all the requirements and states, which are most needed for the upcoming iteration. Every requirement is prioritized into four categories, referred to by the acronym 'MSCW'. Often this is pronounced and written as '*MoSCoW.* These are the *Must Have, Should Have, Could Have* and *Won't Have* requirements. This technique, which is central to DSDM, helps create flexibility and *Agileness* by three tricks:

 ♦ Priorities are set within the framework on iterations which are *timeboxed* – the deadlines are immovable. The team has delegated responsibility as to which *Should Have* and *Could* Have features they will deliver. Of course at the core of their work are the *Must* Haves. If a delivery is to be deployed into live use, rather than as a prototype demonstration of capability, the *business sponsor*, who is the executive responsible for the success of the project, and the team members, which includes key users, should create a joint *deployment plan*. Decisions are set at the lowest level possible so as to reduce the cycle time in decision making and ensure that quality and delivery timescales are met.

 ♦ Priorities are set for each iteration and change as the project progresses. For example, features that are *Should Haves* for one iteration may be promoted to *Must Haves* for the next iteration.

 ♦ Quality is protected: if an essential feature in the emerging solution is not of sufficient quality (it functions incorrectly, is unusable, or cannot meet capacity or other performance requirements) then it can be descoped from delivery for that iteration. Mike Cohn notes that the *could have* requirements items in an DSDM Prioritized Requirements List work as a *feature buffer* which can be sacrificed as required so as to ensure deadlines are met.[28]

DSDM ensures that the necessary governance is in place so that if any *Must Haves* are likely to fail these tests, a Business Sponsor is in place and responsible for decision making. In these cases it is usually necessary to change the deployment plan. Effort is always focused on ensuring that the highest priority features are of adequate quality. Research indicates that on average only 45% of features of technical solutions are used to any great extent, so a ruthless approach to descoping *Could Have* requirements is needed if the overall project is to produce early benefits and have a robust business case.[29]

A Solution to 'Friendly-Fire'

Forward Air Controller engagement scenarios and acceptance criteria were developed with real-life military operators collaborating in the Exploration and Engineering iterations. These tests were indexed against the requirements itemized on the PRL.

For example, air requirements such as interfaces to and from the "Link 16" air intelligence system were *must have* requirements, whereas armored situational awareness systems, such as the Force XXI Battle Command Brigade and Below (FBCB2) system was categorized as being a *Should Have* requirement.[30]

Developing the CIDS in Timeboxes Within Each Increment

Each of the 3–6 month long increments was divided into timeboxes of a month. In each timebox, the team, which included domain experts, was encouraged to get on with the work without interruption. Deadlines were sacrosanct. If within a timebox it became apparent that any of the *Must Have* requirements were at risk, then the team self-organized the redeployment of people away from development of solutions for lower priority requirements. This is the essence of Agility: decisions are delegated to the lowest possible level – to those closest to the work at hand.

A key discipline of Agile is that deadlines cannot be extended. Any issues become evident immediately and a positive attitude towards failed tests is encouraged. It is better to *fail early* and rectify an error, than to hope for the best and carry on regardless. In this case, through a *requirement trading* process the MoD agreed that a few *Should Have* and *Could Have* requirements could be descoped from the PRL. The important factor was that agreement was achieved without any penalties being incurred on the supplier, or any cost or schedule overrun for the customer.[31]

The supplier project manager from General Dynamics led a multidisciplinary team comprising staff members from the other subcontractors (Rockwell Collins and QinetiQ) and also MoD staff and their specialist technical advisors. The MoD designated an overall *Business Sponsor* (responsible for the success of the whole project), and a *Business Visionary* (responsible for decisions on day-to-day issues). Risks were recorded on a *risk register* and linked to items on the PRL to provide a means for prioritization and replanning. Again, the overriding concern was to maintain an iron grip on cost by flexing the delivery of functions to deal with risks as they emerged.

On this project the potential for 'tit-for-tat' negotiations over points of detail and costing were considerable. Trust had to be built up between a potentially suspicious customer not used to an agile approach, and a supplier under pressure to deliver.

The MoD procurement division initially proposed a severe penalty clause to guard against the possibility that the supplier would not deliver all the requirements – even the *Could Have*s. However, a collaborative approach was agreed upon, following the DSDM principles of *fixed cost* rather than *fixed scope*. Any difficulties encountered were to be resolved by *requirement trading*. In effect the project contingency was held in the *Could Have* requirements which could be traded out if unworkable or too onerous.[32]

Laboratory Integration Tests

As planned, at the end of summer 2009, integration tests started to take place at the UK Battlespace Laboratory. The Battlespace Laboratory is an independent body managed and owned by the MoD. It brings together government, industry, and military coalition partners from across the world to collaborate on highly realistic simulations of battlefield conditions.[33]

A test took place at the Battlespace Laboratory at the end of every 3-6 months in line with the development team delivery iteration schedule. The aim was to work towards a final defense demonstration servicing 50 interoperating battlefield positions. This testing was at Technology Readiness Level 6 or TRL6 (explained in more detail later on page 120) and had to be seamless and free of any significant bugs. A realistic demonstration to the military was carried out at the end of each laboratory test to increase their confidence.

Testing was based on a number of scenarios. In agile teams each of these is called a *user story*, but given the special context of the battlefield the team used the term *vignette*. One vignette, for example, was based on a land battle group carrying out counter-insurgency operations. The simulated mission was for the UK to coordinate a multi-nationality NATO attack on an insurgent compound in a desert storm. Proof was needed that the system would be able to provide friendly force ID to all units (including artillery and attack aircraft) in a difficult environment.

The team found that an agile approach instilled a discipline of delivery into the formal test environment at the end of every iteration come what may. An agile approach of immoveable deadlines ensured that intensive use could be made of the Battlefield Laboratory on the expected dates, thus making best use of an expensive and limited facility. A focus on interoperability was the key to the development. Although various items were re-prioritized for each iteration, in the end, the flexibility and discipline of the DSDM framework adopted meant that important requirements were not sacrificed and CIDS and the other battlefield systems all linked up to each other successfully.[34]

Joint US and UK Interoperability Testing

Full coalition interoperability testing with all coalition partners at TRL8 (the highest technology readiness level) was to take place the next year at the next "Bold Quest" coalition Combat ID (CID) capability assessment organized by the Joint Forces Command for 2011. These demanding exercises are aimed to enhance situational awareness, targeting, and minimize "collateral damage and fratricide".

Rather than wait for that event, the MoD decided to carry out a previously unscheduled trial to prove the system at TRL 7 well in advance of "Bold Quest".

So, in Norway, in August 2010, the new UK CIDS system was demonstrated side-by-side with the US CIDS by joint coalition ground and air forces – and all were able to successfully communicate with one another.[35] Both static tests and dynamic tests were undertaken using known positions and mounted and dismounted Norwegian soldiers exercising controlled scenarios.

Over 90 dynamic user friendly force information requests were made from the ground and the air using seven different systems.[36] Throughout the exercise period, the CIDS proved to be highly reliable, providing friendly-force position data within an average of three seconds to within five meter accuracy.

In addition, even though the Danish aircraft had not been specifically prepared for the exercise when they arrived they were immediately able to make successful requests friendly force ID using their Link 16 technology.[37]

Conclusions

In this first of five case studies we have seen how an agile approach delivered a large mission, and safety critical technology solution, and we explored some of the concepts behind agile, and the DSDM framework.

Questions

1. The MoD had indicated their inexperience with agile approaches. What risks did this represent to their business case?

2. What strengths and weaknesses are there in the application of DSDM to the CCID project outlined above?

3. The MoD procurement division was keen to 'nail down' the suppliers to a fixed specification. What may have been their thinking? How would you draw up an agile contract that would fairly hold a supplier to account for poor performance? How would it also ensure that the customer is held to its responsibilities? (More on this in Chapter 2.)

4. The Agile Manifesto Principles expect projects to iteratively deliver working solutions and have a natural preference for shorter rather than longer timescales between iterations (see Table 2).

5. Did the CIDS project meet these criteria? Could more have been done to make the project more agile?

6. Look at the Henson's presentation of the CIDS project plan (see Endnote 38). Compare it with the waterfall lifecycle (see Figure 2). What similarities are there? What differences?

Chapter 2

Case Study at the US Department of Veterans Affairs

With no significant bugs reported ... operation nearly flawless – a stunning and an unpredicted success what are the implications for failing IT programs across government?[39]

Roger Baker,
Assistant Secretary for IT,
Department of Veterans Affairs

Some of the most widespread uses in technology in government are for claims and payment processing systems. Governments and their national economies depend on these mission critical administration systems, their accessibility, and their capabilities. In this case study I will show that these massive systems can be developed and incrementally implemented using an agile approach.

This case study describes how the US Department of Veterans Affairs (VA), implemented a large education claims processing solution quickly and with no major technical bugs. The project was a success, but I include some of the criticisms of the rushed operational implementation. The fast implementation of such a large system would not be without some pain, and it is instructive to examine how these problems occurred and how they were tackled.

In this case, I show how an agile approach provides a natural fit for the need for phased implementation where there is a policy directive that must be implemented urgently. This case examines how attitudes at national audit organizations, such as the US Government Accountability Office (GAO), can sometimes inhibit the adoption of agile. It highlights the need for a deeper understanding of agile concepts in the audit community, especially the focus of auditors on the processes used for testing, rather than the practical outcomes achieved.

This success story is the tale of using an agile approach to rapidly and successfully create the operations needed to implement major pieces of related Congressional legislation. Use of the system LTS has supported VA in delivering over $19.3B in educational benefits to over 760,000 Veterans, Warfighters, spouses and children. The number of claims processed has risen from 200,000 applications a year to about one million a year. Over $5bn is now disbursed annually as a result to those who have served their country.

Background

Historically, VA had experienced significant IT development and delivery difficulties. Individual directors at more than 1,000 sites controlled over 97% of the IT budget. Systems and processes could not share information across the department, and management could not be sure that data backups were being carried out.

On May 3, 2006, the home of a Department of Veterans Affairs (VA) data analyst was burglarized, and an employee's personal laptop and external data storage device were stolen. Stored on this equipment were the names, birthdates, and Social Security numbers of approximately 29.3m veteran personnel and their spouses.[40]

A strategic review decided that from 2007 a policy of centralization of IT would be put in place called the "One VA" policy. Its objective was to ensure security and consistency of data and processes across the organization and to centralize IT. [41]

On June 30, 2008 President Bush signed the Veterans Educational Assistance Act ("Post 9-11 GI Bill") into law. This bill added a new "Chapter 33" to a section of the United States Code. The "One VA" policy helped ensure that an integrated approach to implementing the bill could be taken. The law echoed the original 1944 "GI Bill" (officially entitled Servicemen's Readjustment Act) which was intended to support ex-servicemen and women in education and training after their active service in the Second World War was completed. The 2008 bill offered substantial financial support to those eligible, including payment of full state-university fees, housing allowances and book expenses. VA was responsible for implementing the necessary processes and starting to make payments from August 1, 2009 – just 18 months after the Post-9/11 GI Bill was passed into law.

Not only was time of the essence, but the bill was complex. It had intricate support and eligibility requirements, including the right to transfer benefits to dependents, and a special "Yellow Ribbon" program for support for study at private universities. Right from the start, the need to encompass likely changes and additions was obvious. And indeed, even though the bill had bi-partisan support in Congress and the Senate, it has subsequently been amended and changed several times, including a second version to the bill which widened eligibility to members of the National Guard.[42]

VA not only needed a fast approach to developing a solution to processing these claims, they knew that they needed future flexibility for the inevitable new benefits that would need to be paid in years to come.

The "Chapter 33" Solution

VA had to implement new interim operational processes almost immediately, using spreadsheets, and manual workarounds, together with the existing systems for disbursing monies. A project was set up to automate these interim processes in four interim increments, each delivered at the end of each quarter of 2010.[43]

The waterfall project approach could not have catered for the short timescales for full implementation, and would have left the interim processes running for over a year. An agile approach was needed to develop a system so that VA personnel would handle the complexity of the rules that had to be administered. The project would also need to cater for changes to the details of the regulations as they were agreed during 2010. For example, in 2011 the Post-9/11 Veterans Educational Assistance Improvements Act was passed that required a 60 day turnaround time between approval and implementation into production.

The replacement system was called the Chapter 33 Long Term Solution (LTS). The main problem the team faced was that large-scale agile practices needed to produce traditional Government artifacts and be assessed at gate checkpoints. For example, it met the VA's need for formal independent testing of money systems, and traceability of bug fixes. The implementation of the Chapter 33 requirements was one of the first implemented under VA's Program Management Accountability System (PMAS) which required projects to deliver new functionality every six months or less. LTS was planned to deliver a major feature on average every two to three months.

The project developed and implemented the first two of the four releases of the LTS software on March 31, 2010, and June 30, 2010 as planned. The regional processing offices were provided with key automated capabilities to prepare original and amended benefit claims on time. Legislative changes and housing rate adjustments that happened during the development were also incorporated. All new benefits from the start of the 2010 academic year were supported by the new system, and no significant bugs were reported. VA stated that operation was "nearly flawless" and a "stunning and unpredicted success". It stated that:

> "(Although VA had) one of the worst track records in systems development (as amply documented over the years by the VA's Inspector General and the GAO) we have been able to achieve a stunning success"[44]

This was a large project – $84.6m was spent on the first phase, and the GAO congratulated VA for taking an agile approach:

> "VA has demonstrated key agile practices that are essential to
> effectively managing its system development ... the department has
> ensured that teams represent key stakeholders and that specific agile
> roles were fulfilled ... The department has also made progress toward
> demonstrating the three other agile practices – focusing on business
> priorities, delivering functionality in short increments, and inspecting
> and adapting the project as appropriate." [45]

Impact on Operations

The hurried timescales of the new legislation led to staffing challenges.
No-one knew what the take-up by veterans would be. There were even
predictions that service people might leave the forces early to take advantage of the plan. Over 750 new staff members were hired to process the
claims, but this proved inadequate as they were inexperienced. The interim system did not automate many processes, the office space was
inadequate, and staff turnover as a result was high. In the end VA not only
sanctioned overtime for staff, but actually mandated a minimum of 24
hours of overtime per person per month, including weekends.
A contractor was hired to process over 150,000 other education claims and
staff members were reassigned from other functions. [46]

When claims had started to come in, under the interim processes, the
average time to process a claim was over 80 days, against a target of 24
days. The handling of supplemental claims overwhelmed the call-center to
begin with and the GAO was critical of the advice given to applicants and
the handling of emergency payments. [47] Despite these difficulties, in the
first year there was a payment accuracy rate of 96% against a target of
95%. [48]

Problems with Interfaces to Other Systems

You will notice in this and some of the following case studies, that data
conversion, the creation of smooth data links to other systems, and

performance problems cause a lot of problems in technology projects. In this case, the link to the Defense Identity Repository was deployed seven months late, in October 2010, after many problems, but it was deployed. Interfaces are a common factor in delaying many projects, but are an unavoidable fact of life.

A lesson here is that when planning a project, the data conversion programs and interfaces should be among the first modules to be built and tested, not among the last. This ensures that any problems with existing data can be identified and tackled early on, for data usually takes months or even years to be 'cleaned'. For practical reasons, it is very useful in performance testing to have a full sized database available early in the project. And finally, interfaces are complicated, for example an old system may use a longer format for postal addresses than the new one, causing truncation of some lines of information unless special *data cleaning* programs are developed.[49]

Conclusions

VA managed to put in place the operations to cater for a complex, and changing piece of legislation by using an agile approach. The development progressed at a fast pace, however, there were some problems with implementation which provide a lesson for future agile projects.

The operational teething problems highlighted in this case are not unusual for any rushed project. Most of them derive from the use of the interim system before the LTS was phased in. They show the importance of careful planning for business transition to new ways of working. The problems were understandable, given the speed of implementation which was driven by the need to implement support for urgent legislation, and to do it fast. However, the risks associated with the short project timescales need to be managed carefully. The Scrum method pays no specific attention to interfaces, data conversion, and user implementation planning.[50] To make sure that these areas are integrated into a holistic project approach, a service-oriented framework, such as DSDM, can bring value. It covers the need for focus on interfaces to other systems, user training, using agile to develop new business processes, and how to implement a solution smoothly into Business as Usual/operations.[51] Sometimes an agile project must work alongside waterfall projects, or be part of a large waterfall program of work. This can sometimes be an inescapable fact of life. For example, an existing contract with a supplier may have been drawn up as a result of waterfall procurement. In these cases a superstructure of waterfall project management using standards such as ANSI 99-001-2008 or PRINCE2™ may be appropriate. These aspects of project management need to be planned hand-in-hand with technical development so that the technical solution is implemented smoothly. Where large scale business change is required, a program approach may be adopted to ensure that communications management and benefits management are effective. Relevant program management guidance can be found in the guidance issued by the US Project Management Institute (PMI) in its Standard for Program Management. The UK Association for Project Management (APM) and the UK Cabinet Office also provide useful guidance on strategic governance of programs which has a more external focus than the PMI materials and may usefully be used in conjunction with them.[52]

Despite these teething difficulties, which were overcome, the overall program has been seen as a great success. In the four years since 2008, over 745,000 applications have been processed and $19bn disbursed by the new technology. Senator Jim Webb was pleased with the outcome. He recently said that:

> "The Post-9/11 G.I. Bill is the best veterans' educational program in history." [53]

Questions

1. How was such a large, new operation enabled by the "One VA" initiative?

2. The new system was implemented incrementally. In what ways might this have helped or hindered cut-over from the spreadsheets and other office tools that operations had initially used to process each application?

3. Implementation needed to be in short timescales. Was enough thought given to getting operations ready for the size and scale of processing needed and the number of staff members needed?

4. Look at the more detailed description of the phasing in of the new system provided by the GAO (see Endnote 54). What would a big-bang cut-over to the new system have looked like?

5. Read the GAO's report detailing some other implementation problems (see Endnote 55). Could additional measures have been taken to make implementation smoother for emergency payments and to keep operational costs minimized?

Chapter 3

Case Study at the FBI

One of my arguments is that we've got to have stronger engineering in government. It turns out that in the FBI, the number of really good software engineers is limited, like it is in most federal agencies.[56]

Jack Israel,
former FBI Chief Technology Officer

Many organizations need to integrate their activities and create a database of consistent and instantly available information. It seems logical to spend a great deal of time to create a Big Design Up Front (BDUF), and check it thoroughly before starting to develop a solution. However, as this case study shows, that waterfall approach created a culture of procrastination and delay at the FBI that the adoption of the agile approach eventually overcame. It shows how you can use an agile approach to save failing projects – no matter how large.

This chapter analyzes a situation where the use of a prime contractor did not absolve a government from managing its risks – it merely exacerbated them. In cases such as this, it is not only more expensive, but also more risky to rely on hands-off management of the development team. In this case, a bloated $482m project failed to deliver until the FBI took direct control of development and adopted an agile approach. Moreover, with that smaller, smarter team, they started to deliver.

Here I further the argument that audit recommendations, overlarge procurements, and 'best practice' can be major institutional inhibitors to adoption of the agile approach. Governments must address these factors if they are to become agile. This case provides an example where the US Office of Management and Budget (OMB) and GAO initially reinforced the waterfall culture at the FBI bringing about a massive procurement that failed.

At the end of this case study, I provide some thought-provoking questions that encourage you to re-visit the text. I encourage you to get interactive with other readers and *tweet* your thoughts on these questions using the text #APMFG in your message.

Background

In 2000, the FBI was using old technology – the Automated Case Support (ACS) system – and had to rely upon ad-hoc processes to share documents, photos, and other electronic media. The FBI's handling of the Oklahoma City Bombing case between 1995 and 2001 highlighted the deficiencies of the technology.

On May 8, 2001, just one week before the scheduled date of the execution of the bomber, the FBI revealed to the defense attorneys that it had not disclosed over 700 investigative documents to the defendants. The FBI processed a tremendous volume of material and sent it to the Oklahoma Bombing investigation task force, but in many cases, the FBI did not send material or lost it.

The legal process was thrown into turmoil, and a stay of execution of the death sentence of one month was granted. The FBI came under severe criticism and allegations were made that FBI personnel may have intentionally failed to disclose the information. However, an independent investigation showed that the combination of the "antiquated computer system" and "human error" were to blame. The ACS did not support the critical operational processes, it was over complex, and difficult to use.[57]

The Trilogy VCF Project Is Set Up

The FBI set up a project to build a Virtual Case File (VCF) system to replace the old Automated Case Support (ACS) system as its primary investigative application. The goal of the VCF was to reduce agents' reliance on paperwork and to improve efficiency by allowing agents to scan documents, photos, and other electronic media into a secure, centrally available, electronic case file.

The development of the VCF was part of the overall Trilogy program, approved by Congress in November 2000. Trilogy aimed not only to implement the VCF but also to upgrade the FBI's IT hardware and infrastructure. The requirements for the VCF were to be agreed up-front by experts. The FBI was to commission its build in a massive contract, and, when it was ready, it would be implemented in a full-scale big-bang rollout.

It was a classic waterfall project, with an original planned implementation date for May 2004. However, political pressure was applied after the September 2001 attacks, and the FBI made promises of faster deployment. First, the FBI promised completion for June 2003, then December 2002, and finally (after receiving $78 million of supplemental funding on top of the original $379m) for July 2002 at a cost of $458m.

The Trilogy VCF Plans Start to Unravel

The classic symptoms of waterfall project failure started to reveal themselves. Project plans were found to be unrealistic, and the oversight of project spend was inadequate. Although total spend was being tracked, it was not possible to tell whether the project was over or under budget. However, it became obvious that the project would not meet its accelerated deadlines. A commitment to using unproven *thin client* technology was made, and the design for it to allow web-like access to a central case-management system was deeply flawed. Up-front contracts with suppliers bound the project to this technology. The first step was to be the web-enablement of ACS. In parallel, and before the technology could be proven, both the hardware upgrade and the new functions made great use of thin-client technology. Unfortunately, the project team had not fully explored the security and performance requirements with the users. As these became evident, a total re-write of the programs was required.

Even with the additional $78m of funds, the project missed its July 2002 milestone. Audit reports took a traditional view of what was wrong: more discipline was required. If only processes for tracking and oversight of costs could be made tighter and more detailed. If only more planning and scheduling could be carried out. If only the business requirements had been identified in more detail at the beginning....

The thinking of the auditors was that more detail and planning would have averted the problems. It did not occur to them that over-detailed planning without sufficient real-world feedback was a cause of failure.

The FBI appointed a new Trilogy project executive, hoping that he would recover the Trilogy project using more "structured oversight". Therefore, the July 2002 deadline then was slipped from October 2002, to March 2003 and then to June 2004.[58]

The Trilogy VCF Project Is Abandoned

Unfortunately, the Trilogy project failed to deliver the VCF and $170m was written off when the project was canceled in 2005 after having only completed the more straightforward tasks of hardware and network upgrade.[59]

Auditors applied a waterfall perspective in analyzing why the project failed. Their comments pursued the line of thought that if more detail had been planned upfront, with a stricter set of waterfall processes, then failure would not have occurred. Examples of their conclusions included many possible reasons for the failure:

> "(The project had) poorly defined design requirements, a lack of mature management processes, high management turnover, poor oversight, and significant turnover of project management. 15 different key IT managers over the course of its life, including 10 individuals serving as project managers for various aspects of Trilogy ... and five different Chief Information Officers ... and a lack of a mature

> Enterprise Architecture … a lack of specific completion milestones, review points, and no penalties (for suppliers) if milestones were not met." [60]

However, the one factor that the auditors did not consider was whether even more upfront planning and design could fix a broken waterfall model.

The Second Attempt – the Sentinel Project

In 2005, the FBI was still relying on its increasingly outdated ACS case management system and complicated manual procedures. Therefore, plans were drawn up for a new project to be called Sentinel. The aim, as with the canceled Trilogy VCF project, was to create a web-enabled case management system and to develop it using a waterfall approach based on a Big Design Up-Front. Just as with the previous Trilogy VCF project, Sentinel would take years to develop. Therefore, in the meantime, the users would be given web-based screens to hide the old, difficult to understand mainframe screens. Behind the scenes, data would still be processed by the old ACS system. Despite the new web-based user interface, and a better search facility, no new data capture or sharing functions would be added until the whole VCF was ready.

The project paid very little attention up to this point to planning the necessary changes in business processes to take advantages of the new system. Phase One had been simply the replacement of the displays on the ageing ACS with more user-friendly screens – no significant new functions were to be introduced – it was mainly a like-for-like replacement of features. Jack Israel, the Chief Technology Officer at the time explains that:

> Some called it *lipstick on a pig* because (the screens just) … allowed agents to interact with … ACS's functionality through a Web browser. It was expensive lipstick, about $60m worth.[61]

Sentinel was to be implemented in four overlapping phases: each 12-18 months long, with the last phase to be completed by 2009: [62]

- ◆ Phase one to reach completion in April 2007 to provide a web based portal to the ACS (as previously attempted in the abandoned Trilogy VCF project) and some rudimentary case management and indexing facilities

- ◆ Phase two to implement document management with an electronic records repository with some workflow tool support to ensure correct review and approval

- ◆ Phase three to provide an improved search facility across all the data

- ◆ Phase four to complete the task tracking and reporting functions and transfer data from the ACS and turn it off.

In addition to developing its Sentinel case management system, the FBI also led the inter-agency Federal Investigative Case Management System (FICMS) initiative to ensure the sharing of case management data across agencies. The need for these interfaces, just as with the VA, would cause problems. Upfront work had not thrashed out the potential problems.[63]

However, the auditors were hopeful that the new Sentinel project would address previous attempts to replace ACS with an up-to-date case management system. They felt that the institution of the waterfall lifecycle described in a "Life Cycle Management Directive" would reduce risks. More detailed design and planning would occur up-front, with a comprehensive *enterprise architecture* acting as a detailed blueprint for the future IT environment.[64] The contract was based on a standard National Institutes of Health contract commonly used in US government procurement. The process required the government to assess the suppliers' proposals against theoretical statements of work and project schedules. This type of contract had "proved problematic under Trilogy". Then, the FBI had rewarded the supplier for meeting goals in project management, cost management, meeting the schedule, and technical performance, not for flexibility, or for the achievement of business benefits.

On March 16, 2006, the FBI awarded a contract to Lockheed Martin Services to develop the Sentinel system by December 2009. The total project budget was $425m, made up of a cost of $305m for Lockheed Martin and $120m for the FBI to run a massive *program office* to carry out detailed and prescriptive oversight of the work.[65]

Project control was setup in a traditional waterfall fashion. The specification was fixed at the beginning and spend was allowed to vary. The initial estimates could not be validated, so a contingency of 15 percent overrun in costs was allowed for. The project manager was optimistic and considered this more than adequate since "based on his experience, an 11 percent reserve would be adequate".[66] There was considerable confidence that risks could be averted. So much so, that four of the top five project risks had no contingency plan. It was assumed that little could go wrong, even though the project schedule was based on an early, hypothetical schedule of "dictated milestones" created by the FBI during the procurement – not by Lockheed Martin who actually had to carry out the development work.[67]

The first phase of Sentinel delivered two months late in June 2007 did provide what seemed like adequate "lipstick on the pig". However, it lacked 57 promised features, such as the ability to open and close cases. The project had not carried out the planned data cleansing activities. The data on ACS was still in a mess, and the team had not yet migrated it over into a test database. This was a key task that would have flushed out the technical difficulties in advance of phase two. Despite this, the FBI paid Lockheed Martin as if the phase was 100% complete.[68]

After a few months or so of using the phase one system, some users were beginning to abandon its use. There were many features which had not yet been catered for (such as opening and closing cases), and many users had switched back to using the old system. Usage had declined by 25% in the six months since implementation.

An audit report, issued at this time, however, was optimistic, stating that:

> "The FBI has made considerable progress in establishing controls and processes required to adequately manage a major IT development project such as Sentinel and to bring it to a successful conclusion – if the processes are followed and controls are implemented as intended." [69]

The New CIO Breaks Sentinel into Phases

In December 2008, Chad Fulgham was appointed as the new CIO. He came from Lehman Brothers, and brought a business mentality with him that favored quick results rather than drawn out planning.[70] Fulgham decided to carry out a strategic replanning. Phase One had taken over a year before the first output – expectations now changed, and he now planned for outputs every 3-6 months.[71] The FBI had initiated a Business Process Reengineering (BPR) effort in 2005, but the Sentinel project had not yet taken this work into account. Fulgham now incorporated these changes to ensure that Sentinel would meet the organization's changing needs.[72]

As work started on Phase Two, Fulgham was publically optimistic about progress, claiming that the four increments of phase two constituted an agile approach:

> "This more flexible and agile approach was thoughtfully planned, and further reduces the risk by shifting more of the requirements forward into the program's development.

> "Phase two is now more than halfway complete, and is on schedule and within cost. It will also deliver administrative case management services well ahead of the original schedule.

> "Among the original goals of the Sentinel program were agility, and the ability to make adjustments during the multi-phase, four-year period – both to account for expected advances in technology and to implement lessons learned along the way. By any measure, the *replant* has made Sentinel stronger and more responsive to the needs of users – those FBI employees who rely on cutting-edge technology to help keep America safe." [73]

The Project Does Not Deliver Iteratively

The replanning effort prior to starting phase two had created a gap in the action. Phase One had been completed in June 2007 and Lockheed Martin was only given permission to proceed four months later. The end date for the whole project now had to slip by six months to June 2010, and projected costs had increased by $30m.

Phase Two of Sentinel did not go according to plan. As functions were delivered, the users found that they did not meet their requirements, and the technical approach needed to be reworked again. The end-date of phase two slipped, the cost increased by $18m, and the security and authentication functions were not delivered. Because the new system required a better network infrastructure, some users had reported that it could take up to ½ hour just to login to the system, so an additional $39m was spent to improve and streamline the network. The end-date of the Sentinel project now slipped by another three months to September 2010.[74]

A rigid and hierarchical project reporting structure called a Project Management Office (PMO) had been setup. It was large, unwieldy, and exhibited a huge *optimism bias* in its status reporting. Its bloated $120m budget was spent on inexperienced project managers with general government administration backgrounds. They had received basic training, but had little or no background in technology development. Throughout the project, the reports produced by this PMO, despite being detailed and full of statistics, never reported even one sub-project as being in trouble, even as the project was obviously out of control.[75] As late as December 2009 the FBI was still "expecting to provide capabilities to users sooner than originally planned".[76]

Users rejected Segment 3 of phase two during testing, even though it was theoretically compliant with the FBI's specifications. They required a complete redesign of the screens. Despite these problems, the FBI Project Management Office (PMO) remained optimistic with project status reports showing "a horizontal thermometer, which expressed the project's overall status in red, yellow, or green. From meeting to meeting, the temperature never changed—it was always yellow, trending toward green." [77]

However, the more difficult tasks were left to the end. Important tasks, such as developing the migration processes, were left until fourth and final segment of phase two. Migration was known to be a key problem. Names, addresses, and phone numbers in the old ACS system did not match the format specified in Sentinel's database. In the end, the data migration processes and interfaces took two years to create, and when delivered in 2010 they were still not adequate.[78]

Sentinel Phase Two Is Stopped

Then on March 3, 2010, the FBI decided to reject the deliverables from the fourth and final segment of phase two because of continuing usability, performance, and quality problems. The FBI issued an order to Lockheed Martin to stop development on future phases until the problems were resolved. The FBI could now not be sure that the system would meet user requirements, and could not agree with Lockheed Martin how the project was to proceed. The viability of the September 2010 end-date was called into question.[79]

Not only were some of the essential functions still missing, there were also significant performance issues. These were not just due to poor network infrastructure, but also to poor quality in the coding of the software. In some cases, users could create and use fake identities when signing documents electronically.[80]

In July 2010, more functions were delivered to FBI agents to use, but the system still only had the capability to process four of the 18 forms, and these only partially.

Because of Sentinel's delays and cost increases, in July 2010 the FBI issued a complete stop-work order.[81]

An independent report estimated that completing Sentinel under the current development approach would cost at least an additional $351m on top of the $405m already spent, and take another six years. In addition, the risks of working to an outdated specification now loomed. Some of the redesigned BPR processes were now six years old, technology had moved on, and there had been significant changes to the FBI's work processes that made them outmoded.

The Sentinel system that had been implemented so far was little used by FBI staff. Where it was, it merely resulted in duplication of effort, because data still had to be double-keyed into the ACS. Confidence in the system was so low that its use was officially optional. Between July and August 2010, only 132 new cases were generated in the Sentinel system. This was less than 1% of the 14,831 cases entered into the ACS in the same period.[82]

By now, FBI agents should have had a case management system with workflows for managing their work – instead they were continuing with the same consuming paper-based case management processes that had threatened the Oklahoma Bombing judicial process. The promise of electronic information sharing both within the FBI and to and from other federal agencies to "connect the dots" between cases and suspects had not been realized.[83]

Sentinel Recovers Using Agile Approach

In September 2010, the FBI announced that it would take direct management of the development of Sentinel and use an agile project approach:

> "The FBI made a difficult but sensible decision to develop an alternative plan for completing Sentinel. We examined several options in detail, and selected an approach based on what is known as "agile development" method. This approach will reduce our reliance on traditional contractors and allow for cost-savings by dealing directly with product experts." [84]

The migration of the 8.3m live, cold, and closed cases from ACS to the Sentinel database was in doubt. If it did not work, then ACS would have to remain alive for many years, and FBI agents would have to work with two separate case management systems at the same time. An automated facility to "join the dots" between new and cold cases would not exist.[85]

The existing requirements were analyzed, prioritized, and sequenced to focus on the most valuable requirements with the greatest benefits to agents and analysts.[86]

Within a month, the FBI took direct control of development,

removed all Lockheed Martin personnel from development work on the project, and started to supervise the sub-contractors directly. Fulgham reduced it from over 125 heads to a team of 55.[87]

The project adopted the Scrum Method, with a *Scrum Master* coordinating the development team. This is a role different from that of a project manager in a waterfall project. The Scrum Master leads and enables the team, rather than 'managing' it. They empower a self-organizing team, rather than imposing structure on it.

The original, monolithic requirements document was modularized into 670 separate user stories. The team prioritized each user story in a *product backlog*, each one describing just one end-to-end process that the system needed to do.

Work now started to develop these user stories incrementally. Each cycle of work (or sprint) was two weeks long. At the end of every sprint, all testing had to be complete. The software had to be demonstrated to project stakeholders, and ready for deployment to users if required. [88] 21 sprints were planned to develop all the user stories. Although there was concern that a continual churn of changes could ensue, the brevity of the 10-day sprints kept the danger of uncontrolled changes to what the FBI called "just 9 days of risk". Previously, arguments over change control and *scope creep* took up much more time and effort than that.

At the start of each sprint, the development team identified which stories they were to develop during that sprint – these formed a work plan called the *sprint backlog*. At the end of each sprint, regardless of whether all work was complete, the development team had to test and demonstrate the system. The team could only claim those stories that passed tests as completed. Where a test failed, that user story was placed onto the product backlog for rescheduling into the next or some other future sprint.[89]

The amount of work required to develop each user story was initially estimated as a number of *story points*. These story points were a relative measure of difficulty and size. As work progressed, the team could see how fast they were working, and could start to *calibrate* their efficiency. After a few sprints, it became possible to forecast the rough timescales and start to plan the dates for incremental implementation. This was to be in two increments, with about half the user stories implemented in

September 2011 and the rest in November.

However, concerns were raised about the first implementation being near to the tenth anniversary of 9/11 – potentially a time of heightened security. Therefore, the team carried out additional testing which showed that although Sentinel now had adequate functionality and usability, there were still concerns about its performance and availability. The implementation was then planned to be phased in alongside the standard five-year refresh of computer hardware.[90]

In the *full year to* 2011 (FY 2011) only 52% of the much reduced agile development budget of $32.6m had been spent to build 88% of the system.[91] Jack Israel later commented on this success:

> "Agile is not just a method or a process, it's a way of being. You don't *do* agile. You *are* agile. The FBI has arranged to loan their Scrum Master to other teams to get them trained. Increased transparency has kept stakeholders in sync. Further, stakeholders would modify their expectations, based on the increased visibility of the process." [92]

By June 2012, the revised technical targets had been met, and two releases had been achieved. There was a substantial increase in information sharing of case management information and a resolution of IT problems. $46m had been spent on making progress over the last 12 months, and most importantly, agents were now using the system on real cases. 13,268 agents created 623 documents and made 92,546 searches in the first quarter 2012, against target of 11,000, 550 and 77,000 respectively. The key operational target of 13,200 leads per quarter in the full year 2012 was missed by a whisker (1% short of target).[93]

In the first release, seven functional areas had now gone live, including allowing different user roles, storing attachments for sharing, and automatic routing, workflow and notifications of urgent actions needed on cases. The second release was a fully functional pilot of more functions at selected FBI field offices.[94] User feedback was positive, and full Operational Capability was achieved in May 2012. We will not know the actual business benefits from the new operational processes until the new Sentinel system beds in after the final user of ACS logs off in 2013.[95]

Conclusions

The cost of the initial failed Trilogy VCF project was $170m. The cost of the written off work of Phase 1 and 2 of Sentinel up to the firing of Lockheed Martin was $427m.

The total spend of these failed attempts to replace the ACS system was $597m and wasted 10 years. The agile project, which is now delivering a solution, will only cost $114m for a three-year long project.[96]

Questions

1. The original Trilogy program comprised of three projects: a hardware upgrade, an infrastructure upgrade, and the development of the VCF case management facility. Of these three projects, which seems the most amenable to fixed-price tendering and which was the most likely to benefit from an agile approach?

2. A major criticism of the Trilogy VCF Project was that it was deficient in detailed monitoring of spend versus budget and that it lacked a detailed architecture before work started. These deficiencies were supposedly addressed at set-up for the subsequent Sentinel project. Were these deficiencies really of crucial significance in the failure of the Trilogy VCF project?

3. The FBI originally planned delivery of Sentinel in four overlapping phases. However, at the end of Phase One the start of the next phase was delayed to allow more time for detailed re-planning. Did this delay to plan in more detail reduce the risk of failure?

4. Because of the re-planning, a more incremental approach was agreed to the delivery of Phase Two in four segments. Due to technical difficulties, the implementation dates for these four segments were allowed to slip. Could the use of technical

prototypes and practical targeted pilot usage have clarified the probability of success and the technical fault-lines at an earlier stage?

5. In 2010, the FBI decided to take on the risks of delivery from Lockheed Martin and manage the project directly using agile. Were overall risks actually increased by this bold step?

Chapter 4

Case Study in Queensland, Australia

The Australian Public Service must provide flexible, agile responses to changing realities and government priorities.[97]

Kevin Rudd
Prime Minister, Australia

One argument of this book is that to be agile, governments need to build up their own technical capabilities. They should stop attempting to sub-contract entire waterfall technology developments.

This case study shows how the State of Queensland in Australia has adopted the Scrum method for some projects. It demonstrates how this internal capability can be nurtured, and also shows how agile capabilities are resilient to changes in organization and re-deployment of staff. Later in the book this success is contrasted to the spectacular £1.2bn collapse of a payroll project in another organization in the same state (see page 231).

Background

In 2005, the Minister for Public Works in the State of Queensland, Australia, announced an AU$235m four year program to provide a totally

43

new approach to the provision of social housing.[98]

Queensland has the most dispersed population in Australia. Over 4 million people live in 10 cities, and there are over 70 local authorities. In 2005 the Department of Housing was assisting 240,000 families every year through various programs. But in recent years, affordable private house rentals had become scarce, and there had been significant increases in housing prices. Over 35,000 families were on the waiting list for public housing. Provision of public housing up to that point had been on a first-come, first-served policy. A simple wait-list of applicants for public housing was maintained, and as housing became available it was offered to those who had been waiting longest.

The new policy was for all social housing to be provided through one social housing system. It required the implementation of a priority-based approach. After making an application, and being interviewed, each applicant was assessed into one of four priority bands: *very high*, *high*, *medium* and *low*.

Under this "One Social Housing Policy", housing assistance was to be targeted to people most in need of help, using an integrated register and one common assessment system. The key success factors were that the eligibility and allocation rules had to be consistent across the State, and that existing practices had to be streamlined to improve services.[99]

The Housing Needs Assessment (HNA) Project

Implementation of the processes had to be not just complete within four years, but also all the wrinkles smoothed out. The detail of the new regulations was unclear – many of the mechanisms proposed for implementation were immature. A new housing wait-list management process was planned, and it would require support from a Housing Needs Assessment (HNA) system. It soon became evident that this would be needed urgently and it would be a complex system.

The IT department was based in Brisbane. This small city, the capitol of the State of Queensland, boasts a mild climate and a stable and skilled

IT workforce. It soon became evident that the standard internal waterfall lifecycle would hamper development because of its waterfall nature. Agreement of the detailed BDUF design would be needed before development work could proceed. However the design would not be easy to agree before the practicalities of the solution could be envisaged.

The necessary technical skills existed within the IT department, but without a clear project mandate and documented requirements work on a waterfall project could not start. The existing waterfall practices could not solve this *chicken-and-egg* situation. Which should come first: the design work or the development of a working system? This impasse threatened to derail the politically important switch from a command operation of public housing supply to one based on allocation of scarce resources based on need.

Adrian Royce was working in the IT department and had recently become aware of agile concepts. He proposed that development should adopt the Scrum method and should progress in a series of incremental deliveries. The project should be a collaborative approach, closely involving policy-makers to agree practical new regulations and operational processes.

The work progressed in one month 'Sprints', and at the end of each an increment of the solution was delivered for discussion. A product backlog of wait-list functions was developed, and as requirements became clearer the work accelerated. In Royce's words "The stakeholders knew what they wanted – but not what they needed".

HNA comprised of three main modules: wait-list management, eligibility scoring and links to legacy systems. HNA was based on a variety of new Internet technologies which were adopted at the same time as the team started to use the Scrum method. The team found that the practical nature of Scrum helped them get to grips with the new technology, and work started to accelerate. As they gained confidence, the team became more multi-disciplinary: it grew from 13 to a peak of 68 staff members, comprised of 23 technical staff members and 45 stakeholder staff members.

There was a continuing need for traditional audit and assurance, especially for the housing process that required transparency and fairness of operation. The Queensland Government Chief Information Officer (CIO) mandates the use of the PRINCE2 project process standard for project management. The team worked with the Project Investment Office to track the overall Business Case and report into the PRINCE2 reporting structures. Independent project health checks were carried out without disrupting the team's progress.[100]

The team responded to these demands by ensuring that documentation was up to date at the end of each sprint, and that integration tests were signed-off to standard. The use of 'traditional' approaches to managing the overall project was not seen as problematical to the team.

For example, the mandatory list of outputs expected from the project was defined in a PRINCE2 Project Initiation Document (PID) in the form of a Product Breakdown Structure (PBS). This list of expected outputs then simply became the basis for organizing the product backlog and the prioritization of the work of the three teams. The idea of breaking down the work hierarchically helped in deciding which of the three Scrum teams would be allocated which modules to work on. A key stage in this breakdown is the definition of what constituted acceptable delivery – the Scrum concept of defining what is meant by *done* for each increment. Internal Audit carried out checks that testing had been rigorous and that the products met these formal definitions of quality.

Each sprint of the project was then simply mapped onto each PRINCE2 *stage* of the overall project, which included the necessary BPR activities. The project was governed by a Project Board which signed-off each sprint, and agreed the overall product backlog priorities. A *Scrum of Scrums* comprising the User Project Manager and the Scrum Masters of the three teams used these priorities to co-ordinate each work stream. At the lowest level, each team self-organized its activities, holding *stand-up* meetings at the start of each day to plan day-to-day work, discuss issues, and agree the most efficient way of meeting the overall goals for each sprint.

Issues that could not be resolved via the daily stand-ups and the Scrum of Scrums were recorded as project issues for escalation using a standard PRINCE2 departmental issue management process. The team found that reporting progress against expected budgets was well facilitated by this approach, allowed each Scrum team the room for manoeuver while still complying with the mandated project management approach.

The team found that they did not need complex support tools for the Scrum method, most planning was done on whiteboards, with the product backlog being maintained on spreadsheets.

A Successful Outcome

A Government review carried out in 2008, at the mid-stage of the new project found that:

> "The initiative has delivered successful outcomes to date in terms of the mechanisms and processes put into place to introduce new services, improve co-ordination and increase access and service quality … The Government acknowledges the complexity and challenge involved in designing, developing and implementing the initiative … The process for rolling-out the initiative and getting services functional have progressed extremely well." [101]

Areas of concern were focused on the need for more 'capacity building' (in other words training and staff development) and on:

> "(The problems of success where the) latent demand for services, previously unmet or unarticulated, may now have been unplugged." [102]

The key to success in delivering the technology here was concentrating on making sure that:

- ♦ Documentation was relevant and up to date (rather than comprehensive, but incomprehensible)

- ♦ Regular, incremental delivery of the solution to demonstrate the emerging solution to stakeholders (rather than asking for sign-off of a 'frozen' paper specification before work started)

- ♦ Focus on the correctness of the end-product (rather than the adherence to the processes used in development)

♦ Gaining the confidence of stakeholders was obtained by delivering the essential functions on time (rather than planning supplementary features and then delivering late)

♦ Recognizing the role of a Scrum Master as being one of facilitating the self-organization of a team (rather than the expectation that a project manager will tell the team what to do and how to do it).

Some of the challenges that were overcome were:

♦ Delivery in the short, four week increments was new for the organization. Business analysts now had to build requirements incrementally, rather than producing detailed requirements specifications up front.

♦ Everyone had to lift their game to deliver the outcomes to meet the expectations and intensity of each sprint. All team members had to become committed to team success rather than work as individuals.

♦ The perception that agile practices increase risk had to be overcome. Project Managers were used to planning for every possible contingency before the project begins rather than tackling the highest priority risks head on early in development.

Royce relates that:

> "Top management had expected a classic 'contract' with the team based on a fixed timescale and list of requirements. But as work progressed this understanding of project management changed so as to focus initially on cracking the main technical issues upfront, such as security. We then kept a continuous emphasis on delivering business value early, even if that meant delaying or sacrificing features of less value."

A new initiative commenced, to improve the IT and Scrum skills of government staff and phase out the use of independent contractors.

Growing importance was placed on staff morale and satisfaction. A retention rate of 100% was achieved by staff in the IT department using the Scrum method during this period.

By 2009 the Housing Department had implemented over 30 agile projects. And Adrian Royce was awarded the prestigious Director General's Award in "Recognition of excellence in innovation and improvement".

Subsequent Adoption of Agile at DERM

Queensland is the home to six UNESCO World Heritage listed preservation areas – including the 1,600 mile long Great Barrier Reef.

In 2010 Adrian Royce moved from Housing to the Department of Environment and Resource Management (DERM). This department had responsibility for conservation and management of Queensland's environment and natural resources. It had an IT department three times the size of that of the Housing Department, with a far greater variety of existing, legacy systems.

Royce's role was to act as a coach to help the department adopt the agile approach. The Housing Department had applied agile to new systems development, but DERM had the challenge not only of developing new systems using agile, but also of maintaining and incrementally upgrading their legacy systems. For this Royce has been using complementary *lean* approaches. Each team is free to use its own approach to decision making (such as post-it notes, whiteboards etc.), but at a higher level project issues are tracked using a specialized tool (JIRA) which ensures consistency of reporting and makes amalgamation of an overall management dashboard much smoother. The philosophy of lean approaches, which aim to incrementally improve operations through measurement and feedback, is complimentary to agile approaches, which aim to do the same for development work.

As with the Housing Department, DERM created a hybrid set of governance processes using the PRINCE2 project process standards as a wrapper around agile processes. These documents are agreed between a *Project Executive* who acts as chair of the project board, and is the 'customer' representative, and with the manager of the IT department who acts as a 'supplier' representative. Three other roles support the Project Executive and form the Project Board to whom the Scrum Master/Team Leader reports progress at the end of every sprint:

- ◆ The *Project Manager* (who manages the project on a day-to-day basis for the Project Board)

- ◆ The *Senior User* (who ensures that the products meet user requirements)

- ◆ The *Senior Supplier* (who ensures that the development team meet quality and process standards)

Approvals are needed from three additional governance roles before the project can proceed:

- ◆ Senior Management Board – Directors of IT

- ◆ Executive Management Committee – General Managers across the department

- ◆ Strategic Development and Implementation Committee, chaired by the Director General, and selected General Managers.

Particular emphasis is placed on agreeing how the solution will be delivered and tested. For example, will temporary test computers be required? Is there recognition that development team testing will be supplemented by separate, independent user testing in the case of money systems? Will testing be automated as much as possible to help make re-testing of changed modules fast and efficient? And most importantly: how will continuous integration be achieved so that 'putting the system together' will not be left until the last moment?

Although the agile teams at DERM were self-organizing, they still worked to an overview system architecture to ensure that systems performed well, and were easy to maintain. Building the technical capacity of the individuals and the department as a whole was a key to success. Comments on the system design and aspects of the team's internal thinking in designing certain features were captured in a shared knowledgebase.

Other formal elements of project management, such as the running of a documented *risk register* were also implemented alongside the Scrum team concepts.

As in any Scrum project, each phase of the project was divided into a number of sprints, each starting with a face-to-face planning meeting in Brisbane between the stakeholders from around the State, and the central development team to discuss deliverables for the up-coming sprint. Then the team worked for about a month with daily sprint planning and estimation sessions, sprint reviews and demonstrations to stakeholder. Each sprint was not complete until an integration build was tested and accepted, and minimum documentation (including user and technical documentation) was complete. A 'retrospective' was held at the end of each sprint for the team to discuss how things could have gone smoother, and to agree improvements in their working for the next sprint.

Before any increment went into live use, agreed clean-up activities and formal User Acceptance Testing (UAT) took place with a formal handover 'ceremony' to those responsible for maintaining the running solution. An example output was the StrandNet system which tracks the stranding of marine animals directly input by registered marine agencies, such as Sea World along the 5,100 mile Queensland coastline.

Conclusions

Before its responsibilities were transferred elsewhere in 2012, all new projects at DERM were running Scrum teams and 80% of development teams had adopted agile practices. In 2012 DERM's responsibilities were split and the team dispersed into separate departments. However, the agile skills built up at DERM have not been lost. Because agile does not rely upon a set of rigidly defined processes, when the staff members were reassigned, they took their agile approach with them across into other State departments. The devolved nature of agile approaches creates resilience in skills capacity in the face of organizational changes. Conversely, waterfall approaches which depend on specialists working in teams working in independent silos create brittle organizations that cannot flex and change.

Questions

1. What factors enabled the State of Queensland to develop the HNA system using its own staff members?

2. The Housing Department and DERM both used formal processes as a wrapper to govern agile projects. What strengths and weaknesses do you see in this approach?

3. How can resilience be built into an internal agile capability so that organizational mergers and splits do not degrade that capability?

4. Compare and contrast the agile success stories in this chapter with the description of the big-bang payroll implementation at Queensland Health on page 231. Refer to the report of the Australian Auditor General in this endnote.[103]

5. Could you take advantage of organizational change to identify pockets of excellence and spread agile capabilities?

Chapter 5

Case Study at the UK Met Office

> *Most of us have been frustrated at some time or other by processes or paperwork getting in the way of what the business needs ... We need to strike the right balance. I ask all those involved in project management to use ... the basic disciplines for 'just enough' project management.* [104]

Alan Sheperd
Director, Met Office

The Met Office has combined different aspects of best practice guidance from traditional project management standards, the DSDM framework, the Scrum method and XP techniques. This case study examines which parts of the guidance they found useful and how the hybrid adoption of this best practice led to success.

Background

The UK Met Office provides national weather forecasts, and a variety of commercial services to organizations as diverse as the BBC and super-markets. Among its many roles, it also acts as the World Area Forecast

Centre for the Northern Hemisphere, providing critical weather to the aviation industry (its counterpart in Washington covers the Southern Hemisphere).

Its supercomputer capacity is one of the largest in Europe, carrying out 720 trillion operations a second (equal to 40,000 PCs). The amount of data handled is enormous, and because the weather does not stop, neither does the continuous flow of weather data. Currently, about 20 terabytes of data gushes out every day. To get an idea of the scale, that is 20 million million characters (or bytes) of information a day. This has to be stored somewhere else before the supercomputer's own memory banks overflow. A data ingest system manages the flow of data, indexing it before storing it away on long-term disk or tape storage that needs to be easily accessible to meteorological staff for forecasting and research purposes.

In 2007 the data storage system was running out of space and requirements for faster processing and greater storage capacity were becoming urgent. A project ran from March 2006 to November 2010 to upgrade the hardware. During this time, little progress was made in designing and building an adequate data ingest system, and the need for a replacement was becoming urgent.

The MOOSE Data Ingest Project

In 2009, with time running out, the Met Office decided to use the agile approach to replace the old data ingest system. The Met Office Operational Storage Environment (MOOSE) project was set up, and a replacement system was incrementally phased in over the next 24 months.

The team started by using the Enough Design Up Front (EDUF) approach to identify an overall architecture, and to divide up the system into *chunks* for delivery. Each chunk comprised of small modules, or *units*. Every time a unit was created, or an existing one was altered, it, and its associated *test data* had to be checked into the central *configuration management system*. This acted as a filing system, keeping each version of the code that had been written and its associated unit test data together. The system automatically re-ran the unit tests every time a change occurred, flagging each unit as being in either *green* or *red* status. Automatic *integration tests* ran periodically to report on any compatibility problems. This meant that the team leader had immediate overall visibility of progress and any interface problems.

Other software tools produced statistics on the comprehensiveness of the tests. After all the unit and integration tests were run, it identified which portions of the code were not being exercised by the unit-tests and reported these to the team leader, allowing the team to ensure that all parts of the software had been subjected to rigorous testing.

The team had about six staff members and an agile coach/team leader. They built the system in four to six week increments, phasing in the new MOOSE data ingest software with minimal disruption of day-to-day operations. The phased approach allowed the old system to be retired early, saving about £1m a year.

They followed many XP techniques, which were seen by staff members just *good practice* not *extreme*. For example, the cost and delays associated with having a separate test team was avoided, because testing was being carried out incrementally every time a unit was checked in.

Bringing PRINCE2, DSDM and XP Concepts Together

The idea that the DSDM framework can be successfully used as a *wrapper* around Scrum to make it more accessible to project and organizational stakeholders was the approach taken recently at the UK Met Office. It had created an approach internally called *just enough project management*. This consisted of 21 ground rules distilled from the essential aspects of best practice from PRINCE2 supported by a diagnostic questionnaire to assess the suitability of agile, and DSDM specifically for each project.[105]

They decided which techniques suited their culture and technical needs. For example, not much use was made of the XP concept of pair programming. They found that peer reviewing and structured walk-throughs worked well. The co-location of users was not possible, so the practice of holding a daily stand-up meeting was vital. It brought many of the benefits of face-to-face working, but this did mean that an electronic work tracking system was used rather than the more instantly visual wallboard showing progress and the status of issues.

Just Using the Essential Tools

Open Source software tools were used by the team to support their work:

- ◆ The Trac software tool was used to plan and track progress, and maintain the product backlog. It produced statistics providing the input to plot *burn-down charts*, which graphically illustrated the rate at which product features were being programmed.

- ◆ The CruiseControl software tool was used to provide support for continuous integration. These open source tools were found to be good quality, being subject to intense scrutiny by peers of experts on the Internet.

Although some people expressed concerns about the use of free software rather than branded software, it was easier to allay IT Security concerns about Open Source software than it would have been to get a budget approved and arrange the procurement of expensive proprietary tools. As no licenses were required, there were no problems funding more licenses when new staff members joined the team.

Conclusions

The Met Office faced a problem with the age of its old data storage system, and the data ingest system that fed it. Time was running out. A new approach to *light* control of teams with just the essential controls for management rigor was used to govern the MOOSE data ingest replacement system project. With *just enough project management* in place, the team adopted DSDM as a method that would supply the necessary project controls, and XP and Scrum-like techniques for day-to-day working.

The team did not use expensive, large-scale tools. They adopted free open source tools as and when they needed them. Specifically to support the test driven development approach they had adopted – no new or changed piece of software could be submitted that did not pass its tests. This ensured continual feedback on the real rate of progress since the quality of each piece of software was transparent and up to date.

Questions

1. What formal project processes do you work with that you find useful? Do others find them less useful? Is the time spent negotiating over their use worthwhile?

2. Read more about PRINCE2, DSDM, Scrum, and XP (see Endnote 106). Identify where these four major pieces of best practice overlap. For each area of overlap, propose how you would synthesize a hybrid 'just enough' approach. Are there any areas of these pieces of guidance material that you think go beyond 'just enough'?

Part II

The 9 Agile Leadership Behaviors

On February 11-13, 2001, at The Lodge at Snowbird ski resort in the Wasatch mountains of Utah, seventeen people met to talk, ski, relax, and try to find common ground and, of course, to eat. What emerged was the Agile Software Development Manifesto.

Jim Highsmith, Agile Alliance

This part of the book takes a detailed look at the 2001 the Agile Manifesto and its supporting principles. The Agile Manifesto is presented in Table 1 overleaf.

In the weeks after the Manifesto was signed, 12 related Agile Manifesto Principles were developed focused on the essential needs of agile teams to run themselves effectively from the process perspective of the development team members.

What I propose in this part of the book are 9 Agile Leadership Behaviors which support and enable these principles. These behaviors focus on the essential needs of the project to be run from a leadership perspective (see Figure 4 on page 61).

These leadership behaviors are discussed one by one from Chapter 7 onwards. They are presented in Table 2 alongside the related 12 Agile Manifesto Principles that they enable.

Table 1: The Agile Manifesto (reproduced from agilemanifesto.org)

We are uncovering better ways of developing software by doing it and helping others do it.

Through this work we have come to value:

individuals and interactions	over	processes and tools
working software	over	comprehensive documentation
customer collaboration	over	contract negotiation
responding to change	over	following a plan

That is, while there is value in the items on the right,
we value the items on the left more.

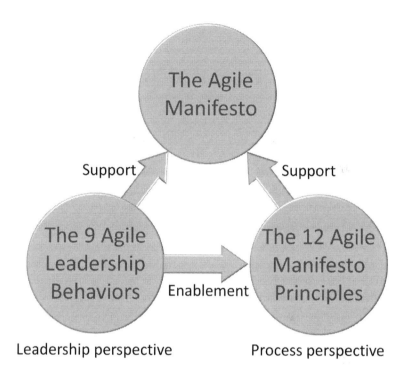

Figure 4: The Proposed 9 Agile Leadership Behaviors Enable and
Support Agile Success

Table 2:   How the 9 Agile Leadership Behaviors are related to the 12
           Principles of the Agile Manifesto

9 Agile Leadership Behaviors	The 12 Agile Manifesto Principles they enable
1. Satisfy the customer	Our highest priority is to satisfy the customer through early and continuous delivery of valuable software – Principle One.
2. Harness change	Welcome changing requirements, even late in development. Agile processes harness change for the customer's competitive advantage – Principle Two.
3. Encourage incremental implementation	Deliver working software frequently, from a couple of weeks to a couple of months, with a preference to the shorter timescale – Principle Three.
4. Get the business and technical people together	Business people and developers must work together daily throughout the project – Principle Four
5. Create trust through leadership and process	Build projects around motivated individuals. Give them the environment and support they need, and trust them to get the job done – Principle Five.
6. Encourage face-to-face conversations	The most efficient and effective method of conveying information to and within a development team is face-to-face conversation – Principle Six.
7. Set targets and reward real progress towards a working solution	Working software is the primary measure of progress – Principle Seven.
8. Pursue simplicity, not complexity	Simplicity, the art of maximizing the amount of work not done, is essential – Principle Ten.
9. Give your teams the space they need to excel	Agile processes promote sustainable development. The sponsors, developers, and users should be able to maintain a constant pace indefinitely – Principle Eight. Continuous attention to technical excellence and good design enhances agility – Principle Nine. The best architectures, requirements, and designs emerge from self-organizing teams – Principle Eleven At regular intervals, the team reflects on how to become more effective, then tunes and adjusts its behavior accordingly – Principle Twelve.

Chapter 6

The Agile Manifesto and its Principles

This chapter explores the Agile Manifesto and its Principles and then outlines the need for people at all levels to adopt the 9 Agile Leadership Principles.

Background to the Signing of the Agile Manifesto

Aspects of agile development have been valued by many in the development community for a long time. For example, taking an iterative approach has been recommended in much of the DOD guidance. But the advantages of incremental development were downplayed by the ideology of 'one size fits all' methods in the 1980s and early 1990s (discussed in more detail in Part III).

In 2001 a meeting took place at which a manifesto was signed which reinvigorated those who were worried about the dangers of waterfall approaches. The signatories of the Agile Manifesto placed themselves against the extreme adoption of BDUF, waterfall, and top-down theoretical designs. They knew that processes, tools, documentation, contracts, and documented plans had their place in most forms of organized work at any scale, but they wanted to emphasize the primacy of the collaborations of individuals and the output of working solutions rather than documentation. The Agile Manifesto was very brief: it was only a few sentences long, and more of a statement of intent than workable guidance.

After the meeting, a set of 12 principles were developed to give a more detailed definition and support the philosophy of the Agile Manifesto. The principles have strong support from *agilists*, but are not well known outside of those interested in agile as a technique, rather than as a business tool. In researching this book, I found that project failure or success generally depends on top management behaviors combined with technical ability. The Agile Manifesto Principles target the team and their technical environment. They do not explain the role of leadership in encouraging and facilitating agile success. Therefore I have analyzed the agile case studies from the perspective of leadership behaviors rather than the perspective of management processes. The 9 Agile Leadership Behaviors that I have identified and their relationship to the 12 Agile Manifesto Principles are shown in Table 2.

You may ask why there are three fewer Agile Leadership Behaviors than there are agile Principles. There are good reasons why the relationship is not exactly one to one. Research by Laurie Williams has identified various small anomalies, duplication and cross-over between the principles. She undertook a major survey to see how well it and the supporting principles had dated. Of the 326 experts surveyed, there was considerable support for the continuing robustness of the principles. Of the respondents, 90.2% considered the principles as more important than any specific agile practice. 100% of respondents found the principles valuable in themselves, above and beyond the overarching manifesto statement.[107] I agree with her conclusion that although the ten year old principles could be polished, they are robust enough for their purpose and well-known and accepted by Agilists. However, since I am now proposing a set of Agile Leadership Behaviors from a management perspective, I have taken the opportunity to incorporate some of her recommendations on agile perspectives in this book.

The Agile Leadership Behaviors I am proposing are typically terser, less repetitive, are easier to remember (being only 9 rather than 12) and less internally focused. In other words, I propose them for the purpose of changing the behaviors of politicians, managers, business people, auditors, procurement staff as well as technical people.

Some have argued that in the new millennium we have entered a *post-method era*. Web development, outsourcing, use of readymade solutions, and cloud-computing undercut the assumption that large complicated methods and procedures are needed to structure the team activities of the developers of technology solutions.[108] Since the 1990s, interest in highly structured complex and prescriptive methods of development has receded. One study in 1998 found only six per cent of private organizations following a method rigorously, with 79 per cent of those not using a method having no intention to adopt one.[109]

So why the resurgence of interest in methods of software development? Especially agile methods?

The trigger that set the agile revolution in motion was the cancellation of the Chrysler C3 project in February 2000 soon after the ill-fated merger of Daimler-Benz. The techniques that now comprise eXtreme Programming (XP) were developed by Kent Beck who worked on the C3 project as a response to the trend towards larger and larger design-led software development projects. Even though use of complex methods had become unfashionable, projects still depended on the concept of BDUF and waterfall lifecycles.

Beck called a meeting of XP practitioners in Omaha to discuss the future of the method. Those at the meeting agreed that there was a lot of common ground between the participants, but no clear solution emerged as to how to make the world aware of these new techniques. In February 2001, Robert C. Martin called a meeting at the Lodge at Snowbird ski resort in the Wasatch Mountains of Utah. Participants included proponents of a diverse number of methods, including Extreme Programming, Scrum, DSDM, Adaptive Software Development, Crystal, Feature-Driven Development, and Pragmatic Programming.[110]

The discussions focused on their distaste of BDUF and waterfall approaches. In the end they found a way of expressing their philosophy, even though when it came to detail they had different methods. They drafted a document they called the Agile Manifesto. It consisted of four short statements in the form "we prefer X over Y".[111] Martin Fowler describes that meeting's objective was to create "a rallying cry to the software industry ... it says what we stand for and also what we are opposed to ... a call to arms" [112]

The manifesto is written in the style of polar opposites – what Beath and Orlikowski identify as dichotomies each comprising of two elements. A *privileged* element is presented in preference to and in opposition to a *deferred* element. They point out that when used to describe development methods, these opposites often prove to be inseparable and dependent on each other. The Agile Manifesto explicitly recognizes this feature by stating "while there is value in the items on the right, we value the items on the left more". If this last sentence in the Agile Manifesto is overlooked, then the statements can be mistakenly interpreted as exclusive dichotomies. They are not. For example, although Agile methods focus on working software rather than detailed documentation of designs, there is still a need for some documents – especially when tracking progress and planning work (see Part II).

The term *lightweight* had been used up to that point as a general description of the different methods that the participants were proposing. That term was discarded in favor of the term *agile*. This was thought to capture the common aspects of the adaptive nature of the related methods represented by the participants, without inferring that the proposed approach was flimsy or facile.

So let's examine the four manifesto statements and their implications for large organizations.

Agile Manifesto Statement One: Valuing Individuals and Interactions over Processes and Tools

This statement orientates agile away from the prescriptive, process oriented structured methods and away from the complex tools needed to follow such methods.

First, consider the preconception of many people that waterfall approaches are inherently superior, if only they are followed strictly enough. At the height of their popularity, these prescriptive, highly structured BDUF methods became widely adopted in governments around the world. The "Structured Systems Analysis and Design Method" (SSADM) was in use from London to Melbourne, from Ottawa to Hong Kong.

The first large scale casualty of SSADM was the London Stock Exchange's Taurus project. Its objective was to radically restructure securities trading in London and introduce fully automated cash settlement. But, after six years and nearly £500m expenditure, the project was canceled.[113] The requirements had been documented using SSADM at a detailed level, but there still was no clear understanding among project staff regarding the interaction of technical, business and institutional requirements. The project was canceled before a single module was implemented.[114]

Second, consider the fact that the Agile Manifesto distances itself from dependency on complex tools. BDUF approaches may employ expensive and difficult to use Computer Aided Software Engineering (CASE) system design tools. The aim of these is to capture a very detailed BDUF analysis and then automatically generate programs. As teams grapple with the inflexibility of updating the detailed designs before programs are generated, they start to bypass the design activities and simply use the CASE tools as glorified programming tools.

Agile Manifesto Statement Two: Valuing Working Software over Comprehensive Documentation

Agile methods are based on the assertion that decisions must be based on evidence that comes from experience. Documents, however carefully compiled and checked, cannot provide evidence of worth. Agile therefore depends on "transparency, inspection, and adaptation". [115] Transparency comes from regular demonstrations of the emerging solution and its proof in early live use. Quality assurance by independent teams is enabled by rigorous detailed testing conducted by developers and user checks before a solution goes into live use. There is nothing un-agile about letting an independent team check that mission critical systems have been tested and are free of fraudulent code. Adaptation is possible because development occurs in short cycles which allow developers to change the design and users to change their minds both without loss of face, or large amounts of rework.

As toddlers, we learn to walk getting regular feedback on the evenness of the ground under our feet. As a child we learn how to cross a road safely, using our eyes and ears to check for approaching cars. As an adult, when we are rushing to work, we may consider stopping to buy a coffee when we smell the aroma coming from a café. It is the natural way that we run our lives, and is also the optimum way to run a project: in short iterations that give feedback.

A good business change project is one that not only balances economies of scale against risks of 'big bang', but also recognizes the need for feedback from real-life implementation to drive changes to targets. Such thinking is often termed *empirical process control*. Its application to complex business changes came out of Shewing's work on continual improvement of quality in manufacturing processes. He argued that more use should be made of data about the products to adapt and improve processes. This idea was adopted by the Japanese in the search for improvements to their recovering industries after the Second World War, and it was later popularized by Deming as a four-step PDSA cycle (see Figure 5). [116]

The waterfall lifecycle neglects the importance of feedback and replanning. It assumes that if enough planning is done upfront, then it will never be necessary to deviate from that perfect plan. This is the *defined process control model*. The Deming PDSA model is an *empirical process control model* – the model emphasizes the need to change the plans regularly using an evidence-based approach. To take full advantage of this theory, we must recognize that:

- ♦ Only an immediate project plan is required in detail – just enough to allow work to proceed to a point where evidence can be gathered on how effective progress is in real-life

- ♦ Evidence must be collected while carrying out tasks – on the effort consumed, the qualities of the outputs, and also on the benefits that the technical solution brings

♦ Effort needs to be put into studying lessons learned – could the work have been carried out more efficiently? Were any recurring problems found during testing? Did the resultant business change produce the intended benefits? Were there any disbenefits?

♦ Decision makers spend time considering the evidence.

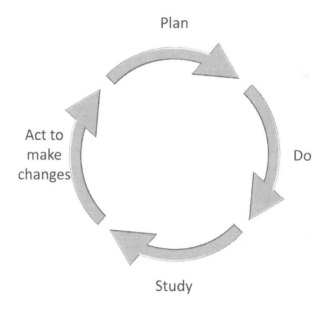

Figure 5: The Plan, Do, Study, Act (PDSA) Model

Most importantly, good leaders accept the inevitability that initial plans will always need to change. Early feedback is needed to incrementally improve the initial overview plans. Techniques such as prototyping, piloting of the solution, parallel running alongside any existing processes, and phased implementation all should be used to provide feedback on the concepts that underlie a project.

Great leaders plan for data to be collected, make enough time to analyze it, and ensure a blame-free culture that allows for easy adoption of changes to plans. At the heart of agile is this concept.

Ken Schwaber makes the difference clear: careful thought is required before choosing to run a waterfall project based on the defined process control model:

> "We use defined processes (in everyday situations where) we can crank up unattended production to such a quantity that the output can be priced as a commodity. However, if the commodity is of such unacceptable quality as to be unusable, the rework is too great to make the price acceptable … we have to turn to, and accept the higher costs of empirical process control. In the long run, making successful products … using empirical process control turns out to be much cheaper than reworking unsuccessful products using defined process control." [117]

The defined process control model expects a specific output to be produced from a pre-determined, exact process laid down at the beginning of the work. Little or no feedback is built in to the process. With empirical process control, on the other hand, regular feedback ensures that the project keeps on track.

In short, we should use feedback and empirical experience to adapt to changing circumstances. We minimize the cost of failure with an iterative approach: the cost of failure is limited to merely the last iteration of work. And the smaller the iterations are, the smaller the cost of potential failure becomes. If the project is high risk, then this theory of Empirical Process Control suggests an iteration length as short as possible. This model shows how mega-projects lie at the opposite end of the pre-planning spectrum from agile projects.

The main determining factor for optimum iteration length is how much you can afford to write off in case the output is unusable. If regular implementation of the output is not onerous, then very short iterations are preferable. If implementation and actual usage cannot be achieved at each iteration, then a proxy measure of success can be used, such as user acceptance testing.

Agile Manifesto Statement Three: Valuing Customer Collaboration over Contract Negotiation

Mary and Tom Poppendieck have identified several traditional engineering contract negotiation approaches as *anti-patterns* for software project management – in other words techniques that are not just a waste of time, but that actually engender harmful behaviors. They criticize detailed work breakdown planning and bureaucratic scope control. They also criticize the use of *earned value analysis* (EVA). This is where the value of an activity is calculated as being equal to the money spent on it (see the discussion about EVA in Part III). These processes often end up being used by the government and the supplier as a means of gaining an advantage in negotiations, rather than working to find common ground.[118]

These specific anti-patterns were evident in the problems encountered in the FBI Sentinel. A great deal of emphasis had been placed on technical project acquisition skills and negotiation. But there was not enough collaboration and discussion between the project managers and the technical experts who could see plainly the technical difficulties of the technology that was being proposed. Project managers had been hurriedly trained, certificated, and then placed into top management positions. The technology experts who understood much better the difficulty of the tasks in hand had to take direction from inexperienced project managers. Their training had consisted of either a nine-day boot camp, or, for the more senior, an eight-week course followed by the PMI Program Management Professional (PMP) exam. The key measure of success was the number of new PMPs, not their ability to lead technical teams to success. Experienced engineers with top flight engineering degrees were placed under their command. This had two catastrophic consequences. First, there was no effective collaboration with the sub-contractor from a technical viewpoint, and poor quality outputs were accepted without any root cause analysis or pressure being brought to bear to improve performance. And second, the planning of work veered towards the easier elements, always pushing back the more challenging aspects for later.[119]

Agile Manifesto Statement Four: Valuing Responding to Change over Following a Plan

A major side effect of pursuing BDUF approaches on large, public sector projects is that of overplanning.

A false security often comes about when the design of every aspect of a solution is attempted before any part of the solution has been built and trialed. This confidence in the design is usually reflected in overcomplicated plans that provide a detailed narrative for the whole of the project, and in a lack of attention to risks and contingency planning just in case things don't turn out as expected. In the same way that CASE tools were built to support ever more complicated and complete modeling techniques in the 1980s, complicated planning tools were developed that supported the perceived need for detailed upfront planning of a whole project. Barry Boehm has described these *inchpebbles* – making the point that they do not provide a helpful way of knowing whether you are on the right track, as good project *milestones* should. These inchpebbles merely lock all parties into an "ironbound contract" with no flexibility in direction:

> "Excessive, prespecified plans overconstrain the development team even at minor levels of change in personnel, technology, or commercial off-the-shelf upgrades. Such plans also provide a source of major contention, rework, and delay at high-change levels." [120]

One study of four large failed software implementations whose costs at project cancellation were between $9m and $112m found long, detailed complicated plans for monolithic big-bang implementation. The contracts based on these plans did not protect the client companies from the risks of failure, but actually helped large consultancy companies extract large fees for longer. [121]

When a great deal of time and effort has gone into detailed long range planning, this can build in a great deal of inertia into a project. Any required change has a great impact on the management products and contracts that have been agreed up-front. The effort required to introduce even the smallest change is enormous, and is resisted. Of importance are the changes that occur in the target environment. In Part I we saw that initial attempts by the FBI to modernize their case management system failed to take into account the BPR exercise that had been underway for some time.

Civil service initiatives such as the UK Technology in Business Fast Stream for young civil servants and the new Major Projects Leadership Academy for experienced senior civil servants may be able to start to modernize the approach to project management.[122] The White House Office of Management and Budget (OMB) has announced a specialized career path for IT program managers, but the job specification only explicitly recognizes a waterfall lifecycle. Even when it is taught, there is always the danger that the agile approach will be segregated as a special technique rather than being the default basis for most technology projects.[123]

An example of the importance of training in collaborative project management skills is the US DOD. There are over 126,000 military and civilian procurement specialists in the DOD, working in more than a dozen different services and agencies. With good education levels and low turnover, the skills base should be very effective at planning and running acquisitions. About 40% of these staff members work with in either program management or systems planning activities.[124]

Since its inception in the 1990s, as a result of the Packard Commission review of the management of the DOD, the Defense Acquisition Workforce Improvement Act (DAWIA) has gone through several revisions. The latest revision in 2006 attempted to increase the quality of contract management by requiring the DOD to establish education and training standards and career paths and setting up the Defense Acquisition University (DAU). DOD-5000 established formal definitions of competencies and career paths for program managers, computer systems developers and auditors, among many other categories.[125]

Good management practices can enable government departments to manage their own collaborative technology projects. An example of how the often inflexible contract negotiation that occurs with prime contractors can be eliminated is the US Social Security Administration (SSA) which now performs nearly all IT program work using its own people, infrastructure and systems.

The SSA enhanced and focused its internal project management capability in the wake of a memorandum issued in April 2007 by the Office of Federal Procurement Policy (OFPP). The memo required each Chief Acquisition Officer (CAO) to develop a workforce policy to ensure agency project managers had essential program and project management competencies. These competencies laid the foundation for the SSA to take control of their own projects.[126] Furthermore, the education program now includes specific support for changes introduced under the OMB's 25 Point Implementation Plan reforms to IT in the UK government. By 2011 the SSA had 85 certificated project managers. The SSA is now proud of its project management capability:

> "Although an objective measure of the PM program is difficult, SSA has had no program failures (and few difficulties) since adopting the program. SSA has also been recognized for superior PM competency during TechStats and other reviews/audits and has been sought out by Federal Acquisition Institute (FAI) and other PM leadership groups for input and participation. Of SSA's 17 major investments on the Federal IT Dashboard, fewer than 20% are *yellow*, compared to 37% of major investments government-wide. SSA has no major investments with an overall score of *red* on the Federal IT Dashboard." [127]

Conclusions

The 9 Agile Leadership Behaviors introduced in Table 2 are an adjunct to and a reflection of the Agile Manifesto Principles. They come from a business perspective that non-technical people will find easy to grasp and implement. Everybody will find these leadership behaviors useful in discussing and explaining the advantages of agile to others, and influencing them to support agile adoption. People who exhibit these behaviors will enable and facilitate agile success, even if they do not know a great deal about the detail of specific agile methods.

If you follow these 9 Agile Leadership Behaviors, you will support your teams in their adoption of agile methods and sticking to the 12 Agile

Manifesto Principles in the running of their projects. It is not enough just to train the technical staff in an agile method, if waterfall leadership behaviors still abound.

Questions

1. Have you experienced the BDUF approach to planning in your professional career? Do professionals, such as accountants, teachers, doctors etc., exhibit these tendencies?

2. Look again at the FBI Sentinel case study in Part I. What features of *defined process control* were exhibited in Phase One?

3. If highly prescriptive technology development methods are dangerous, then should we be wary of agile methods?

4. Read Jim Highsmith's history of the genesis of the Agile Manifesto (see Endnote 128). Condense the thoughts of the participants into a 30 second *elevator pitch* – a brief overview of agile that would convince your top management team or customer to take an interest in the agile approach.

Agile Leadership Exercises

1. Review your diary for the last week. Make a list of the seven most important tasks you carried out, or meetings you attended. Evaluate each task. Which were oriented towards individuals and interactions and which towards processes and tools? In the case of the latter, how could you have changed your approach in each instance to make it less process/tool based?

2. Does your organization reward you and the people around you

for achieving business outcomes, or for creating comprehensive reports? What suggestions could you make to the team to focus peoples' energies on the former?

3. Analyze the last meeting you had with a supplier. Did the discussion feel collaborative or was it a negotiation on points of detail. Think about your next such meeting – could you suggest a better agenda to make it more cooperative?

4. Revisit the latest set of objectives and schedules for your workload. How have they changed over the last few months? Do they still reflect reality? How should they have been changed?

Chapter 7

Agile Leadership Behavior One: Satisfy the Customer

> *Our highest priority is to satisfy the customer through early and continuous delivery of valuable software*

Agile Manifesto Principle Number One

You need to satisfy the people that are funding your projects. You need to take notice of those people who may be impacted by the solutions, whether they support them, or object to them. The obvious aim is to make sure that the people who will use the technical solution, commonly called the *users*, are happy. But that is missing the point. There is a broader spectrum of people that have an interest in the system, and we must make sure that where they have influence over the people funding our work we address their concerns. Often it is not obvious who the 'customer' is at all, and some thought is required as to whom you really are aiming to please. For example:

- ♦ Users: who usually want lots of functions out of a fast, reliable technical solution

- ♦ Bosses: who not only set ambitious goals, but want 'no surprises' along the way

- ♦ Subordinates: who want technical advancement, neat designs, and who may not directly see the benefit of controls and transparency

♦ Maintainers: who will inherit the technical solution and who want it bug-free and well-documented

♦ Sponsor/Product Owner: those in a different division or organization who commissioned the system.[129]

♦ All other stakeholders perceiving an impact from the implementation of new solution, its use, or its final decommissioning.

The old adage is that you can't please all of the people all the time, so your efforts have to be focused on those stakeholders that will be most impacted by the system and also have the most influence over a project – either through direct governance as the boss, or by political or other influence. Some stakeholders may be implacably opposed to the technical solution, for example those who will lose out when it is implemented. The best you can do in these cases is to attempt to reduce the effectiveness of their opposition to the plans.

A successful agile project is one where the customer is the center of focus for the team – both in terms of the product being developed (the *output*) and how it is going to improve the business (the *outcome*).

Waterfall projects are often characterized as *all at once* or *big-bang* projects. The customer is forced to wait for years to see results. Both the US and the UK Government have declared an intention to involve stakeholders more closely as projects progress, but much of the guidance materials still implicitly discourage this.

National audit bodies on both sides of the Atlantic are inconsistent on this issue. If a project is big-bang, it may be criticized for not testing concepts adequately with customers and not being piloted correctly. If incremental, a project may be criticized for moving too quickly and having moved to development before all requirements are agreed with the customers.

In this chapter I describe a method that has had widespread influence in US defense project thinking: Barry Boehm's *Spiral* approach. So much so that it was mandated for military developments in Section 804 in public law.[130] However, many projects that claimed to be using Spiral have merely using it as a cloak to cover a traditional big-bang approach. Later in this chapter I relate the six essential tests you can use to ensure that this does not happen on your agile project.

I also compare the speed and effectiveness of the move to agile project management in the US and UK. We will see that effective direct intervention from a strong Government Chief Information Officer (CIO) in the US has had a profound impact, and that the UK has made progress but has some way to go.

Agile Places the Customer As Top Priority

A comprehensive international survey showed that the first principle of agile has overwhelming support from leading agile practitioners as the most pervasive attribute of success for agile projects. Agile Leadership Behavior 1 corresponds to Agile Manifesto Principle 1, and supports its implementation.[131]

Although the wording of principle 1 assumes that the deliverable from the project is "software", it emphasizes that the ultimate output are positive business *outcomes*, rather than technical *outputs*. Proponents of agile are keen to emphasize that all the principles can apply to non-software developments. For example, in 2007 the phrase 'software development' was used throughout the official Scrum documentation – but had disappeared by 2011 having been replaced by more generic references to 'product development'.[132] Another example of the more generic use of agile beyond systems development are the Case Studies being used in agile qualifications which emphasize the more general applicability of agile outside of corporate IT work. For example, the 2012 sample paper for the APMG Agile Project Management qualification is based on a SME business which needs to prepare marketing materials for a trade fair.

The Evolutionary Approach to Defense Projects

The GAO has for many years been extremely critical of the F/A-22 'Raptor' strike aircraft project. The project to buy 650 fighters capable of evading former Soviet radar defenses ran for 20 years. What began as an effort to buy 650 fighters capable of evading former Soviet radar defenses to escort bombers to targets came to an end in December 2011 with only 195 having been built.[133] From the start, the GAO warned that:

> "(The DOD was) not guided by the principles of evolutionary, knowledge-based acquisition ... and, as a result, (many projects have) experienced cost increases, schedule delays, and poor product quality and reliability." [134]

Instead, the GAO recommended, an evolutionary approach (such as proposed by Tom Gilb) within a Spiral method (such as that proposed by Barry Boehm), should be used. Development cycles should be kept short, and early, practical use should be made of technologies to prove development concepts (see Figure 6).

It is not just technology development projects that can benefit from evolutionary approaches. The NAO advises that:

> "Many ... organizations now regard property transformation as (an) evolutionary process. Evolutionary processes suit organizations that are budget constrained, are subject to regular operational changes, and want to create a sense of staff involvement, learning and ownership."[135]

Government guidance on both sides of the Atlantic has been inconsistent and confusing in this area. In 2001, the dangers of big-bang implementation were recognized by the UK Treasury:

> "Unless approved by a central scrutiny group, no big-bang implementations and developments – we mandate modular, incremental implementations and developments for IT-enabled projects," which included the Chief Secretary to the Treasury[136]

In 2004 another letter was sent extending this guidance "to cover all major acquisition-based projects. [137] However, this guidance was then superseded in 2007 by a new strategic manual to the heads of departments, where the advice was to merely consider "pilot testing before full roll out".[138]

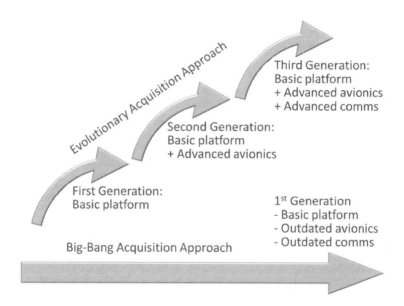

Figure 6: Comparison of Evolutionary and Big Bang Approaches (Adapted from GAO 2003) [139]

Requirements for modular and incremental development were dropped, and a presumption of the big-bang approach implied by an implementation phase only at the end of the project. Furthermore, in 2011 the new UK Integrated Assurance and Approvals guidance described a project model of waterfall design, build, test to be followed finally by implementation, and similarly neglected the advice for incremental development with phased implementation cycles.[140]

The previously acknowledged risks associated with big-bang implementation were also dropped from the list of 'common failings' in government projects in strategic guidance for 'starting gate' reviews.[141]

In 2006, the NAO issued a report emphasizing that late, big-bang deliveries were dangerous, and gave example of successful government case studies that had "avoided the strain on organizational resources and the technical and reputation risks of big-bang roll outs." [142]

The GAO has recently been promoting agile concepts. In one report on weapon systems it urged the DOD to use more realistic timeframes, and to aim to achieve the best with what is available, rather than over specify detail in its projects. Instead of projects that last decades and produce very little, delivery of new defense capabilities should be expected within 6 years or less. Programs are more risky as the delivery timescale extends out. In some cases projects had been planned that were over 15 years long, with costs that grew at exponential rates from the original baseline. The GAO advised that:

> "The DOD should assimilate new technologies into weapon systems more frequently, accelerate delivery of new technology, hold program managers accountable, and make more frequent and predictable work in production, where contractors and the industrial base can profit by being efficient. Too many major acquisitions currently take the opposite approach by seeking to deliver a revolutionary 'big bang' capability in one step." [143]

The GAO has criticized many government and public agency bodies for lack of early demonstration and "knowledge enabled feedback" at early project stages. It criticized NASA of failing to demonstrate technology maturity with realistic models or prototypes before projects are committed to full production.[144]

The US Takes Drastic Action

In the US, Vivek Kundra initiated a comprehensive review of existing technology projects with each department and agency. These Technical Status (TechStat) meetings were long, detailed, face-to-face reviews of all *yellow* and *red* status projects. These reviews were intended to delve deep into an IT project with a relentless pursuit of oversight and either revise the plans or halt or terminate it".

The meetings were jointly held with OMB officials and with CIOs from other departments invited to attend as peer reviewers. To kick off the initiative Kundra attended more than three of these meetings a week, publically issuing memos to agencies where problems were found. At the Environmental Protection Agency (EPA), for example, one IT project was found to be one year late and $30m over budget, so Kundra gave the EPA 30 days to put a recovery strategy in place for the project.[145] In August 2010, for example, he held individual sessions with 13 agency CIOs and identified a list of high-risk projects, for each of which each agency had to submit a proposed improvement plan within 30 days.[146]

The Spiral Development Approach

Since 2003, the US DOD has required acquisitions for advanced technology:

> "To be deployed in the shortest time practicable. Approved, time phased capability needs matched with available technology and resources enable evolutionary acquisition strategies. Evolutionary acquisition strategies are the preferred approach to satisfying operational needs." [147]

This directive stated that the Spiral development process, originally proposed by Barry Boehm, would be the preferred process for executing such strategies. Boehm's Spiral approach stresses the incremental development of the definition of the requirement. A cycle of increasing definition and commitment to a design approach is proposed, where each iteration starts with a risk assessment. The spiral starts off with some outline work on the development objectives, and then risks to those objectives are identified and analyzed "candidly and completely". The highest risks to success are then addressed by the creation of working prototypes in increasing sophistication and operational readiness (see Figure 7).

Each iteration concludes with feedback from experiences in building the solution, replanning, and revisiting the initial objectives (which I have paraphrased in Figure 7 as the 'Business Case').

Since the specific adoption of the Spiral Model in DOD Instruction DOD-5000, Barry Boehm defined six *Spiral Essentials* to guard against "false spiral activity" which can lead to customer dissatisfaction. Some agilists brand these projects as *fragile* rather than *agile*.

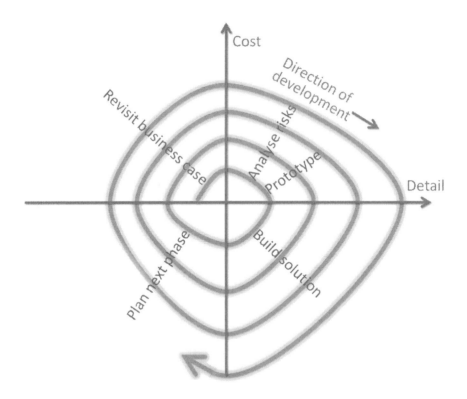

Figure 7: Spiral Model (adapted from Boehm 2001)[148]

Boehm identified six tests to ensure against "hazardous spiral lookalikes" and to keep the focus always on the customer. You can use these essential criteria to ensure success on your agile projects:[149]

♦ Spiral Essential One: Concurrent development should occur of the operational concept, the requirements, plans, design and so-lution. Boehm warns against adapting a sequential waterfall lifecycle. He does identify limited conditions where waterfall may work. For example, if the requirements are pre-specifiable, slowly changing, and shared by all customers.

♦ Spiral Essential Two: The project should be disciplined in ensuring that objectives and constraints are reviewed by the customer at the end of every spiral (and therefore before the next spiral starts). Sufficient governance must be in place to ensure that alternatives are considered. The DOD must be vigilant against inertia and reaffirm a commitment to proceed at the end of each spiral. There is the risk that if any key stakeholders are excluded from technical discussions, or conversely that technicians are not sufficiently involved in risk analysis, then critical risks will go undetected, and unrealistic assumptions will go unchallenged.

♦ Spiral Essential 3: Effort in each spiral should be proportional to risk exposure. Risks can be generated by bad project decisions. Insufficient attention to this is called *project error risk*. Conversely, delays to delivery to the customer may occur by over-analyzing irrelevant items – this is *project delay risk*. As progress is made, the aim is to reduce overall risk, while optimizing the amount of time spent countering those risks. By definition, when the solution is implemented and is successfully deployed and producing benefits, then project risks have been reduced to zero, and what is left is the residual risk of 'Business as Usual' operations. If risks are badly managed then although the project may look like spiral, problems will emerge. Incremental projects that follow this approach are termed *risk-insensitive evolutionary developments*. An example of this is where detailed plans are produced for future spirals without any mechanism for modification after each round of risk review. If the DOD has insufficient linkage between risk management and project planning this symptom may occur.

♦ Spiral Essential 4: Detail of design and specification should be related to risk. The quality acceptance criteria should be only as detailed as necessary to address the risks of not doing so. Boehm points out that one should avoid assuming that a complete, consistent, traceable, testable requirements specification is always required. Too much BDUF increases the risk of delay by forcing solutions to conform to detailed requirements that eventually are discovered not to be what the customer wants. If there is evidence of BDUF in a project, then, Boehm argues, that project is not following a Spiral life cycle.

♦ Spiral Essential 5: Three essential *anchor point milestones* should exist in each spiral of a project at which the customer agrees project objectives, the project lifecycle is agreed and the capability requirements are defined in overview. The three essential anchor point milestones are:

  o Life Cycle Objectives (LCO) Milestone where agreement on the viability of the next iteration of the solution is reviewed from a business perspective.

  o Life Cycle Approach (LCA) Milestone[150] where the project lifecycle to be used is agreed and is linked to a risk-management plan. A decision must be made at each Spiral as to the nature of the development: evolutionary, incremental or even waterfall is appropriate. The LCA must be clear as to whether several spirals may exist between the anchor point milestones, and where in the spiral process they should sit. It must also ensure that evolutionary development is within the context of the many spirals that are required to produce a target solution. Boehm warns that there are risks in sub-optimization by targeting just the upcoming spiral, but storing up problems for the rest of the project.

  o Initial Operating Capability (IOC) Milestone where minimum operational requirements are agreed with the customer. By taking a minimalist approach, the dangers of too much analysis into non-critical requirements are avoided and stakeholder expectations are managed. [151]

♦ Spiral Essential 6: A project should not ignore tasks that surround the development activities. We saw in Part I that there is evidence that the team developing the Education Benefits System at VA overlooked important implementation planning with the stakeholders, such as designing efficient operational procedures and training the users of the new technology. Teams working on technically intensive developments can fall into the trap of ignoring the whole life-cycle, especially customer satisfaction. Non-functional requirements such as security, DOD-5000 governance requirements, and special defense regulations must be taken into account in a holistic plan. The technical performance of the solution must be satisfactory within the actual operational environment, not just in the development lab. Business processes must be considered as must the need for planning organizational changes.

An example of the impact of DOD-5000 and the potential for misinterpretation of the meaning of 'Spiral' development was provided in a Space and Missile Systems Center panel review in 2008. The National Security Space Acquisition Policy (NSSAP-03-01) had provided guidelines for implementation of DOD-5000 for Milestone Decision Authorities (MDAs) for all DOD Space Major Defense Acquisition Programs. In this guidance a specific requirement was that the NSS acquisition team should be streamlined and 'agile', with "short, clear lines of authority with decision making and program execution at the lowest levels possible". However, a large project would still need detailed MDA approval and would not only be required to initiate a project in a waterfall fashion, but also would be required to revisit the MDA to changes required thereafter.[152]

Although Spiral Development was stated to be the key process, the definition of what is meant by the process remained open to interpretation. Definitions of what is meant by Spiral Development (SD) often simply refer back to the Defense Authorization Act of 2003. Peter Hantos warns that:

"A prevailing misconception is that (DOD-5000 defines) spiral

> development, where concept development is the first spiral, technology development the second one, and system development and demonstration is the third one and so on" [153]

This overlaying of a waterfall approach on top of the spiral life-cycle, Hantos warns, is contrary to the concept of concurrent engineering and the risk-driven approach. Conventional risk management involves additional plans to attempt to drive out risk and the creation of alternative contingency plans. In spiral development he points out, the main thrust of the project are mitigation actions. He concludes that the DOD policies are inherently waterfall in nature, even though they state the intent of being evolutionary.[154]

Efforts are continuing to try and make the DOD acquisitions process more incremental. Congress and DOD continue to try to reform the defense acquisition system. The Weapon Systems Acquisition Reform Act (2009) increased the regulation. It required more up-front engineering, cost estimating, and the development of more designs before starting system development. This type of regulation may simply entrench the belief that more and bigger specifications will reduce risk as in the past. This BDUF tendency is a key attribute of waterfall approaches, and often causes bad ideas to be baked into the project objectives right at the start.

The DOD has now instituted annual program reviews which will concentrate on proposing options for descoping and moderation of requirements. But these reforms are still uncertain, as the GAO recently noted.[155]

Evolutionary Acquisition and TSAT

In 2003 the GAO criticized the new $12bn Transformational Satellite (TSAT) project for starting development without detailed designs upfront. They said that more certainty was required of the technology and early designs before commitments were made. The concern was that commitment to TSAT would move funding away from another important program for high frequency satellites.[156]

The objective of TSAT was to enable DOD to enhance defense

information collection – the first TSAT launch was planned for 2011. The GAO criticized the NSSAP-03-01 regulation for allowing the production to start while technology development was still ongoing. The GAO recommended that the DOD modify the policy to separate technology development from product development. The DOD disagreed, stating that the GAO's recommendations would slow down acquisitions, increase risks, and prevent adoption of cutting edge technology.[157]

In April 2009 Robert Gates, the US Secretary of Defense, announced the termination of the program whose projected costs had risen from the original $12bn to $26bn. He announced instead, the purchase of more Advanced Extremely High Frequency (AEHF) satellites which had proven themselves in service.

He also cited problems with the VH-71 presidential helicopter project, which was six years behind schedule and had doubled in forecast cost to $13bn. The only viable solution from the program was for helicopters with a five- to 10-year useful life. He noted that the current VH-3 presidential helicopters were still in operation at 30 to 40 years of age. He stated:

> "(We need) a fundamental overhaul of our approach to procurement, acquisition, and contracting … an acquisition system that can perform with greater urgency and agility … (the problem is that the) procurement and contracting cycle add layer upon layer of cost and complexity onto fewer and fewer platforms that take longer and longer to build". [158]

The GAO proudly announced that as a result of its criticisms over the years of evolutionary projects, and the TSAT project in particular, it had saved the taxpayer $5.3bn by informing Secretary Gates's decision.[159] But, in an analysis of NSSAP-03-01 to instruction DOD-5000, Mark Lorell, in a Rand Corporation research paper, notes that although the system design review and preliminary design review milestones comes earlier in NSSAP-03-01, he argues that there are no other significant differences.[160]

Conflicting guidance is one of the biggest inhibitors to agile adoption, and creates a variety of standards against which audit bodies can criticize the approaches taken. Often it is a case of being *damned if you do, and being damned if you don't.*

The OMB Capital Programming Guide, for example, recommends both incrementalism and BDUF, two concepts that are difficult to reconcile. In some places the guide recommends flexibility and modularity and minimal statement of core requirements.

On the one hand, the Guide says that only once a solution meets core requirements should additional functionality be added. Modular or spiral development should be pursued where possible, and is a 'best practice'. Performance of the solution, it says, should be the objective, not a detailed design specification, and projects should use rapid prototyping techniques[161]

On the other hand, the Guide emphasizes the importance of detailed planning upfront, and the need for detailed requirements to be defined before starting to draw up a well-developed breakdown of tasks (WBS) which should be used to track the detail and cost of each small task performed.[162]

As mentioned previously, the OMB has specific responsibilities for managing the risks of major information systems initiatives, and has required each federal agency to appoint a Chief Information Officer (CIO) to manage IT investment projects. When the OMB was given this responsibility in 2008, it took on the job of closely monitoring a *watch list* of 413 projects, 352 of which were poorly performing and an additional 61 that seemed to be running well, but were at very high-risk of failure. The total value of these projects was a staggering $25.2bn, with 48% having made major changes to their agreed, baselined objectives and plans which increase costs. 11% had been identified as grossly overrunning, but the worry was that this was only the tip of an 'iceberg', and that many problems lay hidden.

The GAO's conclusion was not that a different approach was needed, but that even more planning was required.[163] The OMB recognized that agile projects could be considered as being 'well-run' and they included a small dispensation for detailed up-front planning for modular projects with rapid prototyping techniques and incremental development.[164]

But the emphasis here by both the OMB and the GAO was on detailed cost assessment and low-level monitoring of every task to ensure that no-one deviated from an up-front plan – the opposite of an agile approach.[165]

Each performance measurement baseline is based on an early, detailed breakdown of project activities. These are then closely tracked using EVA to add up the cost of every task carried out and compare it to the original estimate. A deviation of more than 10% from the initial plan is seen as project failure, not a failure in the theoretical estimates, and usually not taken as an opportunity to change direction or scope.[166]

A change of approach, though, is underway. The President's eGovernment scorecard, a measure previously used to track quality of IT projects, has been discontinued. It valued the collection and adherence to detailed planning and collection of accurate project progress metrics above customer satisfaction or early delivery. The OMB criticized this approach because, it said, it rewarded excellent documentation and detailed plans over the actual realization of business benefits.[167] Flexibility and re-baselining were seen merely as mechanisms which were potentially being used *'to mask cost overruns and schedule delays'*. 85% of projects that were added to the watch-list were added because they fell outside tight parameters for documentation and budget management. The process was of little use because it did not pin-point the key problem projects. The OMB could not follow-up so many problems as its predominant mission was to prepare the federal budgets rather than identify the risks of individual project failures.[168]

However, the relationship between poor performance as measured by project objectives and what the scorecard approach defined as 'poor planning' was unclear. In 2008, the GAO found that 326 projects had 'poor planning' but were not assessed as high risk or poorly performing. Conversely, 61 projects had been identified as poorly performing but well planned.[169]

Many projects at the Department of Homeland Security, for example, had made substantial incremental delivery in many of their projects. One project that was criticized was the successful incremental deployment of the Rescue 21 coastguard search and rescue system. The US-VISIT program was criticized despite the implementation of biometrically enabled entry capabilities at 300 air, sea, and land points of entry. The GAO criticized that project not for lack of implementation, but for lacking a "conceptual solution architecture" and for not having followed a waterfall life cycle.[170] It was only in 2010 that the OMB made a clear statement that:

> "Many projects use 'grand design' approaches that aim to deliver functionality every few years, rather than breaking projects into more manageable chunks and demanding new functionality every few quarters ... (the Government should) only approve funding of major IT programs that ... use a modular approach with usable functionality delivered every six months." [171]

Criticisms of Current Approaches in the USA and UK

The USA and UK have both announced major changes in their approach to major projects of work: especially where those projects depend largely on technology and IT solutions.

Although there is recognition of the advantages of an agile approach for incremental development and deployment, the need for leadership by top management is not stressed, and too much emphasis is still placed by those responsible for assurance and audit for compliance to BDUF standards. Agile government needs to be seamlessly implemented by leadership of management and technical experts. Process and standards cannot be a substitute for good decision making, especially when projects are at critical points and need clear objectives and priorities.

For example, the OMB's 25 Point Implementation Plan specifies that a modular approach is expected of projects "with usable functionality delivered every six months", but fails to make clear that the focus should be on delivery of early business benefits, not just delivery for its own sake. Tough decisions need to be made by top management when prioritizing, and if necessary, less important content should be removed from scope so as to focus on meeting 100% of deadlines rather than 100% of the initial specification.[172]

The 25 Point Plan identifies that IT acquisition practices are not currently effective. The only specific guidance on how they should be improved is a recommendation for more 'best practice' guidance.[173] It misses an opportunity to stress the risks of waterfall procurement milestones and *big-bang* implementation, and to ensure a presumption against *big-bang* procurements in favor of incremental delivery and implementation with commensurate milestones.

Similarly, the OPM has released a model set of competencies to improve IT program management in Government and develop an IT program management career path. The competencies need to reflect more the debate and wide acceptance of agile project management for technology development. The overriding importance of achieving benefits from projects, not just delivering outputs needs more emphasis. Benefits realization planning is a cornerstone of agile thinking (see Agile Leadership Behavior 1). Customer satisfaction comes first and foremost. IT project managers need to focus on early piloting, phasing of implementation, and planning the measurement of the improvement of performance of operations. Baseline business performance must be measured and compared with actual results from each increment of project delivery so as to feedback and modify the project approach and objectives in the light of experience.[174]

The OPM competency framework requires knowledge of 'the project life cycle' which it defines as starting with planning and development and moving on to implementation in a later phase. This could be read to imply discrete, sequential phases – in other words a regression in thinking to waterfall life-cycle concepts.[175] In contrast, as I mentioned in the Introduction, from 2014 New Zealand will be turning out IT workers for the future that have been introduced to agile concepts by practical use of iterative development in high-school classrooms.[176]

In the UK the Treasury guidance on 'Managing Public Money' is still the reference work to which all senior civil servants must comply when spending money on projects. The importance of the use of incremental development techniques and phased delivery to provide feedback and steer project strategy is not mentioned, despite these having been identified by the UK Government as some of the main reasons for project failures. The factors listed to consider when planning policies or projects assume that 'full roll out' is the default option, with an implication that pilot testing is optional in most cases.[177] The guidance should require that attention is spent on breaking development and implementation into manageable steps and phasing implementation so as to bring early benefits. An opportunity has been missed in this strategic regulatory document to reflect the advice elsewhere in more detailed documentation that *big-bang* implementation is not the default option that is usually to be preferred. 'Full rollout' in a single phase should be assessed as a counter factual alternative to incremental piloting and phased rollout in the 'Green Book Business Case' required for each project.

Conclusions

The first Agile Leadership Behavior ensures that the customer is at the center of the project. Delivering *outputs* is the short-term focus, but the real mission is improving the business *outcomes*.

The Lockheed Martin F/A-22 'Raptor' strike aircraft project was an *all at once* or *big-bang* project where the customer was told to wait for years to see any outputs. The project was one of many failures which prompted the US Department of Defense to encourage *evolutionary* projects with the customer closely involved in incremental development of a solution.

In both the UK and the US there continues to be conflicting guidance, despite the declared policy for *incremental* and *evolutionary* approaches to projects. The GAO and the NAO need to refine their guidance and auditing approach (see Part III).

Barry Boehm's *Spiral* approach is one incremental approach which can support an agile project. Use Boehm's six essential tests to ensure that your project really is agile. Agile project management in the US Government is spreading quickly, but only has tentative and lukewarm adoption in the UK.

The US Government has changed its culture by direct intervention from a strong Government Chief Information Officer (CIO) and produced several large, high profile agile success stories in a short space of time. The UK has decided on a collegiate approach and has yet to deliver its first large-scale agile project. Although there are some promising pockets of excellence emerging, only about half of the UK Government departments have any agile projects, and most of these are very small scale.

Questions

Read the summary of the 2009 GAO report on defense acquisitions (see Endnote 178). On page 8 of the same report mention is made of the need for "evolutionary business cases". Is this referring to the need for business cases to ensure that projects are evolutionary? Or that business cases need to constantly evolve? Or both?

Agile Leadership Exercises

1. Talk to your customers and all other stakeholders and see whether they would rather wait a long time for a perfect solution, or get some incremental bite-size outputs delivered earlier

2. Identify any inhibiting behaviors exhibited by external influencers such as procurement and audit. Talk to these people and convince them that the effectiveness of incremental delivery and that involving the customer is a better audit measure than documentation checklists

3. Find out what documents are mandated up-front by regulation, and make sure that they are produced – but from an agile perspective

   - Remember: for every piece of government guidance requiring a waterfall project you will probably find conflicting (and probably more recent) advice requiring continuous involvement of users and iterative delivery

4. Do not fight the system – subvert it to create agile success!

   - Remember: generally speaking, everybody is doing what they think is 'best', it is just that the agile paradigm will be a shock for some – lead them through a process of understanding and acceptance.

Chapter 8

Agile Leadership Behavior Two: Harness Change to your Advantage

> *Welcome changing requirements, even late in development. Agile processes harness change for the customer's competitive advantage.*

> Agile Manifesto Principle Number Two

One of the great things about agile project management is that it creates a natural restlessness with regard to the objectives of a project. By assuming that change is inevitable, it tries to seek out that change at an early stage, to facilitate it quickly, and with minimum resistance.

Many projects produce business cases that are so detailed that they become an albatross around the project manager's neck. Changing even minor details of a project's objectives can be fraught with difficulty when faced with the need to keep an overcomplicated business case in line with latest thinking.

The agile approach encourages creativity in thinking in governments. It encourages small, frequent changes of direction rather than only making changes when forced to – which is late, often difficult, and always painful. While, up to now, many technology development projects have adopted a waterfall approach, thus encouraging introversion, we will see agile approaches in the future encouraging extroversion. Waterfall projects rely on commenting on change control documents at a distance, rather than meeting stakeholder face-to-face and collaborating.

Both the US and the UK Governments face challenges in implementing agile project management so as to harness change in this manner. The US Congress must consider what it can do to facilitate an agile approach without tying down government with prescriptive legislation. Both Governments must review their rulebooks and make them consistent with the 9 Agile Leadership Behaviors.

Seek Out and Harness Change

People working on and those affected by government technology development projects react to potential change in three different ways (see Figure 8):

♦ Resisting change

♦ Seeking change

♦ Harnessing Change

There is a risk that projects can burn up sums of money before any benefits are in sight. A waterfall approach can result in a series of feasibility studies and reports, a business case and requirements analysis before any practical development takes place.

A natural inclination of some involved in government projects is to try to manage risk by creating spurious convincing detail in a business case. In the UK, for example, Government departments are required to follow the Treasury Green Book regulations. Over the years these regulations have been widened and deepened. The Green Book guidance was last updated substantially in 2003 and includes recommendations on writing business cases for projects. For example, it gives reasonable advice to recognize and value any 'optimism bias' in proposals, and ensure that judgmental estimates for risks are quantified and shown separately in the calculations.[179] The guidance covers projects that create *intangible* assets such as the technical intellectual property created by software development projects.[180] It is a readable and terse document compared with the OMB Capital Programming Guide, but it still has a tendency to create pressure for voluminous documentation. This often causes early commitment to plans of action based on prematurely agreed large-scale solutions before they have been proven to work on a small scale.

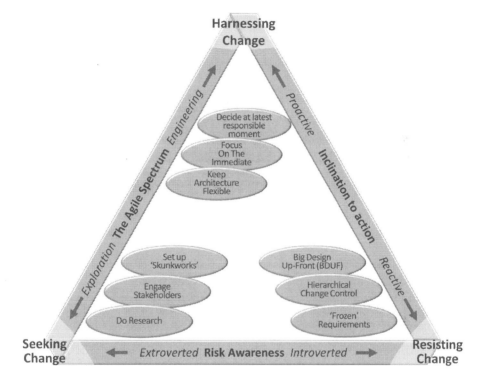

Figure 8: Inertia and Resistance to Changes in Project Direction

The NAO has criticized the regulations for encouraging *spurious precision* used as the basis for major decisions. Often, they warn, the justifications are "pseudo-scientific mumbo jumbo".[181] The NAO gives one example where a hospital project for £746.1m was approved on the basis of such a calculation showing just a £0.1m saving.

The UK Parliamentary Accounts Committee (PAC) is a powerful bi-partisan body of Members of Parliament chaired by a member of the opposition party. The PAC has a powerful role of scrutiny into Economy, Efficiency and Effectiveness of the UK Civil Service. These three "Es" are their definition of *value for money* (VFM). The committee's role is not to find fault with policy, but to examine the performance of the Permanent Secretary of each government department. They are supported in this investigation by the work of the NAO which is not part of the regular civil service, but is independent, and directly funded by parliament. The usual chain of events is that the NAO will carry out VFM audits, with powers of inspection and audit with not only government staff but staff in the private sector supply chain. The NAO publishes a report on each audit stating whether VFM has been achieved. The PAC then calls witnesses to parliament to be questioned. These entertaining events are shown live on webcasts and on UK digital TV. Both the NAO and the PAC have both been critical of the justification of large projects based on artificial business cases:

> "Spurious precision is unproductive ... public authorities need to recognize degrees of uncertainty ... slight adjustments to the calculations, well within the range of error ... (are often made to) ensure cost(s) appear marginally cheaper." [182]

Often the time needed to create this detail creates risk because it closes down the investigation and discussion of other options that may later be seen as superior, and need to be revived (or at least kept in reserve as a 'Plan B' in case the initial project design flounders).

Once this attitude towards the need for detail has started, there is a natural inertia to change. All the careful (i.e. over-detailed) planning that has gone on upfront may start to unravel if any of the base assumptions change. A detailed business case often is fragile, rather than robust. As work proceeds defenses are erected to defend the embedded assumptions. The first defense is to create an even more detailed set of requirements to support the assumptions in the business case. The objective is to *baseline* the documented requirements, and then *freeze* that baseline, not to test it practically and improve upon it. Perversely, this, in conjunction with obscure notation and voluminous documentation, may encourage requirements analysis to be done in isolation from stakeholders.

Bureaucratic Approaches versus Creative Solutions

Orlikowski and Beath have noted the problems from this tendency to prematurely *baseline* and *freeze* requirements. They cite an example from some 'best practice' guidance materials they reviewed:

> "The data administrator, with the help of systems analysts, fed the user views of data into a data modeling process and into the (CASE tool). Appropriate printouts of the models, from the encyclopedia, are given to the user committee to check." [183]

This bureaucratic approach had two self-serving payoffs for the project team, they argue: first there was a release from the obligation to fulfill the stakeholders' real needs, and second it allowed the project team to drive the development in a predetermined direction.

However, as a project progresses there are several threats to the apparent stability of the business case and its supporting requirements. First, outside circumstances may change. Second, hidden requirements may inconveniently start to appear. And third, as development begins, it may become apparent that aspects of the chosen solution design are not workable. These potential changes threaten the investment (both financial and psychological) in the existing Big Design Up Front, and often defensive measures are placed in the way of acceptance that change is needed, and needed fast.

A heavy handed *change control* process may be used that fosters inertia rather than reacting swiftly to necessary changes.

There are often three stages to resistance. First, when a potential change is recognized, an *impact analysis* will need to be conducted to work out what the impact of the change will be. A lot of documentation may need updating if even a small change is made. Second, this impact analysis will be long and complicated due to the large size and number of designs that have already been created, and the complex interdependencies between these designs. So before the impact analysis can start, somebody (usually a change control committee or a project board) has to authorize the effort needed to carry it out. Third, in a hierarchical control mechanism, any effort needed to be spent carrying out that impact analysis will need a documented justification, which will need time for discussion and agreement. The nature of this whole mechanism is to add time and budget to the project, and to discourage and slow down the necessary process of change and adjustment.

Ignoring Risks

Another strategy which may be adapted to those projects that are heavily committed to one course of action, come what may, is to avoid engagement with stakeholders. Several symptoms may be exhibited:

- ◆ An introverted, technical focus to requirements definition that makes the output difficult to understand

- ◆ Large, unwieldy specifications

- ◆ Inadequate stakeholder liaison

- ◆ Lack of real stakeholder buy-in

- ◆ Hidden requirements that will have to be incorporated later at a large cost and risk.

The Agile 'Spectrum' of Responses to Discovery and Change

Agile Leadership Behavior 2 encourages a welcoming approach to clarifications that occur as detail is probed. The DSDM framework, for example, differentiates between 'Exploration' activities during an iteration of analysis, and 'Engineering' activities during build. Both can be built into an iteration of work so that 'Exploration' activities bring to the surface new, previously hidden requirements, and discover detail within existing requirements. (Often agilists use the word *surface* as a verb, and talk about previously hidden requirements *surfacing* when they are discovered by the team.)

The DSDM framework encourages techniques such as stakeholder workshops, and recommends that facilitators of such workshops should be independent of the people present. Mock-ups of the end-solution may be brought to such workshops to facilitate discussion of options. This is especially important at the interface between what the stakeholders would like in a perfect world, and what the available technology can provide. Examples of these mock-ups may be partially working computer programs, scale-size models of buildings, or plans and diagrams. The more realistic these can be made the better.

Specification Prototyping

Partially working models may be developed for the purpose of illustrating the possibilities and restrictions of the possible technology solutions, and often these models are not intended to be robust or of the necessary scale to be implemented – these are 'specification prototypes.

These throwaway prototypes are particularly useful where the requirements are novel and not well understood. Large, detailed written requirements specifications are difficult to critique when the overall shape of desired outcomes and benefits is not understood. This can result in tedious document review sessions where the detail is picked over and corrected for detailed accuracy in logic, while the overall assumptions are still in debate. Researchers have criticized the usefulness of such review sessions when compared with the use of working system models which can demonstrate and bring to life how new processes would work. The aim of such functional prototype review sessions should not be to design the whole system, but to tease out and confirm (or otherwise) the assumptions that need verification. Such prototyping activity can typically cost about 10% of the eventual development effort, but it saves much more in expensive rework later in the software lifecycle.[184]

Setting up of Covert Skunkworks

Another strategy for getting your stakeholders involved, is to set up a *skunkworks*. This is a team room where everybody is working together in close proximity, often covertly without explicit budgets or formal approval from management. Being short of official funding, such teams are often working semi-covertly, housed in ramshackle surroundings that are none too fresh – hence the term.

The term originated from Lockheed Martin, who developed the 'stealth' ground attack aircraft which was nearly invisible to radar. With no red-tape to slow them down, the Lockheed skunkworks developed several prototype demonstrators within two years of being awarded the stealth research contract, and within five years a successful test flight of the F-117 took place. A Lockheed executive explained the success:

> "The skunkworks approach demands the use of a small number of high quality individuals staffing each function. Individuals are given broad responsibility and have substantial workload. Our experience has shown that under these circumstances individual achievement is most often much higher than management's expectations." [185]

Iterative Development

In an agile approach, once a minimum set of general requirements have been identified, a short burst of development takes place to create a partial solution. The objective is to explore the requirements and demonstrate that the technology can be made to work satisfactorily. This is done in a short timescale so as to get feedback on any problem areas as fast as possible. Therefore only part of the overall requirement is tackled in each burst of work.

Three outcomes are possible for each requirement: it may be validated, it may be found to be irrelevant or it may need refinement. Sometimes a requirement may be validated, but found to be of less importance than thought, and so any further work on it may be deferred. Development is repeated in this manner with some outputs not just being delivered for demonstration, but for operational use. Then the cycle is repeated until enough has been delivered, and it is assessed that any further work is not adding much more value.

This iterative delivery is part of the core of an agile approach, but does not define agile in its entirety – as we saw in the FBI Sentinel project, phased delivery of solutions is not sufficient in itself.

Agile terminology may vary from method to method, but the principle and the practice are similar.

In DSDM, development work is termed the *engineering activity*, and the output of each iteration is called the *emerging solution*. In Scrum the outputs are *potentially releasable increments*. Under both methods, each item developed, whether an item on a Scrum product backlog or an entry on a DSDM Prioritized Requirements List, needs a tight completion definition to ensure that the correct quality is achieved. In Scrum each feature delivered in a sprint is described as *done* when it meets a *definition of done* set by the Scrum team. The stricter the quality requirements, the more time will be needed per feature, and therefore less will be attempted in that sprint. Progress on these features will be tracked in the *sprint backlog*. It is not specified in the Scrum manual as to when this definition is agreed, so it is important to agree how and when these definitions of done will take place. *Definitions of done* should only be defined early, or be very prescriptive where this adds value and does not delay a solution.

In DSDM as this definition work is carried out during the Foundations phase of the project, there is the danger that over-specification of quality based on unfounded assumptions may take place. The DSDM guidance does advise that any definition of done work upfront during the Foundations phase should be reviewed regularly throughout the project lifecycle, but leadership is required to ensure that this does not encourage BDUF.[186]

To support Agile Leadership Behavior 2 on large projects, there are three important strategies which encourage adaptation to change rather than denial of the need for change. The next three sections explore these strategies:

◆ Make decisions at the *latest responsible moment* with *progressive fixity*

◆ 'Weave' the requirements and architecture together

◆ Focus on the urgent and immediate

Latest Responsible Moment/ Progressive Fixity

As an agile project progresses, requirements will become more certain during each iteration of activity. This will reduce the waste associated with continually changing objectives and direction. Progress is impeded by stopping and starting work as targets change. Once a feature is started within an iteration, it should be completed as planned for that iteration. It is tempting to 'tweak' and fine-tune the short-term plan. Encourage discussions about requirements at the start of each iteration of development. Get the team members to agree some discipline in changing the features listed in the sprint backlog to protect them from this problem while the iteration is underway.[187]

Early decisions on requirements and solution approaches may prematurely rule out better options. As work progresses, the project team becomes more sure about the solution, and committing time to developing the detail becomes less risky. Decisions should be made at the *latest responsible moment* possible. As each decision is made the design becomes more certain. This is the concept of *progressive fixity*.[188] For example, many details of the design of Terminal 5 at Heathrow airport were left as late as possible, until there was greater clarity about the requirements of the new Airbus A380, which was still under development.[189]

'Weave' the Requirements and Architecture Together

In line with the concept of EDUF, a light architectural framework should be developed which will help large project teams develop solutions with common standards. However, as elsewhere in agile, it is important not to over specify by deciding on the detail of solutions earlier than the development teams need. Bashar Nuseibeh recommends spending time early on in the project understanding not just stakeholders' requirements but also the technical framework. The idea should be to 'weave' these together to discover requirements and technical constraints/opportunities at an overview level. If the project starts with requirements alone, this invariably results in a waterfall development process. Requirements become artificially frozen in time, and constrained architectures handicap developers by resisting inevitable and desirable changes in requirements.[190]

Attention to requirements and technical constraints that generate the greatest risks if left unexplored will help address the three major inhibitors to requirements agreement identified by Barry Boehm: [191]

- ♦ 'IKIWISI' – 'I'll Know It When I See It' occurs when requirements emerge only after users have had an opportunity to view and provide feedback on models or prototypes.

- ♦ Expecting a packaged solution to be configurable so as to meet a theoretical list of detailed requirements. Experience that Commercial Off The Shelf (COTS) solutions are seldom as easy to use 'off the shelf' as expected. Customers must flex their requirements and make their processing consistent so as to ease COTS implementation.

- ♦ Rapid Change – a feature of the modern world, and if solution development cannot accelerate to match the new technology that is becoming available, then changing technology may wash away development work before it is implemented.

Focus on the Urgent and Immediate

The third major strategy of Agile Leadership Behavior 2 is to focus on the solution detail necessary only for the increment that is underway, not on future work. This gives a delivery focus on the immediate timebox of work that will deliver the earliest benefit to the stakeholders. This allows what Rachel Cooper, of Salford University, calls *hard* or *soft stage gates* at the end of each phase. *Stop/go* decisions occur at hard gates, whereas soft gates allow teams to work in parallel, and ensure that the whole project is not stopped dead in its tracks just because of a problem in a single area.

Rules, Regulations, and Managing Change

US government strategy has a specific intent with regard to not just allowing requirements to change, but anticipating and embracing necessary change. In 2011, Teri Takai, the new Defense Department CIO, said one of the biggest challenges is the federal budgeting process and its mismatch with the technology lifecycle:

> "We want to look at agile development and deliverables, but the appropriation process wants to know, 'womb to tomb', how much this is absolutely going to cost. That's a very difficult thing for us to say. It starts from a premise that IT projects are engineering projects, without the people dimensions of how you actually get them in and get them to work." [192]

Takei identified the following inhibitors:

♦ Large integrators not having agile developers

♦ Heavy and slow acquisition practices

♦ Implementation of agile being treated as a training issue, rather than a culture change issue

♦ Timing of the change to agile – government technologists, business people and acquisition specialists and the industry need to change together.

The 25-Point Plan recognizes that the funding model whereby Congress approves specific long-term budgets relating to specific outputs is very wasteful. It proposed the setup of Working Capital Funds (WCFs). These allow each agency the flexibility to re-assigning funding for managing flexible IT funding with revolving funds at agency level. Previously, each budget line was ring-fenced in an inflexible manner against tightly controlled budgets. [193]

Jared Serbu reports that funding has become a thorny issue with some agency CIOs who have identified challenges involved in the OMB reforms. Despite "positive discussions" with members of Congress on the issue, no proposals for legislation had yet been produced on this aspect of the announcement. The key problem, he points out, is that the technology lifecycle and the acquisition process are out of phase with each other. He cited various approaches that have been attempted to get around this problem:

♦ US Customs and Border Protection was moving towards performance based contracts based on business outcomes rather than detailed specifications of outputs. The aim was to build services not systems.

♦ The Department of Veterans Affairs used their pooled budget to fund their 'Transformation 21 Total Technology' (T4) program to provide agile development capabilities within 14 days rather than 180 days (see the case study in Part I for more about the success of their agile Education Benefits Project).

In the UK the Treasury Green Book guidance has been more problematical with regard to the flexible response to requirements that Agile Leadership Behavior 2 is intended to inspire:

♦ The Green Book requires "clear specification of quality standards" at the earliest stage of the project life-cycle and a detailed business case.[194]

♦ It identifies that *procurement risk* exists if the capabilities of the contractor are inadequate, or where necessary changes cannot be easily made. It required that plans and contracts should assume that change will take place, and should facilitate and harness the advantages of changes. [195]

♦ It recommends the use of complex modeling. This, unfortunately, as we have seen from the PAC's comments above, does encourage spurious levels of apparent accuracy. The focus is on how costs will change according to various variables, rather than on how costs can be capped by cutting back on other variables. An agile approach should be taken when interpreting the advice by illustrating how expected benefits would flex if various features of a project are descoped if costs start to escalate. The focus should be on capping funding and timescales and flexing features. [196]

♦ It assumes that an upward drift of costs will occur as more requirements are identified during a project, and that the only remedy is to do more detailed, up front requirements analysis. The agile approach does the opposite. Rather than trying to clamp down in *scope creep*, agile welcomes new ideas, as long as less important requirements are traded out. The Green Book advice can tend to encourage the identification of minor features which constrain the technical design.[197]

♦ It advises that research should take place as a separate step prior to work starting. It suggests comprehensive research covering theoretical work, such as projected trends and published forecasts, and expected technological developments. It places emphasis on making a large commitment based on a substantial first phase of theoretical research. An agile approach would be to test theory at the earliest possible stage by piloting and by releasing small increments of capability, thus providing practical feedback and breaking decisions on the detail of requirements and on the intended design until the latest responsible moment. If possible, models and demonstration facilities should be used to gain real-life feedback. What has to be avoided is agreement of a monolithic design at one gated point based on unsubstantiated economic theory. One should operate with progressive fixity – agreeing designs in a modular fashion no sooner than necessary within the framework of a flexible business case that keeps alternative courses of action open so that the approach can flex according to experience. [198]

♦ It only requires that key assumptions, options and expected implementation issues should be documented, but does not require these assumptions and options to be kept alive and reviewed during the project. A "Business Case Assumptions Register" should be maintained throughout the life of the project, and periodically reviewed. Where an assumption is found to be incorrect, then the business case should be revisited to decide whether a previously rejected option should be reconsidered. [199]

Conclusions

Agile projects seek out change by engaging with stakeholders, carrying out proactive research, and by setting up teams quickly when they are needed based on the people and resources available. They are often *skunkworks* teams that do not stand on ceremony, or worry excessively about their office environment. They just concentrate on doing the work as effectively as possible.

Agile teams do not resist change to project objectives – these are inevitable, and may emanate from policy level – in other words political decision-makers. When administrations change, the shock to the system of what is often a completely different direction must be absorbed. Agile Project Management is an effective way of being able to alter direction when an incoming administration changes policy.

Decisions that will commit to a certain course of action should be taken at the latest responsible moment. Only the immediate problems facing the team that can be solved now are dealt with. Future problems are put onto a backlog of work and dealt with when necessary. This is not procrastination. The solutions to problems are easier to find once related and more immediate problems have been solved. Sometimes problems disappear, and the effort spent in worrying about these at too early a stage is wasted.

Guidance materials, such as the UK Treasury Green Book, have encouraged over-detailed business cases that inhibit the ability of projects to adapt and change. Spurious exactness is exhibited in these business cases, with calculations providing seeming accuracy to several decimal places while assumptions are being used that could be off by a large factor.

Waterfall projects try to suppress change by creating *baselines* of requirements and designs that interlock and depend on each other. The risks of committing to a Big Design Up Front (BDUF) approach can be reduced by using research and development activities using mock-ups, working prototypes and the delivery of partial solutions which can be incrementally enhanced over time.

I have discussed how, in the US, one of the biggest challenges is the federal budgeting process which, effectively, encourages BDUF and detailed plans that have to be followed in detail to release funding.

In the UK, the Treasury guidance also causes a problem. Comprehensive product quality plans have to be in place at the earliest stage of the project. The guidance assumes that change is a risk that should be inhibited rather than accepting change as a fact of life that can be harnessed to our advantage. It recommends complex quantitative modeling, which can encourage reliance on assumptions that are subject to great variances, and these models expect budgets to change rather than an agile approach where delivery scope is flexed to fit within budgets.

Change is inevitable in any project. Often a premature commitment is made to a specific course of action in a business case, with no mechanisms to regularly review the assumptions on which the decision was made. Resistance to change is the norm. The current strategic best practice in both the US and in the UK emphasizes the need for upfront, detailed outcome modeling and sensitivity analysis in business cases. This creates a natural resistance to considering alternative courses of action later on.

Agile leadership is about seeking out necessary changes to existing plans so as to reduce risk, and then harnessing these changes to enhance returns. When necessary changes have a major impact on the business case, it is better to embrace them early in development.

Agile approaches help harness change for advantage. Risks can be seen as opportunities to be proactive and engage with potentially disruptive stakeholders at an early stage. Be vigilant against activities that tend to create inertia and project inflexibility. Chief among these are over-large specifications and designs which have been agreed in too much detail before enough experience has been gained through practical development activities.

Externally focused activities, such as specification prototyping and modeling, and lightly governed skunkworks teams will help reduce the risks of introverted behavior that simply ignores risks and reduces the possibility of identification of unexpected opportunities.

Questions

Read Jared Serbu's 2011 Federal News Radio article (see Endnote <u>200</u>). What are the main points made by the following people cited in that article:

1. Teri Takai, the CIO at the Defense Department

2. Kenneth Ritchhart, the Deputy CIO for Customs and Border Protection

3. Stephen Warren, Deputy CIO for Department of Veterans Affairs.

Agile Leadership Exercises

1. Which of your colleagues exhibits the personality characteristics of a resource investigator? Meredith Belbin defines these as people who are naturally inquisitive and like to find things out. Suggest that this person carry out some research activities into unclear project areas – even if the area that needs looking at is not their specialty. A fresh pair of eyes often sees more clearly!

2. Make a list of anybody who may be affected by your work. This list is longer than just 'users', 'management' or 'customers'. This is your list of stakeholders, internal and external, supportive and non-supportive. List them by their potential to impact your project. Now encourage the relevant people in your team to talk to the ones at the top of the list. Face-to-face.

3. Don't wait for budgets to start getting critical work done – as long as your boss can turn a blind eye, get going and inspire others to get involved. Arrange evening meetings, borrow un-used equipment. Commandeer a room to use for co-location of people interested in your ideas. In other words, set up a skunkworks!

4. Before going into any meeting, think about the decisions that are likely to be made. Put them into two categories:

    - Decisions that need to be made soon: make a list of possible objections to the solution that you think is best, and research counter-arguments to them. If further work is required, go into the meeting with a plan of action that can be approved on the spot.

    - Decisions that don't need to be made at the moment: make a list of objections to these decisions – reasons to delay any premature conclusions.

5. What documentation is mandated for your next piece of work? What is 'just enough, but no more'?

6. Make a list of all the requirements and designs that have been prematurely decided upon on your project. For each, identify which change control mechanisms apply in case they need to change. Go and speak, face-to-face, with those people who would be involved with the process. Remember: don't fight the system, work within it to improve it!

Chapter 9

Agile Leadership Behavior Three: Be Incremental

> *Deliver (a working solution) frequently, from a couple of weeks to a couple of months, with a preference to the shorter timescale*
>
> Agile Manifesto Principle Number Three

In an agile project, transparency of progress is enabled by regular demonstration of parts of the working solution, early integration of different parts to make sure they work together, and incremental implementation at regular intervals. In the past, software projects have been the most obvious candidates for this approach because software can be constructed and dismantled quickly (compared to a building or aircraft development project, say). The trend now is for a wider set of projects to use agile approaches, such as business transformation programs and modular construction projects.

With the right approach, it becomes possible to identify any issues with the design before going too far. Then problems found in the previous iteration can be addressed, or at least placed onto the product backlog for fixing at an appropriate time without holding up the project. As the team plans the next iteration, they are aware of the practical feedback from the previous iteration and can avoid making the same mistake again. Iterative delivery at short intervals can be very expensive to do on many physical

115

engineering or building projects. A waterfall approach to individual stages of a project may still be the best way forward (for example building a sky-scraper). However, iterative delivery is often the key to success on many engineering projects.

Consider the success of the Apollo program. It succeeded in placing a man on the moon in just 8 years by carrying out progressively more challenging missions, one after the other. Initially, a waterfall approach was taken on the project.

A reluctance to change dangerous designs, resulted in a disastrous cabin fire on the launchpad that tragically killed three on the Apollo 1 mission. That first mission was based on a design that was unproven and under tested. From that point onwards, the Apollo program became ruthlessly methodical about feeding back lessons learned from each iteration. Feedback from engineering tests was readily incorporated into the technology for the rest of the program. Working iteratively and progressively towards their goal, on the 11th mission, man landed on the moon.

Rework is not Wasted Effort

Agile embraces the concept of improving a solution by re-working a previously delivered solution. Rework sounds wasteful, but agile embraces this as the concept of *refactoring*. There is no shame in correcting mistakes, as long as this happens in a timely fashion. The idea is to create an initial version so that progress can be made, but with a deliberate intent of not addressing all issues in one go. The concept of refactoring rests on two important premises.

First, that there is an expectation that each technical developer should always reserve some time in each iteration to tidy up any structural defects he/she finds in modules – even if the defect is in an area that is not planned for work in that iteration. Every module should be in a better structure at the end of an iteration than at the beginning. 'Tidying up' the technical solution should take place every time a module is changed. In this way, the solution improves and matures with each iteration, rather than its internals getting more tangled and difficult to work on.

Second, where a deliberate decision is made to leave a technical problem unresolved, or a structure not as neat and tidy as it should be, this is recognized as a *technical debt* and placed as an outstanding item on the product backlog. In this way, known problems are identified and tracked, not 'brushed under the carpet'. The resolution of technical debt can be prioritized and planned into further iterations depending on its importance to the stakeholders.[201]

Using this concept, refactoring is an expectation and regarded as desirable refinement, not regarded as a cost of the failure to deliver perfectly in the first place. Refactoring promises that the solution will not degenerate when it is extended and modified over time, but will become more polished and elegant, perform better, and be more reliable with each iteration. This can also be seen as *embedding maintainability* into the solution lifecycle. Refactoring is a way of incorporating practical feedback into the overall architecture that has been used so far.

At a macro level, refactoring may introduce changes to the overall architecture. If refactoring is at a micro level, in other words a rework of the internals of a solution, the changes in many cases may not even be noticeable by users of the solution, but may improve flexibility for the future and reduce maintenance costs.

Risks exist in this approach, so the team needs to liaise carefully to avoid problems. For example, refactoring the internals of a technical solution that is already working can introduce *bugs* – and these bugs may not be detected by the standard tests that were used on the last version. Informal, ad-hoc refactoring can set the whole team back if the correction of a bug in one module has an unintended impact on another module. It can also be tempting to go beyond the planned scope of refactoring, start to dig deeper and attempt a grand rework of the internal design of a technical solution.

Test driven development is an XP technique where every change, no matter how small, is tested before the next change is made. This ensures that changes are made one step at a time and that if a mistake is made, it is caught immediately, and the source of the error becomes easier to pin down. This continual retesting can consume a lot of time, and so batteries of pre-agreed test data and automated test tools are necessary to ease refactoring. The running of these tests needs to be automated as much as possible to encourage continual and consistent retesting. Risks can be managed by encouraging co-ordination between team members, and between teams.[202]

Iterative working patterns help achieve consistency. Deviations from standards are quickly noticed. Different methods achieve this in different ways. The waterfall approach assumes pre-agreement of detailed theoretical standards by 'quality assurance' teams, and the coercive enforcement of them by independent quality inspectors. A very different approach is taken in XP, where quality standards are agreed by the team and enforced by a natural norming process when pair programming is used. If it is discovered that the quality standards need refinement, the team adopts a more refined approach and spreads the word in an organic way – at standup meetings and by pair working. This is very effective on smaller projects, but once the team grows above a dozen or so people, organic processes need help. The DSDM framework provides a role to help this: the *Technical Co-coordinator* whose responsibility is to ensure that parallel development teams on larger projects work in a consistent way so that the solution is coherent, and that quality is good. A "System Architecture Definition" (SAD) is drawn up before starting to build the solution. DSDM specifically relates this to the IT aspects of design, but there is no reason why the SAD should not cover any aspects of required technology – buildings, communications, machinery, and so on. And, like any other agile product, leadership is needed to ensure that standards stated in the SAD are refined iteratively using practical feedback. The SAD should be a 'just enough' document, not part of a detailed BDUF.

Hierarchy of 'Delivery'

A strength of the agile approach is in the way that it creates a spectrum of delivery. At the one end of that spectrum is the delivery of a non-working model, or mock-up of just one aspect of the solution. At the other end of the spectrum is the full-scale rollout of a tranche of the solution for operational use.

However, when using a specific agile method one must be careful to understand what is meant by 'delivery'. Agilists tend to use the term 'delivery' as a catch-all term – anything on this spectrum is often termed 'delivered', even if it is just a successful team integration test. Defining this spectrum of deliverability is important to provide transparency, demonstrate quality and prove control. But it is only the ultimate delivery of useful, working product and its operational embedding that enables benefits to be realized.

Agile methods, then, often oversimplify the richness of this spectrum. Government cannot just 'ship a product' – it is responsible for delivering outcomes, not technology. The Scrum method is an example of this over simplification. It only provides a binary definition of delivery:

♦ *Done* product – meets a previously jointly agreed *definition of done* or *quality acceptance criteria*

♦ *Done and potentially releasable product* – not just meeting a set of acceptance criteria, but also having the potential for immediate use and business benefit.

The scope of the Scrum method is very much constrained to the internal world of a technical development team. The planning and execution of the implementation of the 'product' is visualized as merely a matter of 'release' or 'shipping' the product for immediate use:

> "The purpose of each sprint is to deliver Increments of potentially shippable functionality that adhere to the Scrum Team's current Definition of 'Done.' Development Teams deliver an Increment of product functionality every sprint. This Increment is useable, so a Product Owner may choose to immediately release it." [203]

Some commentators have suggested that because Scrum is most used in situations where planning ahead is difficult, it can be forgiven for ignoring release management planning and skating over the inherent complexity of implementation. But if we wish to use the method on large scale government environments we must consider the issue of the definition of the delivery spectrum further. [204]

DSDM provides a more useful delivery model. It comes from a project framework perspective that incorporates the mechanisms involved in rollout of solutions, not just their build. In the DSDM framework, iterations target not two, but three levels of *deliverability*:

- Purely *Exploration*, where the stakeholders' requirements are explored through modeling and specification prototyping

- A mix of *Exploration* and *Engineering* where an interactive development takes place to create a working solution which can be demonstrated

- *Deployment*, where the working solution is implemented and business benefit is realized.

Keith Richards suggests that this, among other reasons, explains why, in his opinion:

> "Only DSDM can be used 'as is' for projects. Scrum and XP are product delivery techniques – they have no concept of 'a project'." [205]

But all of these methods do, to some extent, oversimplify the planning needed to meet Agile Manifesto Principle three and deliver a mutually recognizable working solution on a regular basis. Therefore, it is instructive to examine a more differentiated type of hierarchy of delivery. The military defines nine Technology Readiness Levels (TRLs) to categorize delivery:[206]

1. Basic – the lowest level of technology readiness where theory awaits practical implementation

2. Technology concept formulated – some basic principles demonstrated, but still essentially theoretical

3. *Proof-of-concept* – some physical validation of parts of the design

4. Subsystem/Component validation – laboratory environment integration of whole parts of the system

5. Subsystem/Component validation in a relevant environment – technological components tested in a simulated environment

6. System prototype – relevant demonstration – a simulated operational environment demonstration

7. System prototype – operational demonstration – the demonstration of an actual system prototype in an operational environment

8. System completed – technology qualified through test and demonstration in expected conditions

9. Successful mission operations – Application of the technology under mission conditions.

Table 3 introduces the delivery-planning concept, which will help government agile projects demonstrate mutually agreed regular deliveries.

Level 1 Delivery – Specification Prototyping

Level 1 deliveries are useful to elicit feedback and gain buy-in and the confidence of stakeholders – especially at the start of the project. The DSDM framework recommends that a *feasibility prototype* should be used while an *outline business case* is created, but before the feasibility of the project overall is confirmed. This work will, by nature be limited and should focus on the business issues at hand. The objective is not to start building a solution, but to investigate any practical aspects of the solution that could impinge upon financial costs/benefits, and to gain confidence before a full-scale business case is created.

Level 2 Delivery – Demonstration of an Emerging Solution

Level 2 deliveries are not intended for use, but give realistic assurance to management and stakeholders about critical aspects of the solution:

♦ Is the solution 'user friendly'? Is the citizen uptake of the new service that is presumed in the business case still realistic?

♦ Does the solution perform? A set of what are termed 'non-functional requirements' will need to be developed and tested to ensure that performance is adequate.

♦ Is the internal architecture developable and maintainable? It is difficult to ensure that complex solutions will work as intended.

Table 3: Proposed Hierarchy of delivery for Agile Projects

Level	Deliverable	Description
1	Specification Prototype	A working model of some aspects of the solution.
2	Emerging Solution	A partially constructed solution that conforms to technical standards, but still has functions missing required for real-world use.
3	Shippable	A partially constructed solution that could be used.
4	Consumable	A partially constructed solution that is ready for use.
5	Piloted	An increment of the solution deployed and in use in a limited locality, customer segment and/or for a limited time
6	Implemented	An increment of the solution that is in wide-scale rollout/use.

Level 3 Delivery – Having a 'Shippable' Product Ready

Level 3 delivery is simply the 'potential' for delivery. Periodically, a whole solution is built and proven to work – in theory. The stakeholders may not be ready to start using the solution, and other implementation restrictions may exist. For example, the UK Department of Work and Pensions has approximately 10,000 staff working in unemployment 'Job Centers'. Changes to the computer systems must be carefully made in conjunction with staff training, and it is not thought practical to make wholesale changes to processes on a regular basis. Level 3 delivery has the following advantages:

♦ Further feedback can be gathered from stakeholders on the requirements and their priority

♦ Confidence in the progress of the team is increased

♦ The technical infrastructure of the solution can be proven end-to-end, thus reducing the problems of integration of many different components.

However, the delivery of a solution by the development team at Level 3 does not guard against future problems such as:

♦ Whether the solution can be easily implemented and used for full-scale operations

♦ Whether the preparation and training planned for users of the technology is adequate

♦ Whether the user acceptance tests are adequate and have the coverage required for real world use.

Level 4 Delivery – Having a 'Consumable' Product Ready

This delivery level requires user acceptance of the solution, and the delivery mechanisms tested. The delivery is not just 'shippable' from the point of view of the developers, but also 'consumable' from the point of view of the stakeholders.

Setting up delivery mechanisms to make implementation smooth requires activities that Carl Kessler calls 'meta-tasks' – in other words additional planning and development that is necessary not to build a solution, but to build the processes required so that the solution can be implemented.

Dry runs of the product on real life data may take place to show that the new technical solution is usable. Where business rules are unchanged, parallel running can help identify any errors in the running of the new solution.[207]

Level 4 delivery incorporates Kessler's concept of 'consumability': a product needs to be more than just 'shippable', but also 'consumable'. He advises a three-step process to ensure this:

♦ Identify 'consumability meta-tasks': those activities that need to be carried out to smooth the path to a successful use of the solution

♦ Treat consumability capabilities like any other solution capability: implementation and use needs to be formally tested

♦ Set up measures for 'consumability' and continually improve the solution in this respect. [208]

Level 5 Delivery – Piloting the Solution

This level requires pilot running of the solution. The UK Green Book states that:

> "(One benefit of a pilot is that it should) acquire more information about risks affecting a project through (and allow) steps to be taken to mitigate either the adverse consequences of bad outcomes, or increase the benefits of good outcomes.' [209]

The GAO has recently audited pilot projects as diverse as tax collection at the Internal Revenue Service (IRS) and implementation of improved emergency planning at the Federal Emergency Management Agency (FEMA), and has developed criteria for successful planning for pilot projects. These are:

♦ Well-defined, clear, and measurable objectives

♦ Criteria for determining pilot-program performance

♦ A method for the determination of appropriate pilot size and a strategy for comparing the pilot results with other efforts

♦ Plans for data collection and analysis to track the program's performance and evaluate the final results of the project. [210]

Of course, usefulness of pilots goes beyond providing risk management and providing technical feedback to the solution developers. Pilot implementation of a solution can engender transparency because significant stakeholders will be involved in checking that the new way of working really does bring business benefits. Plans for the best approach for rollout of a solution and its speed will be informed by its pilot usage.

Level 6 Delivery – Widespread Phased Rollout

Level 6 is 'real world' delivery, free of the constraints of the theoretical testing of levels 1 to 4, and the limitations of piloting. The costs and benefits of wide-scale rollout and usage can be measured, and the business case tracked. Level 6 delivery should be incremental. An example of an incremental implementation approach was that taken by the US Department of Veterans Affairs (VA), where since 2009 projects are required to have processes to build and deliver incremental functionality every 6 months. A 'three strikes and you're out' policy repeated failure to deliver functionality as scheduled will result in a project being paused – or even terminated.[211] The avoidance of a *big-bang* implementation gives opportunity for early identification of project problems. Carefully used it can guard against the 'scope creep' that can often occur on projects where new features and requirements slowly are added to an overlarge requirements catalogue.

Conclusions

Delivery of a partially working solution provides transparency on the progress of a project – especially if an agile approach is taken which delivers incrementally, and in very short iterations. This will allow for incremental improvement of the solution by refactoring the design and architecture.

You may notice that Agile Manifesto Principle 1 requires "continuous delivery", whereas Principle 3 refers to "short iterations". One should not be too literal in comparing these principles. Principle 1 reflects the ideas behind *lean* development techniques discussed in Part 1. Lean development is almost indistinguishable from *continuous improvement* approaches used in running normal day-to-day operations.[212] *Kanban* is a lean technique that involves displaying status cards on walls to illustrate the planning of outstanding work and progress against schedule. It is simply the Japanese word for "visual information". The idea is that as soon as something changes, whether it be a new issue that is identified, or an existing task is re-prioritized, the cards are changed on the wall, and everybody nearby can see the change immediately.

When scaling up agile techniques for large-scale government projects a decision must be made as to what 'continuous' delivery means, and that requires two factors to be agreed for each iteration. First, the criteria for acceptable delivery, second, the length of time to be taken. Near continuous delivery by very short iterations are most suitable where operations can respond nimbly to change. Longer iterations are more suitable where the nature of operations require periodic releases at longer intervals, or where the build times for the technology are measured in months, rather than days. The important thing is to do this with eyes wide open, and Agile Leadership Behavior 2 requires a presumption towards a shorter length, rather than longer wherever practicable.

VA has required incremental implementation since 2009. Their "three strikes and you're out" policy ensures that project delivery happens regularly. If more than two incremental deliveries are missed, then the project is stopped and considered for major replanning of approach or cancellation.

Agile methods, such as DSDM and Scrum, recognize that 'delivery' does not always imply actual usage. The creation, testing, and acceptance of increments of work results in a type of delivery. It is objective and auditable. But it is not always practical to put every changed piece of software live right now, therefore there is a risk of a lack of nuance over what 'delivery' means, and (especially in Scrum) what the development team's responsibility for implementation preparations are. Implementation is, for most government projects, much more than just 'shipping the product'. For this reason (and others which I will explore later) some agile experts argue that DSDM should be used as a 'wrapper' around delivery techniques such as Scrum and XP which are focused more at team level than corporate level. A useful planning concept is for the development team to target a 'hierarchy of delivery' so that the type of delivery from each increment of work is clear and expectations are set with stakeholders, especially with those tasked with training and implementation of the solution with end-users.

Questions

1. Refer to Ken Schwaber's "Scrum Guide" (see Endnote 213). Read through looking for references to the concept of the "increment", how it is planned, how it is monitored, and how it helps control the direction of work through feedback.

2. Look at the explanation of the *definition of done* on page 15 of the "Scrum Guide" (see Endnote 214). How does this differ from traditional concepts of definition of acceptance criteria?

Agile Leadership Exercises

1. Have you or your team had to carry out considerable rework on something that had taken a lot of effort to produce? What was the trigger for the rework — a quality review perhaps? Or comments from an important stakeholder? Could the team have elicited feedback at an earlier stage? Could you suggest to your team a better way to canvass the right people at the right time in the future?

2. Is there a task you or your team are working on at the moment that is going to be widely circulated and used? Is there a risk that it might not be well received? Suggest using the Hierarchy of Delivery to users to define acceptance levels.

Chapter 10

Agile Leadership Behavior Four: Get the Business and Technical People Together

> *Business people and developers must work together daily throughout the project.*

Agile Manifesto Principle Number Four

One of the key aims of agile is to make sure that the solution being built will be practical, and will bring business benefits. Potential problems are identified as early as possible, with corrective action being taken immediately. At a micro level, this is achieved by a policy of *organic defect detection*. By putting testing at the heart of development, and by carrying out near continuous integration with iterative delivery of the product, we can be sure that the solution will be free of any significant errors. However, even a perfectly bug free delivery may not bring business benefits if it is a solution to the wrong problem. Tom Gilb comments:

> "The intent is to strongly encourage software developers and their stakeholders to communicate with each other about 'what is really needed and valued', and 'what is practical and what works', immediately, frequently, orally, and by demonstration of old and new systems reference points. The intent is that a new system cannot get far, more than one day, off track to realistic usefulness." [215]

At a macro level, then, we need to make sure that we are not only building the solution the right way, but we need to ensure that we are building the right solution. This is why the agile approach places the intended users of the solution at the core of the development team, and ensures that other stakeholders are engaged with as often as possible.

Getting the Business and Technical People Together

In the realm of software development (especially of large systems), it is often desirable for real-world users of a system to be integrated into the development teams. An early approach was Joint Application Design (JAD). This was intended to involve the users of a system by use of formal working meetings called *JAD sessions*. These highly structured events were preceded by the preparation of prototypes of the solution by a specialist JAD analyst. The JAD Session was then executed with a tightly controlled agenda, and the decisions made carefully documented. A separate post-JAD session *wrap-up* phase was carried out by the JAD analyst, producing a refined prototype and supporting documentation for presentation to the executive sponsor.

This JAD approach has been criticized as being a mini-waterfall approach. Many felt that it did not get deep and continuous involvement of users because "managers and users are involved minimally during customization" and that decisions are often merely "distributed to the session participants", ruling out effective collaboration.[216] It was popular among systems professionals because it provided a "prescriptive 'cookbook' of techniques for eliciting information from passive users". JAD was justified mainly in terms of technical gains, principally based on poorly evidenced claims of productivity gains that were made by advocates of the approach.[217]

Erran Carmel argues that the JAD approach was no more than a "consultative approach", tending towards low user involvement in most of the processes. Techniques such as documentation walk-throughs, committee reviews, formal sign-offs and 'liaison' are advised. These approaches leave most of the decision-making power to the 'expert' technical staff, not the users. As such, JAD was used to support the BDUF of a waterfall approach such as Information Engineering where Beath and Orlikowski warned that users were given "a relatively passive role to play during development".[218]

JAD focused on documenting designs, not evolving a working solution. In 2011, the UK Child Maintenance and Enforcement Commission (CMEC) abandoned the use of JAD on its massive waterfall systems redevelopment. The NAO had previously criticized CMEC for "lack of clarity about the functionality of the required system".

CMEC responded by adopting the JAD approach, reporting in 2010 that this would "ensure that the requirements are more comprehensively defined... with the system being developed interactively".[219] However, the use of JAD and iterative development were abandoned when it was recognized that it merely produced "duplicated, conflicting, and ambiguous" specifications.[220]

The JAD approach, then, needed to be improved upon since it proved to be no more than a framework for how to run a meeting, and it maintained the power of specialists over the genuine needs of the business people who needed a working solution.

Participatory Design

The method of 'Participatory Design' (PD) was developed by Pelle Ehn in Scandinavia. There are areas of similarity to JAD, such as use of workshops and visualization/prototyping techniques, but the PD method was a move towards collaborative design rather than consultative requirements elicitation (see Table 4).

Two main themes make PD different. First, the idea of *mutual reciprocal learning* whereby designers learn about the stakeholders' activities and business needs, and simultaneously the stakeholder learn about the possibilities of the available technologies. Second, there is emphasis on *design by doing* rather than documentation. The users and technical developers are expected to experiment with the technology together.

We not only need an effective way of ensuring participatory design, we also need to involve the right people. Not all stakeholders are simply 'users' of a technical solution. Early in this Part of the book, I mentioned five broad categorizations of stakeholders from a project manager's point of view: users, bosses, subordinates, maintainers, sponsors and customers.

Table 4: Comparison of JAD to PD (adapted from Carmel, 1993) [221]

Joint Application Design	Participatory Design
Promise of time savings	Promise of conflict resolution
Design-led development	Collaborative development
Consultancy driven	Workplace driven
Completeness	Empowerment
Time delimitation	Satisfaction delimitation
Structure	Creativity
Stakeholder segmentation unclear	Stakeholder segmentation into users and managers

An effective way, then, of making sure that the right people are involved to create the right solution, is to:

♦ Identify the stakeholders for the coming iteration

♦ Identify their win conditions

♦ Reconcile their win conditions. [222]

Research shows that having a broad definition of what a stakeholder is, and thinking broadly and systematically about their categorization, and therefore the method of engagement will create:

♦ Greater flexibility in adapting to risks and uncertainties

♦ Better discipline in achieving operational capability

♦ Enhanced trust between the project stakeholders. [223]

Stakeholder Engagement in Government

Although Agile Manifesto Principle 2 talks specifically about the need for "business people and developers" to work closely together, there is general agreement in the agile community that any distinction between business user and developer could be a false dichotomy. Decades ago, in the days of mainframe computers, the distinction between programmers and users was clear. In agile teams, business people often bring great technical knowledge into the team. For example, at the British Library a project to start *ingesting* e-journals into the permanent digital store also required the storage of closely related and very complex meta-data (i.e. not just the journal text, but information about the publisher and the authors).

The experts on the Electronic Data Interchange (EDI) standards for this meta-data were not the programmers on the team, but the 'users'. We must also recognize the importance of other technical staff. There may be a statutory accounting need for independent testing, an anathema for many agilists, but IT audit is a fact of life in government. We also need to include strategic planners, user-training specialists, public relations and communications experts and so on.

Thus, Agile Leadership Behavior 4 goes beyond the narrow text of Agile Manifesto Principle 4. We must not only take a broad view, and stress close stakeholder involvement beyond just the community of users of the solution, but also we must engage effectively with those who will be impacted by it.

An example of the catastrophic effect of poor stakeholder engagement, and the production of a fatally flawed technical solution was the failed UK Firecontrol project. It was initiated and run by the Office of the Deputy Prime Minister, John Prescott. After the cancellation of the project, with £469m wasted, Prescott claimed not to have known that there was great resentment among Chief Fire Officers about the proposed centralization that the project proposed in its business case. The aim was for the 46 existing local control centers to be reduced to just nine regional control rooms. A firm of management consultants had already advised against fast centralization, and had instead recommended a reduction to 21 centers. The changes were regarded with hostility by a broad range of stakeholders, including Chief Fire Officers, the Firefighters Union, and the Local Government Association.

When the project was eventually canceled at a cost of £469m, the NAO found that:

> "A major reason why the project had failed was due to insufficient communication and engagement with stakeholders during the initiation and design of the project which led to concerns about its rationale and purpose from the outset.

> "Fire and Rescue Authorities and their Services criticized the lack of clarity on how a regional approach would increase efficiency. The Local Government Association similarly asserted throughout the planning and delivery of Firecontrol that a centrally-dictated, one size fits all model was not an appropriate way to optimize resilience." [224]

In contrast, a major project by the UK Revenue and Customs had delivered 94% uptake of salaried employee tax returns over the period 2007-11 with effective stakeholder engagement applied during a phased implementation of online services. Each stakeholder group was identified and assigned a 'champion' to act as a single point of contact, and consultative groups were set up to liaise with tax agents and industry representatives. Customer concerns were researched and face-to-face events were held to help small businesses and individuals understand the new processes.

Requirements for the new services were prioritized according to stakeholder concerns. For example, as a response to these concerns mandatory filing was delayed, which gave rise to the opportunity to reduce the overall budget of £373m by about 10%. New requirements were proposed and implemented.

Examples of these were free software for small businesses, and *soft landings* of non-mandatory solutions that allowed customers to familiarize themselves with online filing without fear of penalties. Third-party tax and accounting software developers were also identified as important stakeholders and targeted technical information was sent to them to assist them in developing compatible systems.[225]

The GAO identifies active engagement with senior management as a common critical success factor. In a survey of seven large, and successful government IT projects collectively worth $5bn, the GAO found that:

> "Officials from all seven (projects) cited active engagement with program stakeholders as a critical factor to the success of those investments ... stakeholders regularly attended program management office sponsored meetings: were working members of integrated project teams: and were notified of problems and concerns as soon as possible." [226]

The GAO found that the use of multi-disciplinary teams and early involvement of users in defining requirements had created transparency and trust and further increased the support from the stakeholders. In contrast to these successful projects, the GAO has regularly reported on instances of project failures due to poor stakeholder engagement. Examples include:

◆ The Federal Emergency Management Agency (FEMA), where end users were not sufficiently involved in defining requirements for the National Flood Insurance Program's insurance policy and claims management system. The program was canceled in final end-user testing after seven years of development and a budget of $40m, forcing the agency to continue to rely on an outdated 30 year-old system.[227]

◆ The Department of Homeland Security (DHS), which did not allow sufficient time for stakeholder involvement in its planning and had no consistent method for identifying stakeholder roles and incorporating their feedback.[228]

◆ The 2010 US Census where lack of local user involvement in software testing hindered local governments' ability to update address lists and maps accurately.[229]

Stakeholder Engagement in Government

Stakeholders are individuals, organizations, or groups of organizations, which have an actual or perceived interest in a project. Some stakeholders, for example may be very negative about a project, and the best that can be achieved is a reduction of their negativity.

The Guide to the Project Management Body of Knowledge (a US ANSI standard) takes the view that stakeholders need to be "managed by the project manager (as) the lead person responsible for communicating with all stakeholders". The attitude is that stakeholder management is process driven being mainly "distributing information" and "managing stakeholder expectations". [230]

In contrast, the UK Cabinet Office guidance materials on "Managing Successful Programs" (MSP) sees effective stakeholder engagement as a wider function of leadership, not process. An approach is encouraged where top management should demonstrate empathy with and influence of stakeholders, not treating communications as a mechanical top-down process. MSP notes that:

> "Projects that stress the management of stakeholders can lapse into relying on planned communications that are little more than a task list with a bias towards outbound information. This does not sufficiently engage stakeholders, who generally do not appreciate being 'managed'." [231]

In an agile project, stakeholders should be *engaged* not managed. Interactions need to be iterative and adaptive. There is a danger that if a detailed communications plan is set out initially it may become set in stone, and unresponsive to changing circumstances, or to the need for changed emphasis if the project objectives shift.

MSP requires a *Stakeholder* Engagement *Strategy* to be agreed at the start of each major project, and for an associated Communications Plan to be agreed and tracked. MSP provides guidance on running complex, large projects where many sub-projects need to be coordinated to a common business goal. The appointment of a *Business Change Manager* is required who is responsible for ensuring that implementation goes smoothly and ensuring that a *benefits realization plan* is being tracked. [232] The project Communications Plan should recognize different levels of stakeholder engagement, and delegate relationship management to the most appropriate level, so that detailed co-working on specific issues can be encouraged.

Conclusions

Agile principle number four recognizes that business experts are often not the same people who are experts in developing technical solutions. Therefore close teamwork is required if business benefits are to be realized using technology. Frequent and close working relationships are needed between business people and the technical developers – often working in multi-disciplinary teams and/or communicating usually on a daily basis. Face-to-face meetings are likely to lead to the 'richest' forms of communication, but this is often impractical, and web-conferencing using shared visuals can often suffice.

The involvement of the business experts in structured Joint Applications Design (JAD) meetings with a tightly controlled agenda can often merely result in more paperwork and documentation, rather than a continually evolving co-developed solution. Agile approaches require a genuinely participative development approach with stakeholders, with expert business people working on an equal footing and status as the expert technicians who will build the solution.

Project approaches that focus at team level may inadvertently cause a form of 'stakeholder myopia' whereby external stakeholders are ignored. Top management leadership is required to ensure that the necessary stakeholder engagement is facilitated. It should recognize that the most effective communication is two-way, and devolved as far as practical to the grass-roots people. Early, detailed, lengthy, and 'rich' forms of communication regarding a small set of key points of detail will avoid major problems later on. Identification of 'sticking points' where disagreement over priorities or business objectives is important in advance of these detailed meetings – try to find a strategy whereby both sides meet their perceived objectives via 'win-win' resolutions of conflict.

Agile Leadership Exercises

1. How do you plan to communicate with your stakeholders? Which meetings do you have coming up in the next month

with them? If you are planning to email out a report for comment at the meeting then you are in *broadcast mode*. How could you involve people and give them a chance to participate beforehand?

2.   Assess the teams you have worked with recently. Which were specialist teams of staff with very similar skills? Which were multi-disciplinary teams of staff with heterogeneous skills? What were the strengths and weaknesses exhibited by both types of teams? What suggestions for improvements could you make to your team?

3.   Thinking of your team and their interactions, are there any suggestions you could make that would improve their ability to engage with stakeholders in their meetings?

   ▪   Using models?

   ▪   Using working prototypes?

   ▪   Arranging for face-to-face meetings facilitated by someone neutral from outside your team?

Chapter 11

Agile Leadership Behavior Five – Part A: Create Trust (Through Leadership)

> *Build projects around motivated individuals. Give them the environment and support they need, and trust them to get the job done.*

Agile Manifesto Principle Number Five

In this and the next chapter, I will explore how Agile Leadership Behavior 5 engenders motivation and trust – both within project teams, and with the key stakeholders that can make or break your projects. Trust can be engendered through both leadership skills and implementation of just enough process. This chapter focuses on the first factor: leadership skills. The next chapter focuses on motivational behaviors that are based on light, transparent processes. If a process is straightforward, and has just enough structure, but no more, then people will trust each other and work as a team to succeed.

I argue here that good leadership and good process are two different but interdependent parameters for success. Bad leadership will subvert even the best processes for governance project management and technical development. A recent survey into the factors driving the adoption and use of agile revealed that leadership by individuals is the driving force behind agile adoption, not corporate strategy. Resistance within the organization, both from institutional inertia of outdated processes and from apathetic staff members and suppliers, are the key inhibitors to agile adoption.[233]

Disciplined and steady leadership, with clear targets and effective motivation are the bedrock of the *tight* top management behaviors that I propose. These must be complemented by *light* control over teams and suppliers that will use their expert judgment for which they have been employed. Trust has to be exercised in both directions – the team must trust top management to shield them from external forces that would otherwise sap their determination to reach each short, iterative goal. Trust in the team must be demonstrated by top management in allowing them 'off the leash' – the aim is to inspire the team to produce 'surprise and delight' for the stakeholders who will get a solution that is different and better than they imagined at the beginning of the project (see Figure 9).

This diagram shows five major factors that lead to motivation and trust. Each of them, to some extent or another, works in both the leadership dimension and in the process dimension. At the highest level of management, clear leadership is the dominant dimension. At more detailed levels of team management, the process dimension becomes dominant. However, effective leadership cannot exist in a vacuum – good process supports good leadership. Conversely, good leadership needs 'just enough' process. On large public sector projects, effective process adds value where transparency and accountability are vital.

The remainder of this chapter explores the first two of these factors: top-level involvement and governance of project management.

Top Management Involvement

Effective top managers rely primarily on leadership skills, to a larger or lesser extent backed-up by administrative aptitude. At the highest level in government are the political leaders who set policy, which must be implemented at secretarial/commissioner level. The work of the project must be closely linked to the direction set by this top level of leadership. Top management can lead and maintain close involvement with projects in many ways. This will depend a great deal on style and culture. Here I wish to focus on an important aspect of involvement that is more common and widespread and poorly executed than any other: risk management.

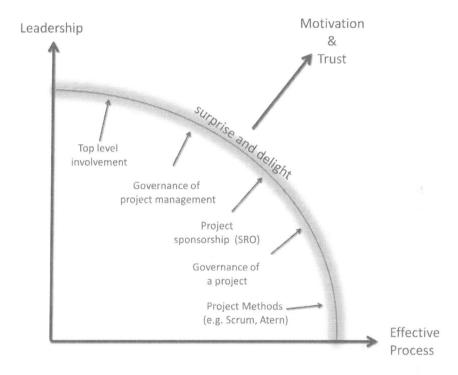

Figure 9: The five factors contributing to motivation and trust

Risk management tends to be a bottom-up driven process, not a top management led activity. By this I mean that often it becomes a case of 'management by risk register', where various bottom-level, known technical risks are identified and tracked individually, without an analysis of how they interact and could cause catastrophic problems.

Let us look at a case of risk management where the interaction between leadership and process was critical: the case of a project document that was leaked to the media, causing a major political row.

In 2012, the UK National Health Service (NHS) was finalizing preparations for a major project to change its organization. Over 90,000 staff would be directly affected. The benefits of the changes were expected to be better health outcomes, fewer avoidable hospital admissions, and a "genuinely patient-centered approach to services". An annual saving of £20bn was expected, and much objected to by healthcare workers.[234]

The project involved a fundamental change to the funding of the NHS which required primary legislation (the Health and Social Care Bill) to be passed by Parliament. This was bitterly fought against by the opposition party. A member of the public had made a Freedom of Information (FOI) request to be provided with a copy of the related risk register that evaluated the proposed reform plans. However, there were two risk registers in existence. An operational risk register and a transitional risk register. The former was authorized for release, but the latter was not because:

> "It was covered by protection for information that relates to the formulation or development of Government policy." [235]

However, a version of the transitional risk register that was at least a year out of date was leaked to Roy Lilley, a blogger who published it on the Internet. It revealed that some risks from the government's policy had been previously assessed as very high probability and impact, notably:

♦ Devolution of the organization being a risk to the NHS's ability to cope with emergencies

♦ Greater costs if greater use was made of the private sector

♦ The danger that the new system would be set up too quickly

♦ Potential loss of financial control. [236]

This case illustrates the importance of top management involvement, review, and leadership in the formulation of project direction. The leaked risk register, which was marked "draft", was over a year old when it was leaked, and was only a list of potential, not actual problems. However, this did not stop it being widely quoted in the media and its contents being used as ammunition by the opposition leader in Parliament at Prime Minister's question time. The position of the Secretary of Health came under intense attack not just from the opposition but also from within his own party, and required the Prime Minister's personal support for the reforms to continue.[237]

The difference between strategic operational risks and transition risks has been widely misunderstood. In many cases organizations focus on only operational risks, even when risky major projects are underway. Table 5 on page 147) gives an overview of how three major delivery departments in the US and the UK manage risk, at the strategic operational level and at the transition/project level.

Both these organizations have adopted the COSO Enterprise Risk Management Framework (ERMF). It was developed by the Committee of Sponsoring Organizations of the Treadway Commission (COSO), which provides guidance on organizational governance issues. COSO has wide support from all major accounting bodies in the USA and UK, and the ERMF has been widely adopted as a standard for managing operational risk. However, it does not have any major components regarding managing the risk from change programs.[238] Change management is often a blind spot not just in such standards, but also the corporate risk management processes set up to conform to them. Weaknesses in overall risk management leadership and policy can result in ineffective recognition of risks to the organization that can come from change programs. For example, the US Internal Revenue Service needed to replace its aging legacy computer systems urgently because they cannot easily support online customer service. A $210m program was set up in 2011, comprised of three large component projects.[239] However, risk management guidelines were not followed resulting in inconsistencies in risk management practices and no consolidated view of risks to top management.[240]

The GAO has been worried about both operational and project risk management in the US government for many years. It has developed its own model for organizational risk management, but has found it difficult to encourage structure in these processes. For example, in 2008 it convened a risk management forum for senior staff from DHS and related agencies. The participants could not reach consensus on integration of risk reporting relationships within the organization, and identified risk communication as the single greatest challenge to using risk management principles. A recommendation was that the Government should develop a national strategic planning process for risk management.[241]

On the other hand, UK Government departments base their risk management approach on central guidance that is given in the Treasury Orange Book.[242] This guidance does not specify a specific standard set for risk management in the Government, but establishes principles for a framework for risk management, suggesting several standards, which could be referenced, namely:

- The COSO ERMF[243]

- The UK Institute of Risk Management (IRM) Standards[244]

- The Australian/New Zealand standard (since ratified in 2009 as an international standard ISO 31000)

- The Canadian government Framework for the Management of Risk (updated in 2010). [245]

Both the UK Treasury Orange Book and the Canadian Risk Management framework explicitly recognize project risk as special. They refer to the need for integration of the monitoring of transition (i.e., project) risks into strategic risk management and give instruction as to where top management can find further guidance:

For Canada:

> "The management of projects ... integrated across the department appropriately for the level of project risk and complexity ... This approach should ensure that accountability for outcomes is clear, appropriate controls are in place to minimize risk ... and outputs and outcomes are monitored and reported ... Ministers have responsibility for the administration of projects in support of the mandated programs of their departments." [246]

For the UK:

> "Risk management is a structured approach to identifying, assessing, and controlling risks that emerge during the course of the policy, project, or project lifecycle. Its task is to ensure an organization makes cost-effective use of a risk process that has a series of well-defined

steps to support better decision-making through good understanding
of the risks inherent in a proposal and their likely impact." [247]

The IRM guidance requires identification of project risks separate from strategic risks and requires their incorporation at the "conceptual stage of projects as well as throughout the life of a specific project."[248]

The Australian/New Zealand risk management standard is now an International Standard.[249] It requires risk management to be an integral part of all organizational processes and "not a stand-alone activity (and should be) part of the responsibilities of management ... including all project and change management".[250]

The UK Department for Work and Pensions (DWP) does not state a strategic policy for integration of change management risk into the monitoring of strategic operational risk with as much clarity as UK Revenue and Customs (see Table 5). DWP's 2011 annual report did not identify any risks centering about its major IT projects. However, some of these are very large, and have huge uncertainties.[251] For example, the Automated Service Delivery (ASD) project was suspended in February 2012 after being used in pilot sites as a proof-of-concept. The ASD was a new system intended to prove the idea of self-service by citizens over the Internet. The project was based on research that concluded that the new online service could expect over 40% uptake from benefit claimants on Jobseeker's Allowance.[252] The project had been set up to develop the system using some agile approaches. Initially progress seemed good. An internal confidential Gateway report optimistically stated that:

> In terms of the use of Agile within Government, DWP also have the
> best current experience via their Automated Service Delivery (ASD)
> Programme.[253]

The team, though, were using a "slightly less lean" version of an agile method based on an "interpretation" advised by consultancy firm Accenture. The system that was delivered was suspended because it was not adequate, and a complete overhaul of the system, which had cost over £15.4m to develop, was announced.[254]

The DWP Universal Credit project is one of the largest IT-enabled projects ever undertaken by the UK government. It aims to change benefits and tax credits for those who are out of work with one universal system. This is in order to ensure that once a claimant gets into work, they will always be better off. At its peak, it had over 750 technical, development, and project staff developing the new systems and operations using a highly tailored version of the Scrum method. It is using a variant of the processes that the ASD project had claimed to be 'agile'. DWP plan to run the first Universal Credit pilot in spring 2013, when the success or not of the 'tailored' version of Scrum that has been adopted can be assessed.[255]

I have focused here on leadership by harnessing the power of risk management processes – this is one very important aspect of how top management should get involved with and keep involved with change projects. Similarly, issue management and decision-making should be led *from the front*, and not managed purely on spreadsheets. One sure way to motivate people is to trust them. The effective and generous delegation of decision-making and the ability to respond to risks and issues to the lowest level possible will achieve much of this.

One such method is a top-down method called 'Failure Mode Evaluation Analysis' (FMEA). Essentially this is a practical activity, best carried out initially in a workshop of multi-disciplinary experts. The objective is to identify major possible catastrophic outcomes and then work backwards to see how they might come about.

For example, one potential risk could be that a project might be delayed due to problems in data conversion. The participants in the workshop then brainstorm various sequences of events (or sub-risks) that could, if they occur together, cause the ultimate *failure mode* – in this case that Benefit *'X'* would not occur and thus undermine the case for the project investment.

Table 5: Three examples of Corporate and Project Risk Management Frameworks used in US and UK Governments

Department	Strategic Operational Risk Management Policy	Project Risk Management Policy
US Internal Revenue Service (IRS) Running Costs: $12bn/annum 107,000 staff	Enterprise Risk Management (ERM) leadership is directed by the Office of Program Evaluation and Risk Analysis (OPERA). Enterprise-wide perspective of risks exists at the agency level.[256] No specific references at policy level to leadership on internal risks arising from change projects.[257]	A tiered governance approach ensures each IT project is governed at the appropriate level within the organization. Potential project risks are escalated as needed.[258]
UK Revenue and Customs (HMRC) Running Costs: £3.7bn/annum 66,000 staff	Implemented a corporate risk management approach in FY 2011. Each business area of the Department has a Lead Risk Champion and Business Risk Partner who support the Executive Committee in managing risk. A Corporate Risk Management function provides central support.[259]	Risk Management Framework includes change management. Risk governance enables a line of sight between the various projects and core business.[260]
UK Work and Pensions (DWP) Running costs £510m/annum 121,000 staff	The Executive Team provides corporate leadership to manage risks and opportunities. Chief Executives of the Department's Agencies and Non-Departmental Public Bodies (NDPBs) are accountable for the maintenance and operation of the system of internal control and risk management in their business areas. Risk Business Partners are in place to support improved risk management in the Department's Agencies and Policy functions.	A Change Delivery Sub-Committee supports successful delivery of the portfolio of mission critical projects. No specific project risk management strategy.[261]

Governance of Agile Project Management

Effective governance of the practice of project management in an organization is a factor that requires leadership by example and just enough process to ensure that the change initiatives are under control.

In 2000, for example, the US Department of Energy strengthened its project management policies and guidance, so as to measure the performance of its projects, and thus improve the quality of federal oversight. The first key area that DOE focused on was strengthening its project management policies and guidance to incorporate industry practices as recommended by the National Research Council. In its 1999 report, the council had urged the DOE to adopt comprehensive project management policies and to emphasize early, detailed planning for projects.[262]

Therefore, the DOE issued a project management order in 1999 followed in 2003, by a comprehensive project management manual, thus instituting the process part of the governance equation.

The leadership dimension was addressed by emphasis on integrating project teams, each major project led by a federal project director. A multidisciplinary approach was encouraged to bring together expertise from project specialists from a central program office, and legal and contracting experts from the Office of General Counsel and other experts in safety, security, and environmental areas.

However, this process led approach had limited impact in some DOE agencies. The National Nuclear Security Administration, for example, had:

> "Not developed a project management policy, not implemented a plan for improving its project management efforts, and not fully shared Project Management Lessons Learned Between Its Sites." [263]

Table 6 presents the 13 Components Identified by the UK Association for Project Management as necessary for effective Governance of Project Management. I have categorized these into those that have predominantly a *leadership* dimension, and those that have mainly a *process* dimension. As can be seen, although eight of the 13 are fundamentally about *leadership*, the remaining five rely upon *process*.

Moreover, there is a great deal of interaction between these principles. For example, principle 3 focuses on the requirement for clarity of change management roles, which in the real world are defined by relationships and behaviors more than documented scoping statements and responsibilities. However, principle 3 depends to a great deal on effective recognition of the need for project structures and organization, which is represented by principle 2.

A quick note on terminology: In Canada and the UK, the term *Senior Responsible Owner* (SRO) is commonly used in government to mean what is generally known as the *project sponsor* or *project board chair* elsewhere. In addition, by *board* I mean the body for strategic decision-making for the public entity concerned. In the US, this might be the office of the departmental Secretary and his/her supporting executive board or top management team (the undersecretaries and assistant secretaries for example). The Chief Financial Officer is often an Assistant Secretary level, but with a direct report in at, effectively, decision making top management level.

Conclusions

In this chapter, I have explored the first two of the five major factors in building motivation and trust:

♦ Top management involvement

♦ Governance of Project Management

Of all the five factors, top management involvement is the one that depends most on leadership skills. It is important when leading a large, complex project that leadership is channeled through effective processes that are light enough not to weigh down the project teams involved. They must be rigorous enough to meet the needs of open and honest transparency.

Table 6: Principles of Governance of Project Management [264]

No.	APM Governance of Project Management Principle	Dimension	Agile implication
1	The board has overall governance of project management responsibility.	Leadership	Top management should exhibit behaviors consonant with the Agile manifesto.
2	The organization differentiates between projects and non-project based activities.	Process	Continuous or incremental change implies a *lean* approach, not a project approach.
3	Roles and responsibilities for the governance of project management are defined clearly.	Leadership	The top management team has a *tight* and disciplined governance approach, intervenes at appropriate points, and is not over controlling.
4	Disciplined governance arrangements, supported by appropriate methods, re-sources, and controls are applied throughout the project life cycle. Every project has a sponsor.	Process	Agile team processes should have clear direction. In DSDM supplied by the *Business Sponsor* at the top level and *the Business Visionary* at day-to-day level. Considering extending or dividing the Scrum concept of *Product Owner* into a strategic *Product Sponsor* and a more detailed and involved *Product Visionary* role.
5	There is a demonstrably coherent and supporting relationship between the overall business strategy and the project portfolio.	Leadership	Top management must work with project sponsors/product owners to emphasize cooperation and coordination between projects and overall strategy.

No.	APM Governance of Project Management Principle	Dimension	Agile implication
6	All projects have an approved plan containing authorization points at which the business case, inclusive of cost, benefits and risk is reviewed. Decisions made at authorization points are recorded and communicated.	Process	Mechanisms are required that keep an overview of all major projects. These mechanisms should comply with the Agile Principles, not require over-documentation, Big Design Up Front (BDUF) planning and other anti-agile processes.
7	Members of delegated authorization bodies have sufficient representation, competence, authority, and resources to enable them to make appropriate decisions.	Leadership	Top management should delegate to the greatest extent that is responsible (the concept of *subsidiarity*), this will demonstrate trust and increase motivation. Teams should self-organize.
8	Project business cases are supported by relevant and realistic information that provides a reliable basis for making authorization decisions.	Process	Business cases should concentrate on analyzing options and emphasizing assumptions and risk, not on justifying one course of action by providing spurious detail.
9	The board or its delegated agents decide when independent scrutiny of projects or project management systems is required and implement such assurance accordingly.	Leadership	Independent scrutiny, whether in the form of 'health checks' or audits should be in the spirit of checking team behaviors and project outputs, not documentation and working papers. (Although proof of adequate testing often must be supported by good documentation. The concept of *agile auditing* is discussed in more detail in a later chapter).

No.	APM Governance of Project Management Principle	Dimension	Agile implication
10	There are clearly defined criteria for reporting project status and for the escalation of risks and issues to the levels required by the organization.	Process	Conventionally, escalation to top management is required when projects go outside their cost, time or quality tolerances. BUT: In agile projects, it is *scope* that is the parameter for flexing – so set Red/Amber/Green tolerances based on whether scope is being delivered.
11	The organization fosters a culture of improvement and of frank internal disclosure of project management information.	Leadership	At the end of every iteration, top management should expect and encourage a *retrospective* meeting to be held. A record is made of lessons learned, and these are used to improve the team processes.
12	Project stakeholders are engaged at a level that is commensurate with their importance to the organization and in a manner that fosters trust.	Leadership	The default position should be that as many stakeholders as practically possible are involved in the on-going design and decision-making – even if some are fundamentally opposed to the project.
13	Projects are closed when they are no longer justified as part of the organization's portfolio.	Leadership	Do not be afraid to stop a course of action if it is no longer justified. If the assumptions in a business case are no longer valid, then consider a different option for implementation. Project cancellation at the right time is a successful decision – allowing a project to continue into failure is abdication of leadership responsibility.

Words such as *empowered*, *motivated*, and *supported* appear at the top of the list of what teams want from agile, together with a shared vision of success and elimination of external obstacles.[265] To provide this, effective governance of project management is required across the organization.

In the next chapter, I will explore the other three factors that motivate the team and all others involved or impacted by a project – those three factors lie more along the process dimension, but still require effective leadership to be implemented.

Questions

1. What are your strengths and weaknesses in motivating people and engendering trust? Are you more 'process' oriented or rely more on leadership skills?

2. Have you selected your team and involved co-workers who can provide skills and behaviors that supplement and support your approach to management?

Agile Leadership Exercises

1. How involved is top management with your team's tasks? Make a list of key people who should be more closely involved. Suggest to your boss/team that there should be some special 'hearts and minds' sessions to brief them and get their feedback.

2. Look at Principles 1, 3, 5, 7, 9, 11, 12, and 13 in Table 6. These are the leadership-oriented principles. Against each of these principles, make a note of an improvement to your organization's approach to projects that you can influence for the better.

3. Suggest that the team should hold a joint brainstorming session with the objective of identifying ways of strengthening the involvement of the project sponsor.

Chapter 12

Agile Leadership Behavior Five – Part B: Create Trust (Through Process)

> *Build projects around motivated individuals. Give them the environment and support they need, and trust them to get the job done.*
>
> Agile Manifesto Principle Number Five

In the last chapter, I explained how agile behaviors engender motivation and trust on agile projects, and introduced the concept that these behaviors work on the two dimensions of *leadership* and *process*. The main argument of this book is that agile leadership is of key significance, much more so than the agile process to be used. In this chapter, I explore the need for "just enough process", and the dangers of too much.

The Dangers of Being Addicted to Process

Dave Morgan describes how the U.S. Department of Defense used agile to replace an aging system for scheduling satellite tracking stations after three failed attempts and $20m wasted. The development team was "addicted to the process" of waterfall software development based on theoretical written specifications. There were fundamental problems with the project organization – the team rarely talked to the customers, and they were on two-year rotations of duty that reduced continuity and commitment. After the three failed attempts to carry out the upgrade, there were only two major alternatives available. First, to replace the failing project with another multi-year waterfall development, or second, to use prototyping, and adopt an iterative approach. The team decided on the latter approach. Although management had approved the budgets, they were unaware that the team had adopted the agile approach. This was a *covert agile* project.

The project manager satisfied contractual and audit requirements by externally delivering the necessary documentation. However, agile "by stealth" was used for team processes. With a target of only 18 months for project completion, a series of short deadlines were agreed, each delivering working software with the appropriate documentation being delivered by a process of 'back documenting' the working solution. The team developed their internal processes as the development went underway. They adapted many ideas from Scrum and XP. After a while the "tense environment based on distrust" had evolved into one based on "collaboration and hope".[266]

The customers were unaware that a new method was being used, they just saw working software, and faster. They were able to interact with the team more effectively face-to-face than through paper specifications. Dave Morgan cites three important lessons for government projects:

- Choose a process because it is going to deliver – not because a method is the latest fad
- Lead the teams to discover a process rather than force it on them
- Ensure frequent customer interactions.[267]

The Secure Government Gateway

Microsoft found that good process could be a very effective way of enabling trust in delivering the £147m UK Government Gateway. It developed the system by giving *slack and empowerment* to the team. The approach to project management combined the essence of agile with the advantages that effective process can bring. Evidence, both anecdotal and from research, shows that attempts to implement a 'perfect' process result, paradoxically, in wasted time and effort. The organization does not react fast enough to the need to modify processes once they are documented and agreed. The result can be a straitjacket for everyone.[268]

The Government Gateway project manager was careful to consider what constitutes an "important" process. These were not selected based on size, value, or criticality, but based on whether documentation of the process added value by reducing the risks of *management error*:

♦ *Tampering* when everything is normal. If a process is demonstrably under control, it should be left alone.

♦ *Failing to intervene when a process is out of control*. In such cases, aggressive issue and risk management are required. [269]

By marrying leadership skills, a clear objective, and agile processes, they developed this high transaction volume application, which has now been adopted by over 70 public sector bodies, running more than 200 secure services. Availability in 2011 was 99.9% for the 2.5m secure information update transactions processed each month.

Only Define Essential Processes

So, rather than aiming for all processes to be comprehensively defined, you should consider which processes are running well, and which are not – and then concentrate on those that are critical. Many attempts to define processes start with the easiest to define – those that are running smoothly already and are easy to document. The documentation then just freezes an effective process in place doing no good, but inhibiting the team's capacity to adapt!

Microsoft also adapted Deming's Principles for Transformation[270] to identify five Agile Leadership Behaviors that can help create trust:[271]

♦ Cease dependence on quality control to achieve quality, instead focus on quality assurance throughout the lifecycle

♦ Training on the job

♦ Drive out fear

♦ Break down barriers between departments

♦ Remove barriers to pride of workmanship, focus management on quality rather than production numbers.

The *leadership* dimension plays a major role not only in creating trust directly, but also in encouraging the implementation of just the right degree of emphasis on the *process* dimension to motivate the team and engender trust from top management and with customers. As we will see in this chapter, these issues can be effectively addressed by the application of leadership through three main factors influencing motivation and trust introduced in the last chapter (see Figure 9) that I will now explore in some more detail.

Effective Project sponsorship

Different methods define alternative roles for who or what a project sponsor is. For example, Scrum defines the role of *product owner* as the decider in critical development decisions. The project sponsor role in government projects may often be called *Project Director* or *Senior Responsible Owner*. In DSDM projects (as we saw in the CIDS case study in Part I), the term *Business Sponsor* is used. Whatever the terminology, the important thing is that someone leads the project and creates a buffer between the often potentially chaotic outside world and the team members, who have to concentrate on the detail of getting a solution right and to plan and execute its successful implementation.

Research from Norway by Knut Samset shows that large complex government projects are prone to risk-negligence and lack of accountability due to lack of effective project sponsorship. These projects are often characterized by complex political drivers and dispersed lines of responsibility. If the project leadership is driven by short-term personal ambitions, then the project may not deliver public benefit, and may fail.

The cure that he suggests is that:

♦ Risk and accountability should be much more centrally placed in decision making

♦ Leadership in risk analysis and risk management should be present

♦ The role of government should be at arm's-length distance from the project

♦ Accountability in decisions should be transparent and measurable. [272]

To achieve this, each project sponsor must:

♦ Take responsibility for all decisions, and yet still delegate to the lowest appropriate level – the concept of *subsidiarity*

♦ Be the key communicator between the project and the outside world for major issues.

The project sponsor on an agile project should lead on major decisions. Minor decisions are best handled by those on the 'coal face' nearest to the users and technology should decide on detail.

In some situations where project start-up has been far from perfect, there may be a plethora of interlocking project boards and investment committees involved. It may take time to unpick these and straighten out reporting lines into a more optimal structure. In the meantime, the project sponsor must relish accountability, not defer to 'approval by committee', and not allow the dispersal of responsibility that could ultimately undermine their authority.

The project sponsor must also communicate with superiors, his peers, and with the project team (see Figure 10). Communications can be seen as the external face of risk and issue management. Problems can arise from above (the strategy/policy level), from below (the technical level), and horizontally (from other projects and operations). Therefore, an effective sponsor should be attentive to all three levels.

Responsibility for Decisions

On an agile project, it is important that the project sponsor makes decisions at the latest responsible moment. An early decision before all the key facts are apparent can close down more optimal technical options that should have been considered. Early closure of differing options is often a tempting tactic. The sponsor is often faced with external expectations (especially from arms of the government responsible for financial approval) to justify the project through a detailed Business Case. Committing to one option in detail at that stage merely creates a superficial appearance of scientific objectivity and precision, when little evidence is available to support the various surrounding assumptions.

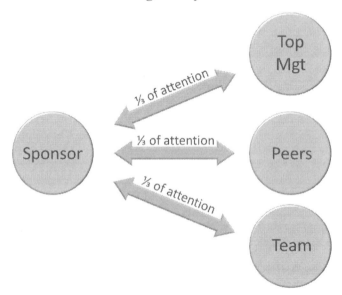

Figure 10: The Project Sponsor Should Be Attentive to Communication at All Levels

Running Parallel and Optional Processes

One major aspect of the role of sponsorship, whether it is carried out by an individual or by an organization, is to organize project processes to run in parallel whenever possible. If one cannot start before another, it creates a *critical* path that elongates the entire project. Delay in the preceding task affects the succeeding one.

A GAO report on the Federal Transit Administration (FTA) and its equivalents in Canada and the UK raised a concern regarding major capital project processes. These were not completed concurrently, and transfer of risk to private sector partners was ineffective.[273] The FTA did not take advantage of the possibility of running processes in parallel, or incrementally. Over the previous decade, the New Starts program had provided over $10 billion for mass transit projects. The problem was that a conventional "design-bid-build" approach was taken. Separate entities were contracted for each sub-project, but much of the integration risk remained within the public sector. This approach was "time consuming, costly, and complex". An alternative incremental approach did exist but little use was made of it. This approach took advantage of *Letters of No Prejudice* and *Early Systems Work Agreements* which would provide the flexibility to cancel a project if it was found not to be feasible after initial work had started. *Letters of Intent* could also be used to allow the FTA to signal "an intention to obligate federal funds at a later date if and when funds become available".[274]

The project sponsors had made little use of this flexible contracting approach. The FTA had only ever issued three Letters of Intent and four Early Systems Work Agreements. Several pilot projects had failed because of a lack of interest from bidders. The problem, the GAO concluded, was that these flexible contracting approaches could not be used with waterfall projects. The root cause, they pointed out, was a lack of coordination and encouragement for flexible project management from senior leaders." [275]

Best Practice Process Guidance Can Enable Agile Adoption

Having sets of guidance materials and standard contracts that stress flexibility and incrementalism can greatly assist the project sponsor and the organization to achieve agility in its widest sense. The provision of project management advice and assistance for mass transit project sponsorship, for example, is provided centrally in Canada and the UK.[276] In an international review, the GAO concluded that these sources of best practice advice helped "foster good public-private partnerships and helped further protect the public interest by ensuring consistency in contracts and serving as a repository of institutional knowledge."[277]

The Sponsor Acting As an Interface

Although the project sponsor is the arbiter for issue resolution and risk management, it is important that this role does not become a bottleneck. A balance is required between firmness and autocracy. An autocratic approach can create two main problems. First, if the sponsor insists on being the main route for communications, this can reduce the potential effectiveness of close co-working between the team and the business and stakeholders. Second, if decision-making is not devolved as far as is safe and practical, it can mean that even minor decisions will need to be referred upwards to the sponsor, thus slowing the pace of development.

An interesting example came to my attention where devolved decision-making became crucial in a developing country. In Bhopal, India, an agricultural advice system was being developed to provide information to the managers of over 500 farms. The project used the Scrum method, and at an early stage, it became obvious that having a government official as a *product owner*, based in the research center, when the researcher was based in the farming community would be problematic. Therefore, a local farmer was appointed as *product owner*.[278] If minor decisions can be left to the discretion of those closest to the detail, then decisions can be made as to which features will be ready or not for each release of the technical solution. These decisions can be left until later, and therefore more flexibility can be retained as to the exact nature of delivery until it is necessary to decide.

Efficient Governance of an Agile Project

In the last chapter, I discussed the importance of the governance of projects across an organization. In some organizations, the *governance of project management* might be widely standardized (for the better or for the worse). Some organizations may just focus on controlling strategic change initiatives.

However, every project must make arrangements (whether formal, informal, consistent, inconsistent, ad-hoc or standardized) for reporting to top management and for making decisions on its various strands of work.

The organization as a whole will make a decision on how each individual project will be governed by top management, and there are two main approaches, which can be used either apart or together:

♦ Project Portfolio Management, and

♦ Program Management.

First, *project portfolio management* should allow projects to run themselves with just the right amount of central oversight. Each project sits within the *portfolio* of change initiatives, some big, some small, some urgent, some on hold. Each project must give evidence that it is still relevant to the organization's strategy and that it is making good progress. This portfolio management may be an ad-hoc arrangement that is not tightly defined, or it may have highly standardized reporting requirements.

Second, *program management* can be used to package together related projects that have common purposes and/or share a common development resource. A *program manager* manages these related projects, coordinating dependencies, resources, and priorities to maximize an overall program business case. This approach can turn into an expensive overhead, however, and UK Cabinet Office guidance advises that it should not be used as a matter of course unless it adds value over and above its additional costs. Many organizations manage a portfolio that is a mix of individual projects and some large programs. [279]

The agile approach taken must recognize top management

requirements for governance across the portfolio of projects, and must also address the governance of the internals of each project. Here, the involvement of the project sponsor is critical. This role will enable the agile project to succeed, or inhibit its flexibility. The sponsor needs to find the right balance between formal channels of communication and control, and the delegation of decision-making and flattening of layers of hierarchy.

Good project governance is a factor that, when done well, can really motivate a team. It should meld together sponsor level leadership with realistic processes for steering the team's direction, reporting progress, and making decisions.

Agile Methods can Motivate and Empower the Team

One of the attractive aspects of agile for team members is that they decide on matters that they are best placed to control. These are typically:

- ◆ Deciding on the optimum technical solution

- ◆ Prioritizing delivery in chunks to gain the greatest benefit in the shortest time

- ◆ Exploration of the interactions between requirements and possible solutions – the 'art of the possible'

- ◆ Quickly responding and adapting to new external factors, whether these are changes in policy/business environment, or new technical solutions that become available during the project

Lack of trust between top management and the team often leads to an unhealthy increase in formal process. Agilists use the term *ceremony* as a catchall label for such processes. The agile approach aims to inspire trust between the parties, reducing ceremony to a minimum. If rules are overused, then cooperation will be delayed as negotiation takes place to agree the rules. People will waste time arguing over and trying to enforce rules entailing what economists call *transaction costs* as an unnecessary overhead to the project.[280]

Adopting Agile Processes at StratCom

DOD Strategic Command (StratCom) is responsible for military space operations, information warfare, and command of the United States nuclear arsenal. [281] Anne Fruhling investigated its adoption of some eXtreme Programming (XP) techniques. She found that while many of the practices of XP techniques are intuitive and straightforward to adopt, some were culturally challenging and met with resistance. Training and expert support would have helped together with clearer leadership of the move to using XP techniques.

There was initial resistance to the some key concepts within XP techniques. For example, *test-driven programming* requires programmers to write code and test it at very frequent intervals. Kent Beck, its creator, explains:

> "Programming and testing together is faster than just programming
> ... the gain in productivity comes from a reduction in the time spent
> debugging – you no longer spend an hour looking for a bug, you find it
> in minutes." [282]

Pair Programming was another XP practice that was new to the team at StratCom. This is a technique where developers write the code for a program together (and of course continually test it together as part of the test-driven programming approach). The idea is that a continual dialogue takes place and the two developers come to a common understanding of the problem. By changing the pairing up of programmers every few hours, ideas spread fast, developers gain a rapid understanding of the solution as a whole, and standards are enforced by the team itself.[283]

At StratCom, these two key concepts of XP met initial resistance. One team did not use them at all. Part of the problem was that pairing up people to program together who are of different abilities can be problematical. For example, if a novice is paired up with an expert, then the programming session will probably degenerate into a tutorial session, and the valuable time of the expert who may have been employed to tackle the most hairy coding challenges may be wasted. When introverts are paired with extroverts, their opinions and expertise are often sidelined.[284] Furthermore, as agile teams should be self-organizing, there will be a tendency for introverts to avoid the practice altogether.

The StratCom teams involved in the research had adopted many agile processes. The teams included stakeholders, not just programmers, they used small increments of delivery, and had a sustainable workload. Researchers identified several lessons:

♦ Teams should be trained in XP before starting to use it

♦ No part-time team members – this can be a problem at project startup when many people are not released fully from previous roles

♦ Good communication between team members can be improved by having regular morning standup meetings

♦ More consideration should have been given at an early stage for the involvement of experts to supply specialist knowledge and skills. For example, at StratCom, although the users were fully involved in making sure that the functions fulfilled the business need, they did not initially have the necessary expertise to explain how the system should be laid out to be easy to use. The development of the search facilities also needed technical database expertise, and the team wasted much time finding out how to achieve certain requirements, when an expert would have solved their problems quickly. [285]

Even though the agile approach had been successful, many stakeholders still felt that detailed pre-planning and documentation would have been better.

This happened despite the fact that perceptions of the quality of the resulting product were high, and that the frequent delivery of new features every two to three weeks rather than every two months was much appreciated.

Anne Fruhling says:

> "While this seems directly at odds with the principles and practices of XP, it might also be interpreted as the lack of recognition of the differences between XP and the plan-driven development approach. Thus, this suggests there needs to be more in-depth agile/XP training prior to execution … and additional mentoring and team lead oversight."[286]

Stephens and Rosenberg's book "Extreme Programming Refactored" is a very readable introduction to XP. Although broadly supportive of XP, the authors poke fun at some of the more extreme statements made by some advocates of XP. They evaluate the practicality of XP practices in an entertaining manner, while making some serious points. They warn against adopting an XP *extremo culture* – seeking out and following more and more radical development processes without evidential basis. They make the argument that some aspects of XP may not work for some people, and they propose a modified version of XP, which is "less extreme" and may be more suitable for a government environment. The conclusion is that implementing XP in an organization is usually a big-bang process, which is ironic since XP is a very incremental method once it is being used:

> "A problem faced by teams wanting to introduce XP into their organization is that XP requires a mind shift in the entire outfit." [287]

This, of course, is true for the agile approach as a whole, not just the XP techniques. The customization of agile techniques by StratCom was not unusual. Many organizations, in government and in the private sector feel that they need to do so. In effect, *à la carte adoption* of agile methods like XP is the norm. Organizations pick out those ideas that are most closely matched to their existing processes. Techniques and processes are not adopted where the method is too challenging for the culture, or where appropriate training has not taken place. In the case of StratCom, two factors were identified as critical. First, a culture that is ready to change, and second, a technical infrastructure that supports efficient development.[288]

Conclusions

In this chapter, I have explored the last three of the five major factors in building trust (see Figure 9 on page 141):

- ◆ Effective Project Sponsorship

- ◆ Efficient Governance

- ◆ Motivating and empowering the team through agile methods.

We have found that the role of *project sponsor* in an agile project is focused on acting as a buffer to protect the team from unnecessary distractions. The sponsor must also make sure that changes in circumstances are quickly incorporated into the work plan, not just for the development team, but also at program and portfolio levels. To achieve this, governance processes need to be both tight and light. Tight enough to ensure that good decisions and made, and light enough to allow the team to execute them quickly and accurately. This concept, and a further discussion on the challenge (and promise) of XP techniques are both examined further in Part III.

The project team can adapt ideas in agile methods to suit the culture of their organization. Agile teams are self-organizing, and if changes to standard methods are required, they should be empowered to make those changes. 'Just enough process' is an effective way of creating trust between the team and those outside who need to have confidence that the project is on the right path.

Questions

1. Section 804 is part of US public law and requires specific development techniques to be used in defense projects. Is it desirable to state in law that particular methods should be used?

2. In the case studies in Part I of the book, we saw process being applied to projects through policy – sometimes through legislation, sometimes through centrally produced guidance materials and sometimes by audit recommendations. Which processes are imposed on your work by centralized policy? Use

the Bemelmans-Videc decision tree to analyze their nature (see page 2 of the reference at endnote <u>289</u>).

Agile Leadership Exercises

1. Identify the main drivers for change from outside your team and talk with your co-workers and team members about ways of managing (and welcoming) the changes that these drivers bring.

2. Identify the expertise in your team and propose ways in which decisions related to these areas can be most effectively delegated to those with this expertise.

3. For your next meeting draw up an agenda of decisions that need to be made and categorize them into:

   - Those for which an immediate decision is vital
   - Those where further investigation is necessary
   - Those where there appears to be only one viable solution, but it does not yet need to be committed to

4. Concentrate your attention on items in the third category above: help the meeting agree the optimum moment to make the decision so as to allow any factors that are unknown at present to be discovered – this is not delay or indecision, it is making the decision at the latest responsible moment.

5. Review the process you use for managing issues – is it:

   - Light?
   - Effective?
   - Good at allowing issues to be resolved at the lowest level possible?

6. Organize a "Failure Mode Evaluation Analysis" workshop to ensure that your risks are identified and managed with a coordinated top-down approach.

7. If there is an existing risk register, get together with several of your peers to 'turn it inside out' by combining several related low impact risks in series to see if their combined potential impact becomes high.

Chapter 13

Agile Leadership Behavior Six: Work Face-to-Face

The most efficient and effective method of conveying information to and within a development team is face-to-face conversation

Agile Manifesto Principle Number Six

We are faced with a complex and beguiling array of communications technologies that we use at work. Email, text messages, video conferencing, wikis, and many other collaboration tools can save us time and effort in getting our own work done. A great deal of information can be efficiently sent to other people involved in a project for them to consider. However, it is often tempting to fire off a few quick emails to shift responsibility elsewhere. Games of email and voicemail *ping-pong* drag down the productivity of all those copied in on correspondence. However, the case studies we have seen show that this is perhaps one of the most difficult aspects of the Agile Manifesto to implement successfully. There are subtle but important benefits of personal body language, but in many circumstances, face-to-face is an expensive communication method. For example, where multinational teams are involved or where expert stakeholders are working in the field, while the development team is at headquarters.

Body Language Increases Engagement

Most readers of this book will probably be familiar with the books of Desmond Morris and Allan Pease that popularized the concept of "body language".[290] The often-repeated statement is that at least 50% of the communication in face-to-face meetings is non-verbal. Additionally, most of this non-verbal communication is involuntary and often treated by the recipient unconsciously as such as more 'truthful' than any words being uttered. Body posture and facial expressions give away the meeting participants' real feelings about a subject. Interest, boredom, support, antagonism, and many other emotions are conveyed by non-verbal cues.

Recent research has shown that the decoding of body language, which had previously been thought of as a central cortex activity, can often be an involuntary neural activity – using ECG and MRI scans researchers have found that these messages are relayed in less than 120 milliseconds. The nervous system automatically looks for congruence or incongruence between facial expressions and body postures. More sophisticated decoding then takes place to interpret further, what the eyes have seen. This information is compared and contrasted with verbal tone, and then, and only then is the text of the language itself taken into account in assessing the totality of the message.[291]

A leadership style that prefers real world contact taps into the rich communications that body language confers – especially those of emotional intensity and building trust. Neurological research to date has concentrated on how the nervous system (not just the central brain) decodes facial expressions. Only 5% of this research has studied total body language, but enough is known to draw some general conclusions. [292]

Bodily expressions are recognized as reliably as facial expressions, and both by-pass higher cognitive functions to inform the listener of emotion before high cognitive functions can decode and interpret the technical information being relayed verbally. Although we talk of *face-to-face* meetings, more information is supplied from body posture than from facial expression. Non-verbal information is ambiguous, and people take into account several different cues to gain a holistic decoding of the messages sent.[293]

Face-to-face meetings are a powerful communication channel. This is because: [294]

♦ Information is communicated faster

♦ Feedback is instantaneous

♦ Non-verbal cues help the person talking to fine-tune what they are saying to make sure that it is relevant to the listener's interests.

Moreover, when there are several participants at a meeting, these interactions are simultaneous and multi-directional. By way of comparison, in a telephone conference where only one person can talk at the same time, there is only one message being communicated at any one moment. For example, consider four people having a face-to-face discussion. Each combination of two people will be continually transmitting and receiving body language to each other. Therefore, with just three people there are six non-verbal 'conversations' going on. With five people present, there are 10 such conversations. Each additional person present in a face-to-face meeting increases the possible complexity and richness of communication through non-verbal means.[295]

So then, this chapter will explain how agile proponents advocate the use of face-to-face meetings. It will also explore some of the practical difficulties of implementing these practices. Government projects often involve geographically dispersed participants, and co-location can be expensive to set up, and travel to meetings can be time wasting.

Use Agile to Get the Team Communicating

The enthusiasm of agilists for face-to-face meetings is embedded in all agile methods. Each method tends to focus on one concept – from formal workshops, co-locating people from a range of technical disciplines into one room, through to the micro level, such as encouraging working in pairs rather than solo development. In the next three sections, I will describe these approaches and then explore how you can implement the ideas within government projects.

Face-to-Face Activities in Scrum

Scrum defines five key activities that involve face-to-face work:

- Sprint Planning Meeting
- Daily Scrums
- Development work
- Sprint Review
- Sprint Retrospective. [296]

At the start of every sprint, a one-day meeting is held broken into two halves: the first half-day to agree on what will be delivered in the coming sprint, and second half-day on how it will be delivered (in what sequence, by whom, and by when).

The Product Owner makes top-level decisions in the meeting, and gives direction on the business priorities via comments on the product backlog – the list of desired features for the solution, each with some relative priority. However, it is the development team and product owner together, who forecast the functions that are feasible for development during the coming sprint. Planning is a collaborative team effort, not the implementation of a 'plan from above':

> "The number of items selected from the product backlog for the sprint
> is solely up to the Development Team. Only the Development Team
> can assess what it can accomplish over the upcoming sprint." [297]

The key concept here is that the Development Team works closely together to self-organize itself in planning the execution of the work.

It should be noted here that there is a divergence in thought between Scrum and DSDM on who agrees the items to be built in an upcoming sprint. Is it solely the development team members (the Scrum approach), or is it a joint decision between the Product Owner and the Development Team (the DSDM approach):

> (The) Product Owner, the Development Team, and the *ScrumMaster*)
> use their knowledge, experience, and understanding of the product

and the requirements to agree a number of the most important items from the *product backlog* to be addressed in a sprint ... The output of the sprint planning meeting is the *Sprint Backlog*"[298]

Another face-to-face concept in Scrum is the *daily scrum.* This is to provide quick feedback on problems encountered in the last 24 hours, assess the speed of progress, and to synchronize the plan for the next 24 hours. The meeting should, Schwaber advises, be *timeboxed* to 15 minutes length, so each participant needs to keep to a very short statement. [299] To encourage brevity, it has become common practice for participants to meet in an area without chairs — these *stand-up* meetings help stop overruns which eat into the day's activities.

Scrum encourages development work to be co-located whenever possible When large developments are required, multiple Scrum teams should be organized in a hierarchy, all working to one master product backlog.[300] In this situation a *scrum of scrums* meeting is then held immediately after all the individual teams have held their *daily scrums*. Ken Schwaber recommends these as a:

> "Mechanism for dealing with the complexity of the dependencies in multi-team Scrum projects... It's just like the Daily Scrum, but at the next level up. The Scrum of Scrums is meant to provide transparency for teams that aren't co-located and don't have on-going communications." [301]

Once the sprint is complete, and delivery has taken place, a half-day *Sprint Review* is held with the Product Owner and key Stakeholders, which checks off the items that have been *done*. It is important to have a shared understanding of what *done* means – and this, of course, should have been agreed upon before at the start of the sprint in a planning meeting. Perhaps only a *proof of concept* was required – a working model of the system perhaps.

On the other hand, a solution might have been required for immediate live use, and should have been tested thoroughly and perhaps delivered via a formal route to thousands of users. The concept of a hierarchy of deliverability I introduced earlier (see Table 3 on page 122) should be applied to help structure the delivery planning process. Progress is not tracked on spreadsheets and memos, but in the daily standup meeting and on kanban wall charts. Project status is reviewed in a sprint review meeting at the end of the sprint, especially:

♦ What went well

♦ Which problems were encountered

♦ How problems were solved

♦ The velocity of progress and a projection for future completion is discussed

♦ Consensus is reached on what to do next. [302]

Just after the sprint review, the development team holds an internal *sprint retrospective* meeting to self-examine its own performance and plan internal improvements. The focus here is on lessons learned about the relationships between people on and outside the team, and improvements to processes and tools.[303]

Debate How the Solution Will Be Implemented

While Scrum says little about the mechanisms of involving the stakeholders, DSDM is more explicit in its advice. A prescriptive approach to set up of the multi-disciplinary teams is an important attribute of the DSDM framework. As with many features of these methods, there is much to be said for incorporating the best ideas from each into your way of working. DSDM requires that a *Business Ambassador* be allocated to work closely and on a day-to-day basis with the development team.

This role is not necessarily a senior one, but one that can interact in a detailed way on features of what DSDM calls the *emerging solution*.[304] The Business Ambassador takes part in the equivalent of *daily scrums* – these are termed *daily stand-ups* in DSDM.

Human Interaction and Technical Progress

A difference between Scrum and DSDM is the explicit emphasis in DSDM on facilitated workshops and the encouragement to use models and non-functional prototypes of the final system during development to get user feedback.[305]

DSDM encourages a facilitative environment, ensuring that outputs are not only practical, but also business-focused. Scrum places more importance on the delivery of a working solution at the end of each iteration, than on the business outcomes.[306] To this extent, DSDM is externally focused on communication with stakeholders, and practical use of the solution in operations, whereas Scrum is more concerned with ensuring that outputs work as agreed with users. A good reason for considering using the two approaches together.

Leadership is needed to balance between these aspects – there is no point in keeping stakeholders blissfully unaware of technical difficulties that may scuttle the entire project. On the other hand, regular integration of the entire solution at the end of each Sprint may not be a very efficient way to progress the project if some aspects of the technology are inflexible and expensive to develop. This is particularly true of the need to interface with *legacy* mainframe technology with which new government technology solutions often has to co-exist.

Many teams do not work face-to-face for reasons of organizational inertia simply due to historical desk allocation, and due to pressures to *hot-desk* and work on multiple projects at the same time. Hot-desking can lead to dramatic efficiency gains on utilization of space, especially where large proportions of the workforce are continually in and out of the office and have meetings off-site. On one client site, I saw accommodation costs halve when it was introduced. However, there is a difference between the proactive decision to work in a temporary desk location, and the accidental placement of staff far from their co-workers. One study analyzed how people perceive their co-workers. It found that members of staff treat colleagues as being outside their own team at distances longer than a fifty foot radius, even if they are in the same project.[307]

Advanced technologies are available that should help people

overcome lack of face-to-face contact. For many years, video-conferencing has been championed, and more recently, computer collaboration tools allowing multiple users to share and edit information simultaneously have been introduced to the workplace. However, researchers have found that these ways of working are not naturally adopted by teams, and that key teleworking concepts need to be accepted by the staff that attempt to work this way:

♦ The acceptance that crucial specialist knowledge is dispersed across the virtual team

♦ A desire to outreach to other team members

♦ A culture that values team performance above individual performance

♦ The desire to apply strong analytical capabilities to make technical progress. [308]

Despite all these factors being in place, research shows that regular face-to-face meetings are a strong leading indicator of success. At team setup, allow interpersonal relationships to form – and not just inside the team, but also between the team and management and with members of other teams. The forming of interpersonal relationships allows the appreciation of the difficulties faced by others and the building of *social capital and trust*. One should not assume that these are enduring and static. Studies show that trust is an evolving phenomenon and is "dynamic and context specific".[309]

Cooper and Kurland carried out a study comparing the governments of two US cities with two private sector organizations of similar size to assess the impact of lack of face-to-face contact among workers on projects.

Of the two public sector organizations, one was a Southern California city employing nearly 10,000 people – not just administrators, but also technical specialists such as civil engineers and systems developers. The other was a large city in the western US employing 14,000 people. Both organizations had implemented structured teleworking over the previous ten years.[310]

The researchers found that a great deal of effort was required to keep communication going between remote and central team members. They recommended that team leaders actively work to find synergies between disparately located workers – matching their different skills to the tasks in hand. The need for formal channels of communication became more important.[311] These factors work against some of the principles of agile – that of self-organizing teams and the importance of informal communications.

Conclusions

In recent years, several trends have pushed us into reduced face-to-face contact on our projects. The use of off-shore teams, teleworking by staff from home to reduce commuting, hot-desking within an organization's main office, or at satellite offices or at buildings of sister organizations are all drivers for reducing the costs of co-location. Technology such as email and video-conferencing has enabled reduction of costs. However, used indiscriminately, these technologies, coupled with the drive for reduced travel time and costs, make for reduced effectiveness of human communication. Face to face communication is also the most effective way of discussing technical information that must be described in documents, for example integrated circuit chip designs, or aeronautical engineering drawings.

The effective leader will build interpersonal relationships early in a project, engendering trust, and creating a common culture, and understanding of the difficulties of other team members. Agile encourages face-to-face working. A balance is required between the cost savings derived from reduced demands for office space and travel time and the inefficiencies that start to creep in when miscommunication occurs.

Questions

1. What communication channels does your team use for their tasks? Could the mix of usages of these channels be changed to make teamwork more efficient?

2.   What changes could be made to increase face-to-face working without large increases in costs? Could costs be reduced by getting your team members to co-locate during a project?

Agile Leadership Exercises

1.   Before each of your projects starts its next stage of work, hold face-to-face planning meetings to:

   - review the list of features to be delivered

   - how the team will tackle the work

2.   Hold your next stand-up in the environment where the technical product is to be used. For example, when developing a new workflow system for tax administrators, hold the meeting in the call center that will be using the new system. Invite a selection of target users to discuss their real-world problems and concerns.

3.   If holding regular videoconferences is part of your organization's culture, then arrange for participants to visit each other's offices for meetings.

4.   When using email, do not use overelaborate grammar or unnecessary jargon. Short coherent sentences will convey meaning more effectively and reduce the possibility of misunderstanding.

5.   When a communication is unresolved after more than one email exchange, pick up the phone and discuss the issue.

6.   If a telephone conversation reveals that basic misconceptions have taken place, then set up a face-to-face meeting to discuss the issue.

7. Hold several, short stand-up meetings over a few days rather than lengthy sit-downs.

8. Hold face-to-face workshops in different locations, hosted by the different parts of the organization contributing to your projects.

Chapter 14

Agile Leadership Behavior Seven: Set Targets and Reward Real Progress

Working software is the primary measure of progress.

Agile Manifesto Principle Number Seven

Targets motivate people. They need to be relevant and measurable. Most importantly, the development team needs to aim at delivering value to the stakeholders, not just the delivery of 'clean code'. Targets need to be collaboratively arrived at, unambiguous, transparent, and they should engender trust by being safe from *gaming*.

I will take these points in reverse order, and in each case compare the agile way of planning and tracking against the traditional waterfall approach.

Engendering Trust by Being Safe from Gaming

Gaming occurs when one or more parties to an agreement take advantage of loopholes to their own advantage. A team leader under pressure may log his team's work on an item as finished by prematurely handing work over to a separate testing team. A project sponsor may placate anxious stakeholders by making elegant presentations on the theoretical advantages of the end-solution, even though the initial prototypes have not worked.

The danger is that the various people on the project become *players*. Rather than working together in a collaborative manner towards an integrated goal, they start to play games with each other to gain a short-term personal advantage, rather than aligning their goals with the team's goals. One of the games played can be that of promising jam tomorrow, rather than bread today.

George Baker warns against the *distortion* of incentives, and the potential problems of attempting to trade-off risk by over-incentivizing. He refers to "The folly of rewarding for A while hoping for B" which leads to distortion of outcomes. If measurements are being used that are not relevant to the real-world project targets, then teams often become risk-averse – sub-optimizing by focusing on short-term output targets rather than real-world delivery. In addition, no matter how many detailed measurements are tracked, it is not possible to measure all outputs. Therefore, the targets will become the focus of activity, no matter whether other measures are more important.[312]

A Stalled Project at the US Department of the Interior (DOI)

The DOI is the largest landowner in the US with 1,672 sites on 500m acres of land and 489m visitors annually. In 2003, the DOI had initiated the development of an Incident Management, Analysis, and Reporting System (IMARS) to provide a centralized incident tracking system. 6,000 staff spread across the nation had difficulty coordinating crime reporting to federal bodies, a weakness already criticized by the GAO.[313]

The number of other bodies that needed access to IMARS information was very large. It included many internal agencies, such as the Office of Law Enforcement and Security, the National Park Service, the Bureau of Reclamation, Fish and Wildlife Service, Bureau of Indian Affairs and the

Bureau of Land Management. It also involved sharing information with the FBI National Incident Based Reporting System (NIBRS), the EI Paso Intelligence Center, the FBI Joint Terrorism Task Force (JTTF) Centers, the DHS Watch Office, The U.S. Court's Central Violations Bureau (CVB) and State, County, and City Governments.[314]

The work started in 2003 with the intent of finishing development by October 2008. However, by April 2010, the project end date had slipped by four years to December 2012.

Costs had escalated out of control. The total forecast cost of the project had increased from $23m million to $42m. The project had under-spent because it had not started many important activities. It often made large requests for funding but failed to manage to get the authorized work underway in time. This 'under-spending' was not money saved, but was simply the result of unattained milestones – spending was substantially below the planned cost and no progress was being made.

Things were so bad that the primary contractor voluntarily quit, and the sub-contractor was terminated for non-performance. An audit found that DOI's planning was poor, that resources were poorly allocated, and that leadership was weak.[315]

In April 2010, the project was reviewed and put under more senior management control. The DOI worked with the OMB using TechStat sessions to review performance and find a solution. The possibility of project cancellation was discussed.

The solution was to shift the focus from plans and theoretical milestones into delivering real solutions. Stakeholder confidence, which had been shattered by the lack of demonstrable progress, would be rebuilt by proving that progress was being made by delivering working software.

On April 29, 2010, DOI decided to pilot a working solution with 500 users by October. This accelerated deployment was successful, across five different offices in seven law enforcement programs in four time zones.[316]

The agile approach they had taken had delivered 90% of the most urgent law enforcement requirements with excellent user feedback on its usability, and several of the aging legacy databases that had been in use had been closed down.

To gain further stakeholder buy-in, and demonstrate real progress, the DOI ran a successful user evaluation exercise with five modules while operational readiness tests were completed. The department did not need to buy and install hardware and infrastructure because the three deliveries using expandable rented *cloud-computing* services that expanded as they were needed.[317]

As this book went to press, the risk rating of the project has been reduced from *high risk* to *moderately low risk*, but challenges remain. Planning is underway for three more deliveries in 2012, and a final clean-up delivery in 2013 aimed at delivering the final 10% of *Should Have* and *Could Have* requirements. Importantly, a Post Implementation Review is planned to learn lessons from the project and to identify and recommend any outstanding actions. The real world benefits from the resulting system, which will be used by over 6,000 members of staff across multiple Federal bodies, will be tracked in an ongoing Operational Analysis exercise. This will compare evidence of end-benefits from the use of the technical solution to the total amount of money that was spent – including the $15m and 4 years wasted in the original waterfall attempt to develop IMARS before an agile approach was successfully adopted.[318]

An Agile Approach to Planning and Tracking

Mike Cohn stresses the importance of acknowledging uncertainty when planning. He breaks this into two types of uncertainty:

- *End uncertainty*: about **what** product features will actually be needed, and therefore which one will actually be built

- *Means uncertainty*: about **how** the product will be built. [319]

In this way, the team avoids the mistake of imagining that features and architectures can be locked down at the beginning of a project. As time passes, Cohn points out, the end and the means become more certain, and the project concentrates on what is actually needed.

This does not mean that we should not bother with plans, but just that we should not bother with plans that go beyond a realistic level of detail. Tom Gilb originally called this the "The principle of highest level inspection":

> "If you fail to inspect the higher levels of planning and goal-setting, then inspection at the lower levels will only serve to confirm errors made earlier! What is put into a design-or-planning process should always have exited successfully from inspection beforehand. You must be prepared to raise the clarity of planning, requirements specification, and design documentation substantially in order to exploit inspection." [320]

Gilb proposes a formal method for identifying strategies and turning them into realistic high-level plans using the Evolutionary Project Management, or "Evo" method and the formal notation of "Planguage". Evo focuses on agile delivery with very small increments of about 2-5% of total timescale. A year-long Evo project would typically have week-long increments based on early:

♦ Identification of the highest priority requirements

♦ Ensuring that the requirements are defined well enough to be objectively verifiable. [321]

A common agile technique for measuring progress is the *burn down* chart, which simply tracks the number of story points remaining to be completed over time. Thus, the line on the graph decreases over time and extrapolates to show when the work is likely to be completed. *Release burn down* charts are for management, and show when work is released and forecast when the project will complete. *Sprint burn down charts* are team facing, and indicate the ongoing progress day-by-day during each sprint. If the line on a sprint burn down chart does not tend towards zero for the last day of the sprint (and it is unlikely to do so unless the estimation has been spot on) then the team will have to decide to change the scope of the sprint backlog.

On traditional projects, a *work breakdown structure* of the tasks and their outputs will have an estimated number of work-days and other costs against it. [322] As work progresses the actual number of work-days and costs is recorded. Once some statistics have been built up the *earned value* can be calculated. This is the percentage of under or overspend against the original estimates, based only on work that has been completed. Partially completed tasks are excluded from the calculation, removing any optimism bias in reporting.

Agile project control turns conventional planning on its head. The features required are allocated *story points* and the team's *velocity* in delivering these story points is calculated. Thus in agile the team's efficiency is calibrated rather than the accuracy of the estimates. An alternative, then, to EVA on agile projects is a technique called *line of balance*. This technique originated at the Goodyear Tire and Rubber Company to regulate factory processes. It ensures that the many activities in a process stay in a sustainable balance and at an even flow. This would be most useful in a large multi-scrum project. Each team's activities can be measured over time showing actual output against expected output of user stories in each sprint. This gives a graphic representation of over and under staffing across teams allowing for reallocation of staff, or more likely, a relocation of user features from one team to another.

The OMB Capital Programming Guide stresses the need for painstaking detail in the collection of enough data to calculate earned value:

> "IPTs must devote the planning time needed to create an adequate Work Breakdown Structure (WBS) at program initiation and keep it current throughout the program execution. Program management use of EVA depends on a well-developed WBS to ensure that a program is completely defined. Program experts, in collaboration with experts in the areas of cost estimating, procurement, risk management, scheduling, and EVA need to develop a WBS as a common framework within a given program, and also among related programs and across an organization's portfolio." [323]

The Guide claims that EVA provides invaluable data:

> "For all levels of the management team … change control, performance variance, cost variance, schedule variance (etc.)" [324]

Alleman and Henderson proposed that this approach of measuring progress against a fixed baseline was easy to adopt for agile methods, and that they had done so in their software development company that worked in "high–ceremony government contracting environments that use EVA". They argue that as formal *artifacts* are needed for compliance with what is often a waterfall contract, EVA is a means of complying with the 'progress-to-plan' approach required.[325]

They see agile developments as unable to forecast future cost and schedule. They argue that this is because of the use of historical *velocity* metrics. Using this is like forecasting tomorrow's weather from yesterday's, they say. However, their argument misses the point of agile – if you fix your team size and keep to immoveable deadlines by flexing scope, then you do not need a forecast of future cost and schedule because it is fixed. EVA will tell you that you are behind schedule and overrunning on cost, even when all the functions the stakeholder need have been delivered, and on time! No schedule variance can be derived in XP because the concept has limited value in an agile environment.

The problem with EVA in the agile environment is that it is the wrong paradigm. It provides calculations of the budgeted cost for work performed. It is not *earned value* but *sunk cost*. Paul Solomon calls this the *EVMS Quality Gap*:

> "A (DOD) supplier is not required to base earned value on technical performance or quality. Technical linkage is optional in the industry standard, ANSI/EIA-748 … EV is based on the quantity of work performed, not quality." [326]

I have often thought that this perspective implies that "Earned Value isn't!" – isn't value and not necessarily earned that is! However, I see the value in collecting essential metrics. The velocity data collected in agile projects can do more than just be used to predicting the project completion data by use of burn-down charts. However, it is possible to use the data that most large US government projects are mandated to produce. Tamara Sulaiman enumerates the circumstances in which this might be needed:

◆ To give an estimate of progress in terms of $ burn to the team members. They will have team burn-up charts showing spend to date, and kanban charts showing feature status, but a monetary view can be an additional useful perspective

♦ If the agile project manager has to keep 'translating' agile terminology for non-Agile stakeholders used to EVA

♦ If working on a defense contract where, typically, 32 different progress reports are required to conform to the ANSI/EIA-748 standard for EVA

♦ To work out when to stop developing any further because the EVA forecasts that return from the benefits of more features is less than the spend required to develop them.

Tamara Sulaiman describes this integration as Agile Earned Value Management (AgileEVM). She claims that it is a light weight approach that compiles the standard metrics that agile projects produce as a matter of course:

♦ Current iteration number

♦ Number of story points actually completed

♦ Number of story points added to or removed from the release

♦ Actual Cost in dollars or hours. It is critical that the actual cost amount used reflects the cost needed to generate the

♦ Completed story points.[327]

She describes how these metrics were used by two Scrum projects. On the first project, the AgileEVM metrics were used to *calibrate* the team velocity in EVA terms. At the end of the first sprint, they proved that the scope (in story points) could not be achieved by the deadline.

The AgileEVM statistics were used in a spreadsheet model to help in requirements trading. They focused attention on the important requirements, and identified outlying features for sacrifice. On a second project, AgileEVM data showed consistency in team output, and this gave the team confidence to calculate a final deployment date. [328]

Conclusions

An agile project's objectives for each iteration need to be based on providing a working solution at an acceptable delivery level. Prototypes and demonstrators have their uses early in the project, but the sponsor needs to raise expectations quickly towards piloting and operational delivery.

Various traditional project management techniques can be used to plan and track progress where they marry well with the agile approach. The AgileEVM method for analyzing earned value is an example of this. It provides traditional EVA metrics based on the data provided day by day from the agile approach.

Questions

Read Tamara Sulaiman's description of the contents of a typical AgileEVM spreadsheet (see Endnote 329). Take a piece of work that you are currently responsible for, and create such a spreadsheet. (If it is not an agile project, then re-imagine it as such for the purposes of this exercise).

1. Where would you get the necessary data to track progress: (budget to complete, iteration lengths, number of iterations planned, number of story points, and start date)?

2. Fill in the spreadsheet for each iteration that has already been completed. Calculate the number of story points completed, the number of story points added to or removed from the re-lease at each iteration, the actual spend in hours and cash.

Agile Leadership Exercises

1. Consider the next task that you and your team have to complete. Get each team member to individually list the targets they think that they are working towards. Then get the

team together to compare their notes.

- Do their perceptions match up?

- Do they match the official, documented objectives?

- Can you come to a consensus about how to make the objectives more specific, measurable, attainable, and targeted?

2. Are the targets that your organization sets for its suppliers safe from 'gaming'?

3. Taking the targets that you have identified above, get your team to discuss each one and analyze what level of *end uncertainty* and *means uncertainty* are present in each.

Chapter 15

Agile Leadership Behavior Eight: Give your Team Space

> *The (team) should be able to maintain a constant pace indefinitely ... continuous attention to technical excellence and good design enhances agility ... the best architectures, requirements, and designs emerge from self-organizing teams ... at regular intervals, the team reflects on how to become more effective, then tunes and adjusts its behavior accordingly.*
>
> From: Agile Manifesto Principles 8, 9, 11 & 12

US Government Health Data Project

In January 2012, the Chief Technology Officer (CTO) of the US Department of Health and Human Services (HHS), Todd Park, asked his agile team to deliver a web data feed before the Third Annual Health Data Initiative "Datapalooza" conference. The new and improved HealthData.gov website had to include:

♦ Datasets from agencies across Federal government to provide open data on national health

♦ Special brainstorming and sharing of new applications

♦ Crowdsourcing to encourage aggregation of new datasets

♦ The ability for other developers to write their own applications to directly access health data

♦ A new content management system to load information faster. [330]

The initial problem was getting the right people together to create a cross-functional team. This took two months, leaving only time for five sprints – two week scrum sprints being the planned approach. The Scrum Master used the idea of a *minimally viable product* (MVP) to make sure that delivery would be made before the June conference. Low priority requirements on the product backlog were planned for delivery after the conference to ensure that the tight deadline was met. [331]

Beta.gov: a Self-Organizing Team

The total cost of setting up and running UK Government web services in the decade to 2011 was £479m. The expense of these services rose up to about £30m/year towards the end of this period. [332]

The public-facing website was run by DirectGov and the business facing-website by Business Link. The organizations running these websites used traditional project thinking, and the costs and inflexibilities reflected this. (Please forgive the varying use of capital letters and periods in organization and website names in this chapter, but I am just using the actual titles of these websites and project names, which varied over the 2000s and into the 2010s as trends in naming fluxed!).

However, the old DirectGov organization had already incubated a small team working in a very different manner. They were delivering a new portal for delivery of digital government services called alpha.gov, and they built it in just 10 weeks with only 10 staff and £327,000. The team did not follow either a waterfall approach to delivering the required breakthrough in technology, nor did they follow a specific prescriptive agile method. They followed the principles of Scrum, but were not dogmatic in its application. One of the many interesting things about the way they worked was that they used the opportunity of the frequent *retrospectives* at the end of each sprint of work to reinterpret how to use Scrum rather than slavishly following the manual.[333]

An example of this adaptive behavior, happened just before the fifth and final sprint was about to begin. The team decided that agreeing on a fixed list of priorities would not be flexible enough. The alpha.gov team needed to use the kanban planning method rather than using computer spreadsheets or planning software because they found that the necessary work was varying dramatically almost hour by hour. They had to deal with a number of *bugs* that became apparent when the fully sized implementation was being prepared. They also found that a number of other Government departments had 'woken up' to the fact that the alpha.gov site was really going to happen (many had expected it to slip).

Francis Maude, the Minister for the Cabinet Office, had authorized the live release of the alpha.gov website for general access to the public to try out the new facilities and provide feedback. He had been very close to the work that had gone on and was very involved in the technology.

The alpha.gov team was working as part of the "Directgov" organization that was responsible for converging 95% of the public-facing content of central government websites onto a single, reliable platform with a consistent user-friendly interface over the three-year period from 2008 to 2011. However, in many cases, the government did not close down the old departmental web servers, and duplication continued. Moreover, the web publication software that had been setup for Government officers to use to publish content onto the web was coming to the end of its life. In 2011, the rest of the world was moving onto Internet Explorer version 9 ("IE9"), while most UK Government staff members were still stuck on a ten-year-old version ("IE6"). This was creating extreme inflexibility and expense for web publication and a growing disconnect between the Government, working with old technology, and citizens working with new technology, such as smartphones and tablet computers.[334]

The Government Digital Service (GDS) was established in 2011, headed by Mike Bracken, who had moved from the Guardian newspaper where he was head of Digital. GDS set up a successor project to alpha.gov, predictably called beta.gov, with the aim of implementing a new strategy of *digital by default*. The aim was to implement all information flows to and from users of Government services by Internet. GDS planned to convert old services over time, while implementing new services digitally right from the start. No paper forms required. No letters required by post. Safeguards called *assisted digital* would exist for the *digitally excluded* who could not access the service on the Internet for whatever reason.[335]

The Delivery of Beta.gov

The GDS beta.gov team grew to twice the size of the alpha.gov team, and it quickly delivered the new website for public access on January 31, 2012. There were two Scrum teams: One concentrated on further conversion of DirectGov public-facing information, and the other created a *wide and thin* conversion of the old content still rattling around on departmental websites.

Prior to the setup of GDS, DirectGov had preceded its website launches with high profile marketing activity. This had created expectations of large step changes at each project delivery point. The GDS team now decided to release changes incrementally, and without fuss. An example of such a release was the Inside Government beta release. GDS made this available for six weeks in Feb 2012 to collect feedback from other Government users. It had many innovative features, including:

- ◆ A responsive design with variable page layouts taking advantage of the latest web browser capabilities

- ◆ Consistent layout and look and feel for all Government web pages – no matter which Department

- ◆ A consistent approach to policy definitions in the substantive content

- ◆ Lookup by topic and clear statement of ministerial responsibility

- ♦ A special "Overseas" section to pool information on the UK Government's international interests and policies

- ♦ A custom built publishing engine to replace the obsolete *content management* system previously used by Government staff

- ♦ Special functionality to cater for Cabinet reshuffles, elections and *machinery of government* changes (where departments are merged and split)

- ♦ State of the art analytics to show where people are looking, what pages they access and in which order, including diagrams to make the understanding of the statistics clearer. [336]

A second example where the team members self-organized and decided to try a new approach was in the usability testing. The traditional approach would be to agree on theoretical quality criteria for usability in advance of development, and then inspect the web site to see if it had been created according to those standards. The team chose a more practical approach called *summative testing*. This used large panels of trial users to measure how user-friendly the system was. GDS worked with a specialist supplier who organized hundreds of these test users to access the system pages remotely over the Internet. Their use of the system was tested using the 30 key *needs* that the system had to fulfill, from finding a school holiday date, through to finding details on powers of attorney in family cases. The test system tracked each user's actual use of the system to see how many people managed to find the right information, and how long it took them. Error rates were reduced by a quarter with the first release of this new system.

A third example of how the team organized their work was the conversion of the existing content from the old DirectGov website to beta.gov. First, a *Pareto* analysis was carried out that identified which areas of the website were popular, and which areas were the equivalent of a web graveyard of unused pages. The team recognized early on, that the old web site had become bloated, with many aging pages that related to one-off campaigns and special projects that had no benefit. For example, a defunct campaign to recruit firefighters did not need conversion. Neither did obsolete information about a new motorcycle safety standard. Many of these pages were not related to core government business. At the end of the analysis, only 1,000 core pages were selected for conversion to beta.gov. The team insisted that content experts should work alongside the beta.gov team in reworking those pages. Efficiency increased when the co-location started, because the developers could ask questions and demonstrate ideas first-hand to policy and organizational experts.

The team re-organized itself again after delivering beta.gov. It scaled up again into a three-tier *scrum of scrums* with over 100 people, including some external experts under the direction of the GDS *Scrum Masters*. There were 16 teams organized within six sub-programs, all under the direction of one *Proposition Director*, who was, in effect, the ultimate *product* owner. The major roles were:

- *Product Manager*: one per team – controlled the product backlog and kanban charts for that team. Each of the six sub-programs also had a more senior product manager who juggled priorities between the product backlogs for each team in that sub-program.

- *Fact check coordinator*: a special role provided a single point of contact where there was a discrepancy between two pieces of content.

- *Technical Architect*: an additional role given to the product manager for the *publishing platform* team. The TA was responsible for providing a consistent publishing engine to all the other teams and rolling it out into all Government departments.

The aim was to move to a flexible cloud-computing contract, and away from the existing managed services contract for the hosting of DirectGov. The scope widened to include not just the decommissioning of the public-facing DirectGov content, but also the Business Link website, aimed at the business user. The aim was for all major UK Government websites to run as one service for the first time. Mike Beaven of GDS explains:

"We have a pretty established and successful agile software delivery engine ... a firmly established way of working beyond the core delivery teams, and lean/agile methods are used across GDS in a variety of teams. However, we need to interact with other projects to be accountable when we spend public money. That gives us a challenge in terms of needing heavier processes and being able to articulate what we do in good old milestone, cost and risk ways." [337]

GDS maintained a light, but effective program *box* around the agile project teams. A project management office (PMO) created the necessary standard statistics and reports needed for departmental portfolio reporting, while allowing teams to decide how to control the delivery.

Beaven pointed out that the important thing is to allow "different methods for different areas of managing delivery – one size does not fit all." [338]

Other Agile Projects at GDS

The conversion and upgrading of government services and information under the alpha.gov and beta.gov initiatives was only part of the GDS remit. Other activities included:

♦ The e-petitions project, which was built using an agile approach. It has demonstrated the importance of using *open source software* which is available without license fees and has allowed the e-petitions program code to be shared with other governments "from as far afield as the governments of Montenegro and Chile"

♦ The assisted digital team, mentioned briefly above, puts in place safeguards to ensure citizen access to Government *digital by default* services. Rather than digital being merely an alternative to paper information exchange it will be the primary channel. The assisted digital team investigates the requirements for different people in an agile manner. Rather than attempt a detailed specification up-front, GDS carried out a wide collaboration exercise with organizations already providing assisted digital such as the

Post Office and the public library service. This included 16.1% who had never used the internet and millions of disabled adults.

Francis Maude took a much closer interest in agile project management concepts than previous politicians did. He encouraged team self-organization and planning. He said that:

> "Already we have seen the beta launch of gov.uk which signaled a new approach to providing services based on real user needs rather than internal Government processes and traditions ... This is the new model for digital service provision and ... we will transform many existing Government transactions in this way. For the first time in Government we are using agile, iterative processes." [339]

Conclusions

In this chapter, we have seen how self-organizing teams can quickly address changing requirements. Agile Leadership Principle 8 encourages you to give your team space to organize itself, and delegate decision making as much as possible.

Having light controls over the detail of the development team requires a corresponding restraint, consistency and tightness in top management governance. In Part III of the book, I discuss the need for this combination to achieve *light-tight* management of agile projects.

Questions

Read Chapter Three of the UK Civil Service Reform plan published in June 2012 (see Endnote 340, page 18 onwards).

1. Comment on the objectives of "Action 8" on page 18 and its support for the agile approach.

2. The "Red tape challenge" on page 20 refers to elimination of unnecessary data in Management Information (MI) reporting.

Which data could you eliminate from your MI reports to enable your teams to work more efficiently?

Agile Leadership Exercises

1. Hold a workshop with your team to review the existing team structure with the objective of reviewing all formally defined roles. For each role ask the team:

    *   Does this role need to be formally defined because it has authorization or 'ceremonial' duties?

    *   Other roles: do these need to be defined at all?

    *   Does the existence of an organization chart help or hinder team flexibility?

2. Describe the sequence of activities that you and your team carry out in meeting your medium to long-term objectives. Discuss this sequence with your boss to discover decision points where the team needs to get approval or ratification of their decisions. For each of these decision points pose this question to yourself:

    *   Is the decision best made by the team without approval?

    *   Could minor monetary decisions be made at team level? For example, if project budgetary tolerances are set at zero dollars, even minor decisions to buy expertise or tools could be delayed.

    *   Could those who make the decisions be involved in earlier discussions, so as to be able to make final authorizations more quickly?

Chapter 16

Agile Leadership Behavior Nine: Pursue Simplicity

Simplicity – the art of maximizing the amount of work not done – is essential

Agile Manifesto Principle Number 10

The agile approach creates a tendency towards light, targeted use of technology to provide key benefits. It does this in three main ways:

♦ By removing marginal features from upcoming development work

♦ By eliminating the tendency to add unnecessary design features to a paper BDUF specification

♦ By focusing on the immediate concerns of stakeholders.

This immediacy and short-term focus in the agile approach counters the tendency of many to look too far ahead to the 'next job' rather than concentrate on current work. In this chapter, we will see how one large, over-complex project was cut down to size by a change to an incremental implementation of a simple solution.

USDA puts its Email on the Cloud

In 2008, USDA employed over 100,000 staff, carrying out a range of functions – from crop insurance to food safety, from agricultural research to animal health. However, there was one common requirement: the need for reliable, consistent, and cost-effective e-mail system and shared calendars.

Each of the 29 bodies under the Department was responsible for organizing their own email systems and computer networks. A classic case of *sub-optimization*. Each network had its own dedicated staff and was managed differently. Necessary data dissemination was inhibited by the reliance on local email address books that could not be shared. Meetings were difficult to set up, as the calendars of the invitees were often not visible to the meeting organizers unless all the participants worked in the same department.

Across USDA, the average cost of email was approximately $156 per user per year, over $15m a year when all costs were added up. Different versions of email software were being used from one unit to another. This caused problems when staff transferred departments. It also introduced the risk that one day a disaster might occur and it might be found that not all the necessary backups had been taken. Or, more likely, even if the backups were available, they would not restore the data properly.[341]

Faced with this organization-wide problem, the Department assumed that a large, complicated solution was needed. A single, centrally run *enterprise e-mail system* was planned. Each of the 29 or more existing email systems would be merged into a single enterprise system. Despite the fact that its core competencies were in agriculturally related administrative work, USDA planned to set up and run the *enterprise e-mail system* itself. It planned to employ specialist senior managers and contracted expert technical consultants. It would house the computers in its own premises and be responsible for all the security and disaster recovery procedures.

From the beginning, the federated components of the Department resisted this single *one size fits all* solution. They were used to running their own affairs, and each had 'special' requirements of their own that had to be met before they moved to a new system.

Because capital budgets were tight and the new enterprise e-mail system was going to serve so many customers, storage was going to be tight. Staff members were only going to be offered a small mailbox, and would need to continually delete old messages or use inefficient and complicated archive facilities to store them in case they needed to refer to them in the future. The miserliness of the storage, combined with the problems of conversion also meant that staff would not have access to more than two weeks of previous emails once they started to use the new system. A staff member would have to make a special request to retrieve old emails from their previous system.

The planning for migration to the new enterprise e-mail system grew increasingly complex. The addition of extra storage and processing power had to be synchronized with the switch-over of staff members from their old email systems.[342] As work got underway, and more technical difficulties became evident, the USDA Chief Information Officer (CIO) researched the possibility of moving the email services based on *cloud-computing* instead (see page 227).

Suppliers had just started to offer cloud-computing email services. These offered more functionality, greater storage, increased reliability, and flexibility. Costs would increase smoothly as new users were added. The *cloud* offered consistent and reliable recovery if disaster struck. After some research, the CIO decided to take this route rather than continue with the project to build the complex enterprise email system. There was still planning to be done, but now the focus was now on business decisions, not technical decisions.

The move to the cloud computer solution was a great success. It provided mailboxes 25 times the size of the planned enterprise e-mail solution, with easy access to additional capacity if required. Previously unavailable facilities, such as *chat, web collaboration*, and *video conferencing* could be added as required.[343]

The new system cost only $96 per user per year – a $6m per year saving over the previous decentralized email approach. This is a good example of how the incremental agile approach was used outside of its usual narrow focus on software development.[344]

Conclusions

We have seen how the USDA overcame barriers to the implementation of a single email system by removing local requirements for unusual features and exceptions. Plans changed from a large, complex design to the purchase of a simple, standard commodity. Stakeholders accepted the new solution because they could see the benefits of its stability and in its use of new technology.

Questions

Read more about the USDA switch-over to cloud-computing (see Endnote 345).

1. Buying the *software as a service* reduced the technical preparation required, but what technical responsibilities still remained with USDA.? (For example, see page 4 for an explanation of the difficulties encountered with setting up the internal security *firewalls* at the 21 agencies.)

2. There are seven lessons learned in the report (see page 5). How many of these relate to technical decisions and how many are business migration planning factors?

Agile Leadership Exercises

1. Talk with your technical expert to identify the seven most challenging tasks that lay ahead of you or your team.

    ▪ For each task, work together to quantify the amount of effort required for that task, and also the risk that the chosen solution may not work.

    ▪ Select the two largest, and riskiest tasks, and brainstorm alternative approaches that reduce the effort and risk

2. Identify the major outputs expected from you and your team for the next six months. Work with your stakeholders to identify the business benefits that will ensue from each output. Then, hold a workshop with your team to work backwards from each benefit to see if some other, simpler set of outputs would lead to a similar benefit.

3. Discuss delays that you have experienced to expected schedules with your boss and your peers. Jointly:

    ▪ Identify any dependencies between tasks or resource bottlenecks that caused those delays

    ▪ Agree ways of 'softening' these 'hand-offs' between teams. For example, by putting people into a multi-disciplinary team that would decide for themselves how to most efficiently allocate resources or run tasks in parallel.

Part III

The 6 Barriers to Agile Success

Project management in public services has a checkered history. Some large projects succeed, but far too many are late, have massive cost overruns, and many are canceled or produce no benefits.

In this final part of the book, I examine the six barriers to agile success and discuss how to overcome them:

- ♦ Chapter 17: Addiction to process

- ♦ Chapter 18: Mega-project mania

- ♦ Chapter 19: The lure of Big Design Up Front

- ♦ Chapter 20: Traditional procurement and Contracts

- ♦ Chapter 21: Can we legislate for agile? The DOD experience

- ♦ Chapter 22: Traditional Audit Approaches

Chapter 17

Addiction to Process

A well-functioning team of great individuals with mediocre tools will always outperform a dysfunctional team of mediocre individuals with great tools.[346]

Mike Cohn
founder of Mountain Goat Software

Organizational development should stress the importance of people and leadership, not a constricting process model. If the leaders of the organization see process as the primary driver of culture change, then the resulting culture will value process over people – the opposite of the approach called for in the Agile Manifesto. Elizabeth Thomas has branded this reliance on documented procedures as an 'addiction to process' – an addiction that agile can help break.[347]

However, commentators such as Rakitin have articulated concerns about the intent and the impact of the Agile Manifesto:

> "(Not) using a process gives (hackers) the freedom to do whatever (they) want – spend all (their) time coding – (these) programmers don't write documentation – (they) work out the details once (they) deliver something. On-going design at development time ... has become an excuse for putting off design until the last minute ... a disaster in the making for larger (projects) – planning as something you can do on the fly ... is a recipe for disaster on projects of any significance." [348]

His main objections are based on the possibility that some will see the Manifesto as a license to ignore the 'items on the right' (see page 60). Processes and tools, documentation, contracts, and plans still have their place, even on an agile project. The Manifesto clearly states that a balance is required between the practical and the theoretical elements of planning and execution. When in doubt, it suggests, the presumption should be in favor of, say *'individuals'* over *'processes'*. I propose that the most effective way of countering the dangers of anarchy that Rakitin warns about, is not to rely on the use of agile best practice alone (although that has value), but to ensure a focus on agile leadership.

As we have seen, the Agile Manifesto Principles provide an underpinning that moves the manifesto from being a statement of intent, to a concrete influence of team process. By encouraging business and technical people to work together, trust is engendered and inefficient communication is reduced. Motivation is increased because, as the solution emerges, it is continually tested, improved, and demonstrated to be working. Rather than a desperate run towards a long distant milestone, a baton relay in stage at a fast, but measured pace is encouraged.

Decisions should be delegated to the lowest appropriate level, thus reducing the risk that the project will go off track.

The Apparent Paradoxes in Agile Processes

The Agile Manifesto exhibits four features, which on first glance appear to be paradoxes:

- ◆ Tight control over the overall project, but a light touch when it comes to giving direction to a team

- ◆ De-emphasis on documentation but a high value on comprehensive, thorough testing with detailed audit logs

- ◆ Lack of written process within the team, but a stress on rich and immediate communications

♦ Informal liaison, often unseen, across disciplines and organizational units, but high transparency of the plans and actual progress.

It is the perception of paradoxes in the agile manifesto that have been identified as the main inhibitor to uptake – both in commerce and the public sector. Agile processes are not plan driven but instead drive the re-finement of a plan. Realistic, detailed plans exist for short-term activities, but plans further out into the future are more in overview, and all plans are subject to revision.[349]

Agile processes are self-managed rather than imposed. Communication is not channeled through a hierarchy, but directly between team members and those that they need to speak to. This requires senior management to relinquish aspects of detailed control. They must recognize that team members are usually in a better position to make detailed business and engineering decisions than they are.

Agile Organizations

Sridhar Nerur argues for a shift from command-and-control in organizations to leadership-and-collaboration. The project manager's traditional role of planner and controller must change to one of facilitator and coordinator. Organizations must accept that not all detailed knowledge can be codified and documented – Agile cuts down on the overhead of bureaucracy, reducing documentation.[350]

Authoritarian project management needs to be replaced by a cooperative social process of communication and collaboration. Many technical experts are accustomed to solitary activities and many failed projects have allowed development teams to work apart from business people.[351]

However, the perception propagated by some enthusiasts that only above-average people can use agile is self-defeating. If agile can only be used by an elite, then skills shortages and the dangers of exclusivity may affect morale of non-agile developers and create barriers to adoption. [352]

New ways of expressing the effectiveness of processes in an organization are needed. Especially those that encourage flexing of the processes to fit the capabilities and competencies of people and the characteristics of each project. [353]

Light-Tight Governance Enables Agile Approaches

Davies and Gray contend that conventional management of change tends to be light at top management level, but that, conversely, individual projects tend to be tightly controlled. They call for this conventional wisdom to be turned on its head. They argue that exactly the opposite approach is required for success: tight management at the top level to achieve a highly consistent approach across a broad program of work, whereas other aspects are lightly managed to provide flexibility.[354]

Agile can provide a framework for introducing this *light-tight* management. For example, DSDM specifically differentiates between tightly directed teams and those that are *self-directed*. Self-directed teams develop rich communications channels and are able to demonstrate the evolving solution in shorter increments – there simply is not enough time to control fast-moving teams with a bureaucratic process. These teams take initiative rather than directions.[355]

Effective organizations exhibit *tightness* at top management level by ensuring consistency in the control of the company-wide portfolio of projects. For example, when combining reports from many sub-projects up to the larger portfolio level or when there is a need to reinforce some specific organization-wide objective.

And these effective organizations exhibit *lightness* in control of the detail of the work of teams. Where the implementation of overall targets (for example, health and safety) can be achieved in many different ways, each project team in these organizations is individually responsible for the specifics of how these should be achieved. Imposition of standard approaches will be counterproductive – it is better to provide an objective, and encourage each team to find their own route.[356]

So, organizations that are effective at governing their projects use *light-tight* leadership behaviors. However, the three other, dysfunctional combinations (*light-light*, and *tight-tight*, and *tight-light* governance) occur frequently, and are usually present when large projects break down and fail (see Figure 11).

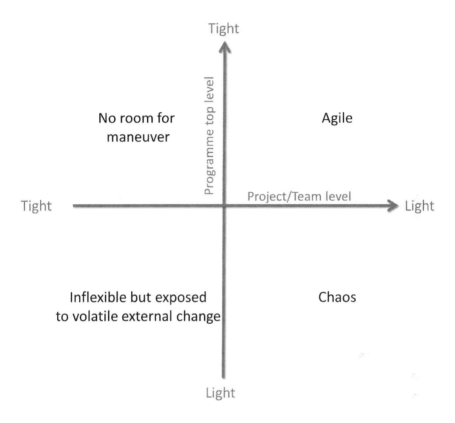

Figure 11: The dimensions of control

Chaos: the Light-Light Model of Control

Projects often come into being without a conscious decision to get organized and are passed from one top manager to another until they find a comfortable home. These are typified by a combination of inconsistent leadership coupled with an ad-hoc approach to planning. These projects fall into the category of *light-light* control. In the early stages of a project when requirements are starting to emerge, the business case is unclear and often only top management is involved in discussions on alternative solutions, and do not involve their staff. *Lightness* is evident at all levels. Often there is only a small team working on the project at first, usually at 'policy' level. Control of these small research teams seems simple enough, and often projects go through initial stages of work and start to grow before top management considers bringing some discipline and structure to the governance of the project. One government review in Canada found this to be a factor in underperformance and failure resulting in:[357]

♦ Project conception that results in unwise approaches

♦ Unsupportive project environments that contain barriers to success

♦ Project participants who lack the necessary qualifications or experience.

The approach to be taken on a project is often decided upon before a governance structure has been agreed, and in many cases the business case is an after-thought. In the case of the UK Government's Work Programme the NAO found that:

> "The Department (for Work and Pensions) devised the business case for the Work Programme after the main decisions had been made and before data about the performance of existing projects was available. No alternatives were considered." [358]

In the UK and Canada, a gated review approach is now in place to try to create a tight approach to governance for all large projects.[359] The problem in the past has been that reviews have been carried out too late to improve project start-up. A major review across UK government projects found that a major risk was from projects entering the process after the business case has been prepared in the first of a series of pre-defined decision *Gates*. Most (63%) of project boards never bothered with a business case Gate Review, and a sizable minority (41%) did not review at the next Gate (Delivery Strategy) either.[360]

Inflexibility: the Tight-Tight Model of Control

Organizations that have experienced the chaos of light-light control sometimes react by moving to the polar opposite: *tight* controls at every level when managing change. One means of attempting this focus on process is by using the Capability Maturity Model Integration (CMMI®) model.

The CMMI model is based on approaches to continual improvement of processes by Crosby, Deming, Juran, and Humphrey. The main assumption in the CMMI model is that "the quality of a system or product is highly influenced by the quality of the process used to develop and maintain it".[361] It is claimed by many, including the US GAO, to contain the essential elements of effective processes and enables the user of the model to measure the degree of *maturity* in processes involved in governance of projects and technical development (see Table 7).[362]

Table 7: CMMI Maturity Levels[363]

Level	Maturity Level
1	Initial
2	Managed
3	Defined
4	Quantitatively Managed
5	Optimized

The UK Department of Work and Pensions (DWP) has placed a great deal of emphasis on its adoption of the CMMI model, becoming officially accredited in 2008.[364] However, this 'improvement' in internal IT procedures did not help its operations to reduce error and fraud. Mistakes made by staff processing benefits in FY 2011 remained critically high at estimated £1.1bn in overpayment and £500m that should have been paid to the needy was not.[365] Problems with its IT projects continued with high profile projects such as ASD being cancelled (see page 145) and the Work

Programme IT system leaving the department open to a £60m risk of fraud. DWP remains the only UK central government department with qualified financial accounts. [366]

In 2011 the US GAO issued no less than 10 reports that used the CMMI process model as a reference for measuring the 'maturity' of organizations.[367] Although they repeatedly note in these reports that the CMMI model is "highly regarded and widely used guidance, they do not provide any evidence base to justify it as a driver for efficiency and effective processes.[6] In their own recent report on the critical factors underlying successful major acquisitions, they admit that after more than a decade of increasing volumes of best practice guidance, legislation, and increasing calls for CMMI compliance:

> "IT projects (still) too frequently incur cost overruns and schedule slippages while contributing little to mission-related outcomes" [368]

The very existence to CMMI accreditation has caused problems. In one case the winning bidder for a NASA contract for ground systems and mission operations services lodged an appeal with GAO against the award of the contract to another bidder on the basis that it did not have the CMMI accreditation, even though it was not a requirement of the procurement.[369]

The US IRS has implemented CMMI, with a massive resultant increase in overheads. A recent GAO report noted that the IRS was now spending $174m (15% of its program budget) on support activities to run these procedures. A much higher proportion than is normal for a federal department, and yet the GAO could not link this spend to any specific improvements in output. Problems still remained, including:

♦ One project that was 70% over cost due to unplanned requirements

♦ Weaknesses in information security

♦ Over-optimistic plans for the new mission critical CADE2 tax records system

♦ Poor tracking of overhead spending, with over 50% of the

bureaucratic overheads of running CMMI itself being mis-categorized. [370]

Michael Spayd, a former CMMI assessor stresses the cultural misfit between the agile approach and the process maturity mind-set:

> "It's certainly true that culturally speaking, CMMI lives most easily in a control culture, where the idea is really to minimize risk by emphasizing predictable, repeatable results" [371]

Theoretically, Spayd says, it is possible to implement CMMI without using the waterfall approach or BDUF. But most organizations take a process-driven route to CMMI achievement without any nuance. In most cases it simply reinforces a waterfall culture, rather than helping it to become agile.[372]

The latest research from Forrester shows that CMMI take-up is reducing, and that most respondents firmly place CMMI in the same category with waterfall techniques, with only 13% pursuing that model.[373] Many organizations start up the CMMI mountain, but very few stay balanced at the top, in an optimum position There are four reasons why so many problems exist for the adopters of the CMMI model in government (see Figure 12). These are: [374]

♦ It is difficult for many organizations to make the necessary investment up front to develop and document effective processes if the returns are not immediate and obvious.

♦ Although many organizations have reached CMMI level 3 (of managed processes), CMMI level 4 is a potential *vale of despondency*. More processes become documented, and yet more quantitative measurement takes place. However, this produces little benefit until the processes start to become optimized, which is meant to happen at level 5.

♦ Organizations find it difficult to optimize, and the process of 'becoming mature' may overshoot. The rollout of CMMI project can push the organization over into what I call "CMMI level 5½", where processes are over-documented, over-measured, too broadly prescriptive and difficult and expensive to change. Finding the sweet spot of CMMI can often turn into an expensive and forlorn search for the holy grail of CMMI level 5.

♦ Any great investment in organizational maturity is at risk from organizational changes which split or join together portions of different departments. Organizations which are highly dependent on process maturity tend to have brittle and inflexible responses to organizational changes that are thrust upon them.

We saw in Part II that Microsoft had decided only to implement *just enough* process in their development of the Government Gateway – they had decided not to try and implement CMMI level 5 for this very reason.[375]

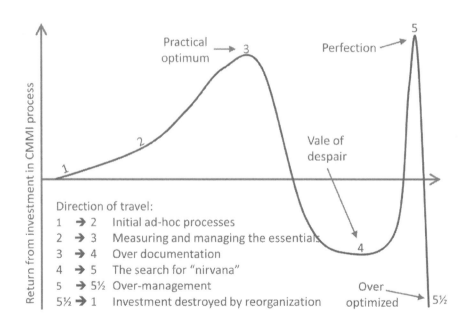

Figure 12: Problems with CMMI *overmaturity*

An example of over addiction to process at the expense of efficiency was the failure of phase two of the Sentinel project which was salvaged eventually by the adoption of an agile approach. The then Chief Technology Officer, Jerome Israel, still feels that the process was right, they just didn't have enough of it:

> "The FBI's engineering strength was weak—we didn't have the engineering talent to pull off a major project like Sentinel ... (So) how can government agencies assure Congress that taxpayers' IT investments will be successful? ... If the DOD rates software development companies according to CMMI, why not apply a similar model to government agencies?" [376]

Spayd rejects this argument:

> "There's a fundamental assumption in the CMMI that processes can be repeatable, and that they are predictive processes, basically not empirical processes. That is the fundamental flaw in the CMMI, and that's actually why I don't personally believe in level 4 and 5. They are ridiculous and do not create value." [377]

And a further weakness of the CMMI approach is that unexpected reorganizations become difficult and very expensive in process-bound organizations, as the NAO recently pointed out:

> "There have been over 90 reorganizations (in) central government departments ... between May 2005 and June 2009: over 20 a year on average. We estimate the gross cost of the 51 reorganizations covered by our survey to be £780 million, equivalent to £15 million for each reorganization and just under £200 million a year. Around 85 per cent of the total cost is for establishing and reorganizing arm's length bodies. (Staff and information technology cost £473m)." [378]

Turner and Jain examined whether a partial implementation of CMMI could work alongside the agile approach. They consulted with both CMMI proponents and agilists. They found that the CMMI experts could be sub-categorized into a *conservative, by-the-letter group* and a *liberal, concepts-oriented group*. They also found *conservative agilists,* who were extremely rigid in their definitions, and *liberal agilists* who saw value in comparing, matching and hybridizing methods. The conservative sections on either side of the argument found little to agree upon, and divided into two separate camps. However, the liberal groupings generally agreed that there were some components of CMMI that supported and complemented agile (see Table 8).[379]

Table 8: Components of CMMI and their possible support of agile[380]

CMMI elements that may conflict with agile	CMMI elements that may support agile
Objectively Evaluate Adherence	Ensure Continuous Process Improvement
Collect Improvement Information	Manage Configurations
Stabilize Sub-process Performance	Train People
Establish Quantitative Objectives for the Process	Provide Resources
Plan the Process	Identify and Involve Relevant Stakeholders
	Assign Responsibility

The four CMMI elements that most agile proponents found most difficult to see as agile-friendly were those that most 'tightly' controlled the detailed work of developers through documented process. All the agilists disliked the idea of a "process mafia that checked on how the developers developed". They felt that it would be expensive and distracting if detailed processes not associated with customer objectives were recorded and analyzed. On the other hand, the agilists were split over whether defined processes for continuous improvement, rigor in configuration management, and up-front planning were, or were not anti-patterns to the agile approach. Overall the researchers concluded that:

> "It is evident that while there are significant differences, the 'oil and water' description of CMMI and agile approaches is somewhat overstated ... It is our belief that there is much in common between the two world views, and that the strengths and weaknesses are often complimentary." [381]

A recent example of *tight-tight* project management in the UK Child Maintenance and Enforcement Commission (CMEC) within the Department of Work and Pensions (DWP) led to the abandonment of an agile approach on a critical project.

The track record of IT systems implementation at CMEC and its predecessors was appalling. CMEC was set up to take over the work of the Child Support Agency whose IT systems were grossly inaccurate. CMEC's job was to track down absent parents, enforce child maintenance payments and pass these on to the responsible parents. A new database was built to address this problem but it was scrapped when it could not take on the data from the old system. Then a third system was developed, but it was so poor that an extra 600 staff had to be taken on, at an annual cost of £43m to manually handle claims that the new system still could not process.

So, a fourth system was planned. Costs on the project rose from £149m to £275m and the incremental approach that was promised was abandoned. Two key factors were at play:[382]

♦ Management planned a *big-bang* delivery of all functions of the new system from April 2010. As with so many big-bang projects, the management realized after a time that full implementation all at once was unrealistic, and belatedly (and at some expense and further delay) decided to change to a phased implementation.

♦ The project approach was inconsistent and unintegrated. One team worked using a requirements list and followed a traditional waterfall approach. A second team used the JAD approach (discussed earlier in Part II) that they claimed was agile to develop extensive prototypes. The two teams worked in isolation. Two sets of overlapping, conflicting and ambiguous specifications were constructed. (One source claims that over the 90,000 requirements were documented.) [383]

Another recent major IT project within DWP also had significant delays caused by 'tight-tight' project management in a CMMI environment. A major IT system was required in 2011 to make £1bn a year payments to suppliers to the new "Work Programme" applying automatic safeguards against fraud and error. However, DWP delayed work from starting until it decided on a detailed BDUF specification.[384] Delivery of the complete system was then planned in one 'big-bang for autumn 2012, leaving large amounts of money subject to the possibility of fraud and error (at least £60m by March 2012, rising by £20m for each month of delay).[385] DWP decided, again belatedly, to split implementation into more manageable portions: the error and fraud functions earlier and the management information and reporting functions later.[386]

Inflexibility: the 'Tight-Light' Model of Control

Some commentators have wryly commented on enforced implementation of management processes as *anti-patterns* of inefficiency – that is, processes that actually worked to increase risk and decrease efficiency. Michael Finkelstein, tongue in cheek, even proposed levels of 'immaturity' (see Table 9).

Table 9: Finkelstein's irreverent suggestion for measuring 'immaturity' levels[387]

Level	Immaturity Level	Characteristic
Zero	Foolish	Negligence
Minus 1	Stupid	Obstructive
Minus 2	Lunatic	Contemptuous

This effect can be perceived in large organizations that attempt to control the detailed work of teams without attending to deficiencies in management control and organizational behavior.

> "All immature organizations (in contrast to Level 1 organizations) fail to recognize that their management is severely awry. They believe firmly that a technical fix will solve all their problems. For these

organizations management issues almost never appear at the top of key priority issue lists." [388]

At *level zero*, Finkelstein suggests, organizations subvert attempts at the individual and team levels to work together to be productive. Lightness in management attention will result in ill-informed and badly thought through decisions. Top management may change implementation plans and pull the rug from under the feet of the solution development team.

At *level minus one* the organization actually works against productivity. Finkelstein says that they may "sincerely believe that they are assisting", but the result is obstruction – solutions are actually prevented from being developed, let alone implemented.

At *level minus two*, the obstructions are so systemic that they can only be the result of cynical manipulation so as to increase the cost of development and maintenance through development inefficiencies and solution unreliability.

Although Finkelstein was not proposing a serious analysis, the paper itself simply reflects a presumption that process maturity is a 'good thing' and that those adopting a different stance are deliberately being obstructive. However, researchers on organization change have suggested that what appear to be destructive behaviors of those obstructing change, are actually adoptions of alternative models of behavior that make sense to those exhibiting them. In other words one person's 'pattern' may simply be another person's 'anti-pattern', and vice-versa.[389]

Agile: a Light-Tight Control Model for Success

In the early stages of a project when the business case is developing, top management must exercise self-discipline, especially when solutions are beginning to emerge. Attempting to put in place appropriate decision making structures after a project has already started creates unnecessary risks.

Options for the intended solution may have narrowed down to just one approach. This often results in a business case that merely attempts to justify a pre-ordained decision, and fails to explore other options. These other options may be revived later in the process when the preferred approach proves problematical. If some of the assumptions in the intended approach are flawed, and problems are encountered when building a solution, or feedback from testing and piloting is negative, then some of the previously discarded options may need to be revived.

Similarly, the development route to be taken, for example whether to use a COTS solution or build a new solution from scratch, should be analyzed and any assumptions carefully tested and revisited as the project progresses.

Early adoption of 'tight' top management processes will help set up a project environment that enables, not constrains teams, and the necessary skills can be brought to bear on the problem through thoughtful appointments and appropriate procurement of suppliers.

The use of a gated review approach is useful, but it is in the early stages pre-business case and pre-procurement that benefits are greatest. Late, heavy-handed use of gated reviews to fix poor strategic decisions by imposing detailed management processes on solution development teams will simply result in further entrenchment of 'light-tight' controls.

Certain aspects of process approaches, such as CMMI, may support an agile approach – especially those that help management proactively work to support the development team to success, rather than strangle them with inappropriate red tape. The two mistakes that are most likely to risk the objectives of *light-tight* control when implementing CMMI are unthinking adherence to process, and inappropriate measurement of team effectiveness.

As we saw on page 190, agile approaches do produce useful metrics that help track progress and improve productivity. There are claims that these measures can be successfully adopted within a CMMI and EVA approach without endangering the maturity level of overall management process, and without imposing a non-agile approach on the development team.

Most importantly, top management must be careful not to believe that technical decisions can fix strategic problems. Changes to requirements can and will happen and should be embraced and exploited by solution developers. Inflexible and expensive change control procedures can slow down the adoption of necessary changes, and make that those changes late, expensive, and painful.

Curing the Addiction to Process in the US

In this section I will outline the claims for agile success made in the first year after the Vivek Kundra's 25 Point Plan was published. The plan itself was intended to "shock the system", and shake up the counterproductive processes that had led to so many project failures. This attempt to cure the government bodies of their addiction to process kicked off with several major initiatives to put in place technologies that complement agile approaches. These included:[390]

- ♦ Cloud Computing: an approach to buying and running IT services that allows the customer to immediately and incrementally purchase extra capacity, or slim down usage as demand changes, without the need for long, drawn out projects or procurements.

- ♦ Shared Services: centralizing IT databases and standardizing on run-of-the-mill business processes, such as personnel management, purchasing, invoicing and accounting. This does not just save money, but also focuses IT development on value-added projects, rather than catering for unnecessary variations in local practices.

- ♦ Upgrading project management skills: Introducing innovative approaches, including agile, by the creation of a new IT project management career path. Breaking down barriers to adoption of agile by requiring integrated project teams, rather than silos of specialties and by collaboration on creation of best practice guidance.

- ♦ Aligning the acquisition/procurement process to IT lifecycles:

making sure that specialized IT acquisition professionals can support agile approaches, and facilitate the use of small, innovative technology suppliers.

♦ Influencing Congress: aim to change legislative frameworks that are 'anti-patterns' to agile development.

♦ Restructuring the Investment Review Boards (IRBs) to implement the "TechStat" project review model. Kundra criticized the previous approach as follows:

"Many current IT projects are scheduled to produce the first deliverables years after work begins ... (because) projects designed to deliver initial functionality after several years of planning are inevitably doomed ... typical IRB meeting agendas currently set aside two hours to review the entire IT portfolio, far too little time to adequately review dozens of technical projects." [391]

The UK Also Starts to Quit Addiction to Process

In 2011 the UK Coalition Government published its IT Strategy. The UK focus was similar to the US 25 Point Plan: to reduce costs and to increase flexibility in public services. The plan was greatly influenced by the Institute for Government whose 2011 report, "System Error", had recommended two major changes:

♦ First, the adoption of the concept of *government as a platform*, by the creation of a shared, government-wide approach to driving down costs and increased interoperability

♦ Second, the rollout of agile project management throughout government.[392]

The IT Strategy planned 19 separate strands of technological change, one of which was the adoption of an agile approach. The Government announced plans to use flexible framework contracts, rather than the large fixed price contracts that had so often ended up as anything but fixed in price and length. It was perceived that the tendency for massive contracts favored an oligopoly of large suppliers. A target was set for 50% of all large IT developments to be running using agile techniques by 2013.[393]

In 2011, in the very early stages of the implementation of the new UK Government IT Strategy, the NAO investigated the planning and set-up activities. Their report was optimistic, but found that there were no clear measurable targets in the strategy and no system to measure its impact. They warned that because there was no overall plan to support the strategy, progress could be hindered through lack of resources.[394]

However, one year later there was still little evidence of the promised increase in use of agile approaches. 10 departments had not yet started any significant agile projects, and in those that had, agile adoption was patchy. Significant progress was reported in only three areas:

♦ The massive Universal Credit project was underway using some agile techniques

♦ The Government Digital Service had released alpha.gov and beta.gov websites (as discussed on page 194)

♦ Significant training of staff in agile had been carried out at the Maritime and Coastguard Agency.

When the Government produced a statement on progress towards the IT Strategy in June 2012, the only agile project cited as a success was the successful, but small-scale, e-Petitions project which, although it had collated 16,000 petitions successfully, was not a large-scale delivery project.[395] In a response to that statement, the IFG published a report from their research into progress. They interviewed all significant Government CIOs and their procurements staff, and representatives of IT suppliers – both large and small. They found that progress towards using agile approaches has been slow.[396]

They noted that the US has effective direct intervention from a strong Government Chief Information Officer (CIO). In the UK they found that the implementation of agile and the strategy overall was poorly coordinated, incoherent and still without clear objectives or success criteria, despite the warnings in the NAO report of the previous year. The IFG noted that although senior leaders in government and in technology suppliers supported the concepts proposed in the 19 strands of the strategy, they were not convinced about the approach to implementing it:

> "The IT strategy did not ... adopt the (previous IFG) recommendation that 'platform' and 'agile' should be driven by a strong, independent CIO – instead (it relies on a) CIO delivery board. CIOs should question whether they are genuinely improving the ways that they are working in areas such as agile, or whether they are just attaching a label to projects to get a tick in the box." [397]

The IFG found that there were concerns that the agile projects that were underway were "often very minor projects running on the fringe of the departments" and that "in some areas projects may be being labeled as agile without having really changed the way in which they were run." [398]

Large and Complicated Processes

A strand of the UK strategy that crucially depended on agile adoption was the drive to achieve greater efficiencies through the economies of scale of Shared Service Centers. Several of these had been set up by the previous administration to provide centralized services to Government departments to reap massive economies of scale.

However, rather than buying simple accounting software and implementing their new business model in an incremental, phased and agile manner, these shared services were set up using a waterfall mentality. They bought huge, complex systems that would take years to bed in. The Enterprise Resource Planning (*ERP*) systems they purchased from SAP and Oracle were meant to be set-up by non-programmers by the alteration of look-up tables and parameters. However, experience shows that this work has always been fraught with difficulty. They took a substantial amount of effort and skill to set-up, and came with unexpected difficulties. Their "tremendous generality and enormous complexity" make them prone to "glitches and low performance". Not only are they often "nightmarish to implement" but also "difficult to maintain".[399]

Potentially these ERP systems can bring about efficiencies, but their complexity encourages unnecessary customization. Standardization is difficult to achieve unless led from the top:

> "A thirst for customized software and a lack of mandation means seven years on, shared services aren't delivering value for money ... the cost to establish, maintain and upgrade these systems is high. ... two centers now intend to totally re-implement their existing systems with simpler, standard software, despite the significant investment already made ... it is not clear why such expensive solutions were bought. Other smaller and simpler accounting packages were not looked at to see if they may have provided the required functionality" [400]

The spectacular $1.2bn failure in 2010 of a botched big-bang payroll implementation by IBM at Queensland Health is an example of these problems, and contrasts with the agile successes in other departments elsewhere in the State of Queensland documented in Part I of the book. The new payroll project was based on the SAP COTS package and was implemented using a waterfall approach, based on formal change control of an inadequate BDUF. Parallel runs against the old system were not carried out and it went live in a big-bang fashion. The government had to make emergency loans to thousands of staff left unpaid in the months after implementation. Two years later overpayments still affected nearly all of the 78,000 staff, requiring 200,000 payment adjustment entries to be applied manually every month.[401]

Conclusions

This book argues that management control and agile are not incompatible. Some proponents of process maturity argue for *tight-tight* control – tightly defined processes for management and tightly defined processes for development. Some proponents of agile place themselves at the extreme end of both spectrums. They wish to divorce themselves from management control completely: a *light-light* model. But this model could be a dangerous road to chaos.

The agile approach provides a successful model of *light-tight* management which offers the best of both worlds: enough freedom being given to the development team and its expert abilities, combined with effective engagement with corporate governance.

Questions

1. Which aspects of your organization's management process maturity enable or inhibit your project's effectiveness?

2. Which patterns of behavior in your current work do you see around you as negative 'anti-patterns'? Imagine how these behaviors could be perceived as constructive and useful from a different perspective.

3. How was your current work initiated? Is there a business case? When was it drawn up? Were alternative options considered? Has it been reviewed and fine-tuned since?

4. The incoming administrations in both the US and the UK wanted to cure their respective government departments and agencies of ineffective addiction to process. Compare and contrast the TechStat approach (see Endnote 402) with the Delivery Council approach used in the UK (see Endnote 403).

Chapter 18

Mega-Project Mania

We know why projects fail, we know how to prevent their failure. So why do they still fail?[404]

Martin Cobb,
Treasury Board of Canada Secretariat

Government has a variable history of success in managing projects around the world. The sheer scale of some projects is staggering, as is the lack of information about spending on activities that often come to nothing. Some governments, such as those in the UK and France have highly centralized, integrated processes, such as levying sales taxes or administering driving licenses. In other federated countries, such as the USA and Germany, substantially sized non-Federal authorities try to control budgets on single massive run-away projects. In the State of Victoria in Australia in 2011 forecasts to complete the top ten projects had more than doubled from AU$1.3bn to AU$2.7bn.[405]

Centralization of administration through change projects promises the possibility of large economies of scale. The natural tendency is for large, monolithic projects to be initiated. Large, complex, bloated project structures often fail to identify the major risks to delivery. Even risks that are recognized are often not quantified or managed proactively.

Risk management often becomes a sanitized activity. It can be reduced to mere cutting and pasting of spreadsheets updated by specialist risk managers away from the governance structures and the key decision makers. Management must actively balance the benefits of scale against the risks that over-scaling creates (see Figure 13).[406]

First, mega projects are often justified based on the promise of savings from economies of scale. The cost for each unit of delivery is expected to reduce as the size of the project being considered increases. Notice from the graph that savings through economies of scale flatten off quickly – the costs of running mega-projects grow almost as fast as any savings are achieved through increased size.

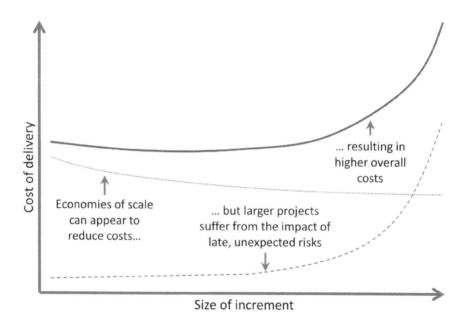

Cost of delivery

Economies of scale can appear to reduce costs...

... but larger projects suffer from the impact of late, unexpected risks

... resulting in higher overall costs

Size of increment

Figure 13 The impact of risk as the time between deliveries increases

Second, notice that the hidden costs of rising risk increase dramatically with size. This is because the importance of a risk depends on two components: the probability of it happening and its impact if it does happen. Larger projects will have risks which are more difficult to predict and they will also have a higher impact if they occur. This is a double-whammy effect that gives rise to an exponential rise in likely cost from hidden risks as project size increases.

Conversely, agile behaviors tend towards doing small chunks of work.

Agile projects are smaller, and have lower overall costs – once risk is taken into account.

The more complex the system the more inevitable is change. Typical waterfall approach software projects experience a 25% change in requirements over their life. Larger projects experience a 35% change or more in requirements. Not only this, but the number of these changes is less predictable in large projects. Large projects suffer from more variability in scope than small projects.[407]

Consider waterfall mega-projects: any slight savings achieved through economies of scale are more than wiped out by the costs of counteracting the risks. If management were to consider the risk-weighted costs, a smaller, and more optimum project size would be chosen.

Flyvbjerg attributes the popularity of large projects in the early 2000s to the *mega-projects paradox*:

> The irony is that more and more mega-projects are built despite the poor performance record of many projects … The main causes of the mega-projects paradox are the inadequate deliberation about risk and (secondly the) lack of accountability in the project decision-making process.[408]

Efforts to transfer risk to sub-contractors through contractual penalties cannot reflect the true cost of business failure that the client is exposed to – not just additional costs incurred, but the late or non-realization of benefits. Despite efforts to transfer responsibility, the client ultimately must bear and pay for the risk when a mega-project runs into trouble.[409]

Can more layers of assurance help?

One of the first edicts to be proclaimed when the new coalition Government in the UK took office in 2010 was to reverse the decision made in the 1980s which progressively devolved project supervision away from the center of government to individual departments.[410] The Cabinet Office Major Projects Authority (MPA) was established and carried out a review of all large IT contracts. More than 300 IT projects were reviewed with many being put on hold, including the National Id Card project.[411] This initiative was driven by the policy aim of reducing the Government's public funding deficit. A special focus was placed on IT projects which were perceived to be over-centralized and overlarge.[412]

The reviewers now had a problem – many large projects were underway and needed to continue, and no better alternative for their management had been agreed. Therefore it was decided that a traditional milestone review assurance approach would be used – but this time mandatory and with centralized scrutiny. These improvements in control focused on more detailed budgeting and assurance health checks based on check-box assurance. Some efficiencies were planned by attempting to eliminate duplication of assurance activities through a mandatory Integrated Assurance and Approval Plan (IAAP) for every large project.[413]

This approach to throttling back the size of projects was mainly focused on reducing consultant usage and killing obviously failing projects, such as the £469m Firecontrol fiasco which gets several mentions in this book.[414]. On-going centralized project review was still subject to the same set of Gateway control processes as had been in place for at least 10 years.[415] This waterfall Gateway review approach had failed to stem the number of failing projects, and an agile approach was not explicitly part of the IAAP.

Another problem was the continued reliance on Gateway reports. These reports were confidential between the reviewing team and the project sponsor, and because of their secrecy they could not be requested under the UK Freedom of Information (FOI) legislation.[416]. The original objective of this secrecy was to encourage robust criticism that might have been stifled if embarrassing facts were made public. However, the contents of each report were often widely distributed within the government, so the conclusions were often not clear and were usually overoptimistic. One report stated that the reports were ineffective because of this lack of robustness, and that they were "considered unimportant by Senior Responsible Owners".[417] One example was leaked onto the Internet in 2011 which contained an optimistic appraisal of a project that went on to fail (see page 145).

Although claiming compatibility with agile approaches, no specific guidance on implementing agile in Government was made[418], and in continuing with 'more of the same' the guidance did little to ensure that projects were of optimum size and did not specifically address the following major weaknesses:

♦ Big-bang delivery is a shock to steady-state operations

♦ Risks are unquantified and as a result unanalyzable

♦ The pointless pursuit of certainty through detailed planning

♦ Solutions being over-specified before the problems they are meant to solve are understood

♦ The technology being divorced from the stakeholders.

Big-Bang Delivery from Mega-Projects

The 'Big Bang' approach is often a side effect of the drive to reduce perceived costs. If all business change is packaged into one delivery on one date this appears to reduce costs – all user training is expected to take place at one time, all testing is planned to be done in one short, sharp phase and therefore development time is saved.

Assuming that big-bang implementation is the best way forward is a convenient simplifying assumption for management and technologists alike. However, with a big-bang approach at the end of a mega-project, the staff members in operations have to suddenly change all their working practices at once and start using a new system, often riddled with bugs and with vital functions missing.

To avoid these risks, many individual organizations, such as the US IRS, and the UK Revenue and Customs, have started to base their change strategies on making changes in increments (albeit in the case of the IRS cases in rather large increments). [419]

But only recently has the UK Government pronounced a 'presumption against big bang projects'.[420] And there are three major ways in which big bang can be avoided:

First, a pilot project can be implemented before committing to national rollout. This can help, but only if the pilot is carefully chosen and there is sufficient time to assess its impact so that the future direction of the project can be influenced. All too often pilots are badly conceived. In the case of the "Pathways to Work" project in the UK the NAO found that:

> "The pilot evaluation sampled people who made an enquiry about claiming incapacity benefits – not those who actually went on to claim ... and it did not pilot its proposed contractor model." [421]

Second, phased delivery reduces risk, and the additional costs of phased delivery are usually recouped several times over from earlier delivery of benefits. For example, the UK tax authority, HMRC consulted stakeholders and was congratulated by the NAO for deliberately phasing in the introduction of online business tax returns over a period of three years.[422]

Third, incremental delivery of change can be exploited to reduce the pain and cost of big bang. An example from India illustrates this problem. The devolution of grant making facilities to Kerala State was sudden and ill-prepared. An audit of the situation by the national audit organization in India (CAG) found that if an incremental approach had been followed, then the problems of training at local levels would have been avoided.[423] Incremental delivery focuses on matching delivery to the capacity of the business for change.

Risks are Unquantified

Projects often drift into being – from an initial concept they rapidly gain a life of their own. One regularly encountered criticism is that investments are committed before enough depth of analysis is complete. The counter-argument is that if one waits for analysis to be completed one would never start work, and nothing would ever get done.

In a recent study claimed to be the most extensive ever undertaken, Flyvbjerg and Budzier analyzed 1,472 projects (of which 92% were public projects). They identified that one in six had cost overruns of over 200%. Moreover, the impact of time overruns of 70% on these projects led to unexpected spectacular losses. These 'Black swan' projects included the cargo and flight information system project at the new Hong Kong airport that reportedly cost the economy $600 million in lost business in 1998 and 1999. [424]

Detailed best practice guidance on risk quantification for projects has been available for many years. Attempts have been made to raise the profile of governance of project risk, however, project risk management still does not appear on the radar screen of corporate good governance in either the private or public sectors. [425]

Unrealistic Expectations for Certainty

When faced in everyday life with a task that has inherent risks, such as setting out to drive to work when bad weather is forecast, we naturally think of changing our behavior to reduce risk. For example, we might decide to work at home that day, or perhaps set out after the bad weather has passed by. We do not expect to reduce risk by making a list of roads we are travelling on and adding up the exact distances. However, once a direction has been set on a project we all too often see the symptoms of increased analysis and planning as an attempt to reduce risk.

Methods for assessing the inherent risk of the project objectives exist. These methods typically focus on areas perceived to contribute most often to project failure, and then measure the profile of each factor within the project in question. In the UK a Risk Potential Assessment (RPA) form is used to assess major public mega-projects.[426] The recommended response to high risk projects is for the Cabinet Office to apply an extra degree of checking to the project, rather than to work with the project management to change the project approach in order to reduce the inherent risk itself.

The GAO has attempted a strategy of trying to increase large project success through the dissemination of information and best practice. Analysts such as Paul Strassman have noted that despite an accumulation of how-to guides, project success rates have not improved.[427] Over-prescriptive, detailed 'best practice' checklists have not helped. Each item on such a checklist seems unobjectionable and logical, but often priorities between these mandatory commandments may be conflicting. Each expansion of a set of best practices adds to the enormous number of rules and stipulations that should be adhered to. Strassman points out that as these rules have expanded, the number of GAO reports detailing information management failures have also increased:

> "What GAO misses is exactly what has been at fault with the Government's information management practices. The increasing volumes of congressional diktats, legislative directives, Inspector General guidelines, General Services Administration rules, and departmental standards manuals have not improved performance as systems complexity keeps increasing. GAO has worked the problem from the wrong end. They have tried to induce excellence by adding to an already unmanageable volume of requirements that define best practice and methods ... they over define inputs instead of allowing agencies to commit to performance objectives that deliver measurable end-results."[428]

Solutions Specified Before Problems are Understood

Project managers often make an attempt to head off the twin threats of unknown risks and over-assurance by trying to tie down the requirements too early and in too much detail.

Ironically, such attempts to reduce uncertainty by detailed description of solutions often increase the risk of addressing the wrong problem. The rush to design a solution is compounded by early involvement of specialists with experience in (and an agenda to use) specific technologies, and with a lack of interest in solving the users' problems. Always using the same staff and suppliers to work on project definition and setup may seem a low risk approach. But, often this will only tend to repeat the errors of the past, and little fresh thinking will emerge. Overspecification can take three forms:

   ♦ First by following Doran's criteria: objectives should always be Specific, Measurable, Assignable, Realistic and Related to Time

(SMART).[429] Too much emphasis can be placed on being 'Specific', leading to a branching out of strategic objectives into specific requirements – away from key areas into secondary issues that are not necessary for success.

♦ Second, detailed requirements often morph too early into designs. Early teachings in structured systems analysis recognized this tendency, and advised against jumping early to conclusions as to the required processes and technologies.[430] In Part II I mentioned the UK Government SSADM method as an example of a waterfall design approach which deliberately split requirements from solutions and *logical analysis* from *physical design*. [431] Such methods became unwieldy as systems became more complex in the 1990s, and these techniques waned. As COTS solutions have become more popular there has been a tendency to assume a particular implementation process or technology and then to write the requirements in terms of what that solution would look like. It is difficult to justify the use of a method that requires extensive 'logical' analysis, independent of the probable solution. It can save time to incorporate assumptions as to the technological solution into early requirements analysis, but the risk is that options are not fully explored.

♦ Finally, specifications can become gold-plated. This most often occurs when there are diverse groups of stakeholders with diverse objectives and their own special methods of working. Without adequate stakeholder management, consultation, prioritization and central adjudication on priorities, a set of requirements can be built up that satisfies everyone but pleases no-one. In the Firecontrol project, cited for different reasons elsewhere in this book, the high-specification regional fire and emergency buildings added greatly to the cost impact of late delivery of the IT system. And that system had been overcomplicated by lack of consensus on core requirements from those running the 46 existing control centers.[432]

The Technology is Divorced from the Stakeholders

Although it may seem obvious that the technologists working on a project should ensure that the solution is closely aligned to the stakeholders' needs, real engagement and understanding is often lacking.

In 2011 the GAO reported on the cancellation of the NextGen insurance policy and claims management system at FEMA after 7 years and $40 million had been spent. Stakeholders had not been involved in requirements gathering and the system did not meet user expectations. FEMA now struggles on with an ineffective 30-year old system.[433]

Cross-government projects need the support and active engagement of multiple stakeholders across departments and agencies. As mentioned in Part II, 'ownership' of a project should not be treated as a simple issue. Usually several parties have to make an investment to make a project feasible, and many projects become unviable because a hierarchy of control has been put in place that does not recognize the need for co-ordination between parties with potentially diverging interests.[434]

Conclusions

The decisions on size and delivery strategies are the most important that can be made when setting up a project. All too often it is enticing to solve all the world's problems in one fell swoop. Objectives are set out to please the project sponsor without any consideration of priorities or attempt to prune back marginal objectives. By trying to please all the stakeholders the lowest common denominator sets the bar for acceptance of mandatory objectives too low, and the list of requirements becomes bloated.

In large organizations, this tendency can be aggravated by procurement practices that favor large mega-projects. Marginal reductions in overall costs that are gained by organizing work in massive procurements are not matched by the hidden costs of failure. Risks are considered to have been 'transferred' to the supplier simply by virtue of huge penalty clauses in contracts for failure to deliver.

However, the risk of not gaining the expected business benefits cannot be transferred – it always remains with the Government, and having over-long periods without any 'proof of concept' increases the cost of failure.

In this chapter we have seen how the drive for ever greater economies of scale is based on a flawed economic rationale. Mega-projects that plan for all changes to be implemented as *big-bang* is a risky approach, and the risks of being large scale quickly outweigh the savings. Big-bang projects seldom deliver at lowest cost because they tend to delay implementation until everything is ready at the same time. This not only militates against any quick wins, but also escalates risks that would otherwise be manageable. Further, we have discovered the benefits of an evidence based approach to identifying real-world solutions at an early stage using the discipline of short iterations of delivery. The risks of the Defined Process Approach are reduced by the use of the Empirical Process Approach. Under these circumstances an approach with small iterative steps becomes the optimal.

Questions

1. We started this chapter by introducing the concept of 'optimum project size'. What is the optimum project size for your current project? Has the hidden cost of risk been assessed in an attempt to moderate project size?

2. What other reasons can you think of for pruning back projects that have very wide, all-encompassing objectives?

3. Think of previous, successful projects you have worked on. What aspects of PDSA iterative development were exhibited?

4. Look at the IAAP diagram that the UK Cabinet Office has published (see Endnote 435). Make a list of the positive and negative aspects of the project lifecycle it assumes. Is this model suitable for reviewing agile projects?

Chapter 19

The Lure of 'Big Design Up Front'

Procrastination is the thief of time.

Mr. Micawber
from "David Copperfield"
by Charles Dickens

Big Design Up Front (BDUF) and waterfall approaches go hand in hand. Where one is assumed, the other follows. There are institutional reasons why these approaches are often followed in government development projects:

♦ Top-down approaches are very appealing to hierarchical organizations

♦ Having detailed specifications appears to simplify procurement

♦ The sign-off and baselining of each progressive stage of a project appears to give certainty to the making of progress

♦ Advisors and consultants to large organizations may be motivated to tell the client what they want to hear, especially if it results in protracted strategy studies and analysis

♦ The use of approaches which produce a copious audit trail of documentation is appealing to bureaucratic organizations.

The Origins of BDUF

It is difficult to imagine today the influence that James Martin had over the development of IT practices in the 1980s. Bill Gates's Microsoft was still a sub-contractor to IBM, and Steve Jobs had left Apple and was spending his wilderness years trying to sell the ill-fated NeXt computer. The name on everybody's lips at the time was "James Martin" – the 'Guru of the Information Age'.

Martin had an amazing influence in selling the IT industry the waterfall model of planning, detailed specification, build and test. From his seminal 1983 book entitled "An Information Systems Manifesto", through to his huge 1,000 page, three volume work "Information Engineering", he convinced many that the way forward was to carry out extensive strategic reviews and build comprehensive designs before starting any practical work – in other words he convinced many people that a Big Design Up Front was a precondition for success.[436]

And now 30 years later, Martin has given away $150m of his fortune to his alma mater, Oxford University.[437] He lives in luxury on his private island in the Caribbean,[438] and is still writing books – adding to the over 100 that he has published over the last 50 years.[439]

In the late 1960s programming was maturing from a semi-amateur, part-time occupation into a profession in its own right. The programmers became more ambitious with their projects, not just writing payroll and accounting programs but stating to automate other business critical applications, such as stock control and invoicing. As the scope of the programs increased so did the size and complexity of the programs that they were writing. As they started working in larger teams the need for a method of coordination of their work became apparent.[440]

An approach to this organization was first suggested in a modest paper by H.D. Benington back in 1956 as a way of formalizing the development of software using a waterfall approach.[441] The resultant problems of using a waterfall approach have been picked over many times over the years.[442] Benington himself recognized the problem that operational testing (or 'shakedown' as he termed it) could take an indefinite time, and that total costs could never be predicted with accuracy.

Benington's paper was the seed of an emerging paradigm – early restrictions of the size of computers and lack of sophistication in tools forced a waterfall approach which continued to be adopted even as these performance restrictions fell away.[443]

In 1970 an influential Institute of Electrical and Electronics Engineers (IEEE) paper Winston Royce declared it to be "fundamentally sound". He advised that some additional features needed to be added to address most of the development risks: [444]

♦ Carry out early work to "assure that the software will not fail because of storage, timing and data (performance) reasons".

♦ Create a pilot model, test and use it about ⅓ of the way into the project to find "trouble spots in the design"

♦ Carefully plan, control and monitor testing which occurs "at the latest point in the schedule when ... alternatives are least available, if at all".

♦ Involve the customer so that "he has committed himself at earlier points before final delivery."

Despite Winston Royce's advice that an early prototype should be used, his emphasis was that the creation of 'quite a lot of documentation' was a priority, thus sign-posting the way for the move towards design work being seen as an output in its own right, above and beyond the production of working software.[445]

His recommendations should be seen in context. He was giving advice for programmers creating small, but mission critical pieces of software written in difficult to read *machine code*. His expertise was in development of software for spacecraft leading up to the successful 1969 mission to put a man on the moon – no mean accomplishment. However, his specific context, that of documenting small modules life-critical software as part of a complex mechanical control system, was soon lost, and was taken up as general advice for all software developers.

Programming on mainframes in those days was a slow and tedious process. Getting users to commit very early to a theoretical specification could save programmers a lot of time, as long as the specification was correct. This need to ensure correctness of mainframe specifications was a very strong influencing factor in the development of formal techniques in governmental organizations.

As the size and complexity of software development increased in the 1970s governments latched onto waterfall approaches with eagerness. They cast aside Winston Royce's insights into the value of prototyping and the importance of continual feedback. Standards such as DOD-STD-2167, SSADM and Merise were developed in the US, UK and France respectively. As discussed earlier in the discussion about the failures of the London Stock Exchange Taurus project (on page 67), SSADM and Merise focused on activities, not outcomes – teams were rewarded for creating volumes of beautiful, interconnected diagrams, not for creating solutions for users' problems. These methods concretized the ideas of popular works by Yourdon, Sarson and Gane and Tom DeMarco which were only intended as techniques for stimulating thinking, not as standards.

In the UK the SSADM method added Ted Codd's ground breaking mathematical ideas on data structures to create what became a rigid approach to requirements development.[446] A major study by Middleton found that:[447]

> "SSADM helps to give the appearance of administrative control over the complex process of software development ... It has failed on two counts. First, it is based on a waterfall model of software development which is appropriate for only a small number of projects. Second, due to its flaws, complexity and lack of empirical base, it is not an effective way to raise skills, or direct the efforts of inexperienced software developers." [448]

By the mid-90s these methods had reached a high-tide mark of acceptance. Middleton carried out an in-depth investigation into 15 public sector organizations and several private sector companies found that the structured approach was neither suitable for large systems, nor for the development of small PC based systems. None of the projects using this approach had delivered on time or to the users' needs. The standard defense of the proponents of the method argued that this was simply due to insufficient rigor in their use, and lack of tailoring of the method to the situation. However, again and again these approaches led to technical problems emerging very late in projects causing disruption and unexpected cost. After several years of work on these projects there were often no tangible results and the users had completely lost confidence in the process. In the case of small projects, the method was either disregarded, or tailored beyond recognition, and many had started to use prototyping or incremental development.

The assumption behind SSADM was that it would establish firm requirements at an early stage. But this pre-requisite is difficult to meet because users often do not know exactly what they need or what the technology can achieve. Changes to requirements were continually needed as the users better understood the emerging solution and developers gained an understanding of the detail of the business and as external circumstances changed. The staff members who were being asked to use the method remained unconvinced until late in the process because the method was theoretical. Evidence that the method actually delivered benefits did not exist, and poor results seemed to suggest the opposite.

Using CASE Tools to Control the Problems of BDUF

Problems that the early users of these structured methods encountered were widely put down to two factors: one, the paper mountains of documentation that they generated and two, their tactical nature. The designs produced were criticized as only being specifications for individual software modules, without a grand view of the end-to-end system.

Two solutions to the problems of BDUF were proposed by James Martin. First, in association with Texas Instruments Corporation, he developed a Computer Aided Software Engineering (CASE) tool called the Information Engineering Facility' (IEF) to record the detailed documentation and ensure that cross-references were automatically updated. Second he created a strategic method called Information Engineering to encourage analysts to document a whole organization in complex diagrams and designs which would be typed into the IEF tool.

IEF fastidiously documented designs from strategy to detail, and then generated mainframe computer programs automatically from those details. Martin proclaimed that the end of the programmer was nigh!

Alongside the IEF, Martin's big-scale, top down Information Engineering method required a detailed waterfall of analysis and design activities. There were five steps to Martin's waterfall: Information Strategy Planning (ISP), then Business Area Analysis (BAA), then System Design (SD), then Construction and finally Cutover (together known as CC). The initial phases of ISP and BAA would typically take months to complete, after which more experts would be drafted in to spend months, and sometimes years on SD. Many customers gave up at this stage, not having seen any practical output from this work. Others, who persevered, found that the resultant systems that were generated at the end of the process would only work on mainframes, not on the more efficient and flexible personal computers and mini-servers that were becoming available.[449]

The high point of CASE tools was in 1990. As IT departments remained fixated on use of mainframes, end-users became increasingly frustrated and started to buy and program PCs and mini-computers of their own. This revolution in *end-user computing* started to eat into IBM's revenues, so it attempted a last ditch attempt to lock customers into the dying mainframe technology. This new method was called AD/Cycle, and was the last significant attempt to create a waterfall structured method with an associated complex and expensive toolset. AD/Cycle was abandoned after just two years in 1992 and signaled the death of the Information Engineering approach.[450]

Although he had belatedly become interested in iterative development, Martin's voluminous writings on Rapid Application Development (RAD) only contained a few pages on the topics of prototyping and timeboxing which are vital for iterative development.[451] In fact, worries about the usefulness of outputs from RAD developments were a prime motivator for the development of DSDM.[452]

In an influential paper, Beath and Orlowski noted that Information Engineering was ideological in nature, not evidence based. They accused Martin of using a patronizing tone towards users who they say were "portrayed as naïve, technically unsophisticated and parochial". They note that the amount of action expected of users in the analysis stages was actually only about 2%, far below the level of user participation and collaboration promised by the method.[453]

Many empirical studies conducted found either very little or no productivity improvement from the IE code generation process. Some research at the Ford Motor Company in the UK showed an 85% improvement in output when they switched from using SSADM paper specifications to using Information Engineering supported by the automated IEF tool. However, it is not clear whether this was just due to the dumping of the old method rather than the adoption of the new method and tools. It was certainly much less than the 300% improvement that Ford was promised. It has not been publically disclosed whether the $9m exercise plus additional on-going training, expense of skills acquisition and recurring license fees gave a positive return on investment or not.

Usage of the IE method and the IEF tool began to wane because feedback from the users involved in these projects was poor. IT departments also started to baulk at the incredibly high recurring license fees for the IEF tool together with its very restrictive licensing and dependency on costly mainframe technology.[454] Various attempts to revive interest in the Information Engineering approach were made, but most companies discovered that it was quicker and cheaper to program directly into the mainframe rather than draw all the diagrams first.[455]

Using Better Techniques to Solve the Problems of BDUF

With interest in IEF fast fading, Martin took up an interest in another form of BDUF called Object Oriented Analysis and Design (OOAD).[456] In structured analysis, documentation was produced in two volumes: a data definition and a process definition. In writing a program a developer would have to constantly cross-reference between the two. OOAD was an attempt to integrate these processes and data analyses under one documentation standard. As with the previous structured methods OOAD was initially proposed as a modest, user oriented, approach,[457] but its use was developed by proponents into grander and grander schemes until a new BDUF approach was born called the Unified Modeling Language (UML).[458]

Research shows that UML has a clear benefit where the functional correctness of small but complex systems is paramount, which confirms Bennington's original thesis. For checking the internal logic of these systems it has its uses, but most practitioners now believe that its use should be limited. There is a significant learning curve to its adoption, and no time savings in development have been found in the research into its use. Indeed, for simpler tasks the researchers on one study found that "the time needed to update UML documentation may be substantial compared with the potential benefits"[459]

Barry Boehm is a critic of the continuing use of complex modeling. He has stated that "most published object-oriented analysis and design (OOA&D) methods inadequately address the critical aspects of system performance".[460]

A three year experimental study agreed that the benefits of UML were marginal at best, but concluded with the hopeful statement that:

> "The potential benefits of UML in the mid and long term are probably larger than what was observed in this experiment." [461]

Conclusions

The rise and subsequent fall of the most extreme waterfall approaches occurred from mid-1960s through to the early 1990s. The growth of the use of PCs during the end-user computing revolution, and what is now common usage of complex systems by everyday folk over the Internet has meant that non-IT professionals have appropriated control of areas of IS development that once were the sole preserve of the IS elite. If BDUF is a busted flush, what then for waterfall project management? What we have in this second decade of the 2000s is an *inflexion point*. We have reached a situation where we cannot continue with waterfall project management for technology developments.

Questions

1. Identify problems that you have seen in the past when a top-down approach to designing a solution is taken? Has it resulted in BDUF? Was a working solution produced?

2. In your current organization, are there certain processes where requirements are agreed in detail up-front before development of a solution commences?

3. Does any project you are currently involved in have elements of a waterfall approach? If BDUF is a pre-cursor for waterfall, how could your organization reduce these risks?

4. Read Middleton's critique of SSADM and its proposed adoption as a European standard (see Endnote 462). What are the main objections to SSADM that he cites?

5. Read Beath and Orlowski's entertaining critique of Information Engineering (see Endnote 463). What features of IE do you think helped to fuel the end-user computing revolution?

Chapter 20

Traditional Procurement and Contracts

> *Agile projects rely on decisions based on mutual trust. They are therefore well suited to in-house projects. But the faith they ask customers to have in service providers makes them ill-suited for external developments.* [464]

Alistair Maughan
Partner, Morrison Foerster

Governments have successfully set up and managed their own agile projects. In Part I we saw how the State of Queensland, Australia implemented housing application and referral processes using their own employees. I related how the FBI turned around the failing Sentinel project by taking the project back under their own control, and employing specialist contractors directly where needed. The GDS in London built the beta.gov technology using a similar approach.

However, when the technology used is of a very advanced nature or where the project is a one-off that needs a very large number of development staff, and quickly, then procurement of a solution under supplier management would be an attractive option – if it can be made to work.

This chapter looks at traditional procurement and contracts, and examines the barrier to the agile approach that they present. This barrier has three major facets:

♦ Lack of incentives to 'play the game' for mutual long-term benefit past the end of the immediate contract

♦ Legislation, especially in the European Union, that forces 'open competition' based on BDUF requirement specifications

♦ Lack of clarity over what an adequate 'agile contract' looks like.

Solving these three problems will be an area of major research in the field of agile project management over the next decade as governments struggle to find the optimal approach for engaging with third-party suppliers for complex technology developments.

Game Playing in Contractual Relationships

In 2008, the Federal Communications Commission (FCC) auctioned off 1,099 licenses to telecommunications organizations for use of the 700MHz radio bandwidth across the USA. The FCC predicted vast economic benefits from a smooth take-up of new Fourth Generation (4G) services. It was a complex auction. The 4G radio bandwidth had become available for other uses after the transition from analogue to digital television. This was a much sought after range of radio frequencies. It has much better properties than Third Generation (3G) cellular mobile phone frequencies because its radio waves can penetrate buildings and walls easily and cover larger geographic areas. The value at stake in the 2008 auction was huge. Preparations for the auction were complex, and the final bidding process took place over a two-month period during which bidders could see the bids of others, and raise their bids accordingly. In the event, the auction successfully raised over \$18.9bn.[465]

This was in stark contrast to the failure of one of the first radio frequency auctions, which was held in New Zealand in 1990. The government there was embarrassed when the sale went badly wrong. In one case a license was sold for only NZ\$5,000 when the winning company had been willing to bid up to NZ$7m. The auction only raised NZ$36m overall, rather than the NZ$250m that the government had expected. The problem was that the bidders had been required to submit the entirety of their bids simultaneously. Bidders did not know how many lots they would actually end up having to pay for, and so they made conservative bids, and only on selected lots. The lack of competition for one license allowed the successful bidder to buy it for only six dollars.[466]

Getting to a fair price

In economics, there is a theory that in a perfect market with perfect competition, then supply and demand will balance and converge on the *market price*. This is called the '*Law of One Price*'.

If, then, a government buyer commoditizes the supply of services as much as possible, and involves as many bidders in an open procurement as possible, will the Law of One Price be assured? Unfortunately, not often.

Bulow, Levin, and Milgrom have described how they used advanced game theory to help one company to underbid the incumbent operators of advanced wireless licenses by an average of 33.8%. As a result, SpectrumCo became the second largest license holder overnight. It underpaid for its licenses by an astonishing $1.1bn.[467]

Over-stressful tendering can create two major problems for suppliers. First, suppliers are wary of exposure to overbidding. Problems occur because bidders would like to supply complementary services but do not want to bid high on one unless they know whether they have won another related service. Resource constraints also constrain suppliers from bidding on too many lots, and often they end up under spending. Expensive internal resources set up and ready to start work can be left unutilized if bids on several lots fall through.

What can make a procurement agile?

You can make sure that the outcome of a procurement is agile by applying the same 12 principles to the workings of the relationship with the supplier as you would to those with the project stakeholders. Especially important is point four in the Agile Manifesto:

"We value customer collaboration over contract negotiation." [468]

With the waterfall approach, procurements often end up with the buyer, the supplier, or both regretting having entered into a contract in the first place. Agile procurements aim to find the sweet spot where both sides win.

Figure 14 shows the outcomes in four quadrants of combinations of *win* and *fail* for the two sides in procurement. The worst situations are typified by procurements where the process itself does not result in a contract. The project is then stalled without a supplier, with no sight of any of the expected benefits happening any time soon. The suppliers who bid have wasted their time and resources supplying proposals that are not accepted by the client. Even worse, procurement may result in a bad contract being drawn up that results in a painful project – painful for the buyer because the outputs are often not what were required, or that the outputs are so expensive that they are greater than the resultant benefits. In the worst case, expensive litigation can ensue.

A case in point is the UK Firecontrol project previously cited. The main contract to supply the Firecontrol system started late and took two years longer than expected to complete. The relationships in the project between the IT supplier, EADS, and the government were painful to say the least. The Government and EADS failed to provide timely information to each other. A lack of interim milestones undermined the Department's ability to hold EADS to account for delivery and conversely the delays to delivery led to cash flow difficulties for EADS which created further strains in an already tense relationship. Both sides were locked into the deadly embrace of a non-agile contract. The Government took legal advice and found out that it was unable to terminate its contract with EADS without incurring substantial compensation payments provided for under the contract. And EADS in turn was unable to deliver against a final key milestone for mid-2011. In the end, the contract was terminated and the government received a settlement of £22.5 million from EADS – little cheer considering that £469m was eventually written off.[469]

The disadvantages to the buyer of being in the *fail/win* quadrant are clear. This is where an un-economic price is agreed, changes (during build and maintenance) are difficult to implement and expensive when they are. It may seem that the supplier should be happy with this result, but there is often a sting in the tail for the supplier.

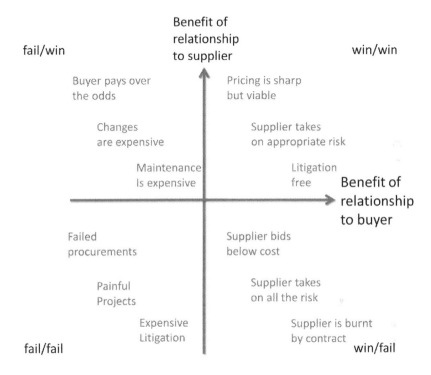

Figure 14: Getting to a *win/win* situation in agile procurements

The next time that there is a procurement, the buyer is wiser, or at least thinks so. Tables are then turned – a *win/fail* may occur where a supplier is browbeaten into submitting a bid at a suicidal level. The supplier may take on risks that it cannot control and the may end up losing substantial sums of money. These situations can seesaw back and forth from procurement to procurement, with the buyer or the supplier in turn being burnt on each subsequent contract.

An agile procurement will result in a much higher probability of a *win/win* outcome. The pricing of the accepted proposal should be realistic and allow the project to be run in a co-operative manner. Each side can concentrate on the risks that they can reasonably be expected to control, and the supplier has the flow of money needed to fund the work. Both sides can demonstrate to their own stakeholders the benefits of entering into the deal.

In the next section I will return to the lessons that can be learned from game theory so that you can achieve these *win/win* outcomes. There are two levels at which game theory helps. First, I will consider the game playing within the confines of the procurement, and second I will consider the effects of future (and prior) procurements on the procurement in hand.

Why Public Procurement in the EU is not Agile

with Susan Atkinson

The European Union (EU) was originally founded as a Common Market to encourage trading and economic activity between the member states by reducing and eliminating trade tariffs. By the mid-1980s considerable progress towards achieving these aims in procurement had been made in the private sector, but the public sector was lagging far behind. The results of a survey conducted in 1985 in five member states (Belgium, France, Germany, Italy and the UK) showed that whilst the import penetration rates for the economies as a whole was 22%, the comparable figure for the public sector was just 2%. [470]

The public procurement policy and practice of the member states was identified as a significant obstacle to the free movement of goods and services in the EU. Public sector bodies tended to favor national suppliers at the expense of foreign suppliers, thereby sheltering markets from competition and distorting trade patterns. This finding led to the body of EU public procurement law which today governs the procurement by all EU public sector bodies of goods, works and services. There are three sources of EU public procurement law: procedure, principles and case law.

The EU public procurement directives set out the legal framework for public procurement. Member states are mandated to implement these directives into their national law. Broadly speaking, the public procurement directives set out four different award procedures: open, restricted, negotiated and competitive dialogue. Any public sector body must follow one of these procedures when procuring goods, services or works, subject to certain limited exceptions. Each of the procedures is based on the following key stages: advertisement, pre-qualification (except for the open procedure), invitation to tender/dialogue/negotiation, dialogue or negotiation (competitive dialogue and negotiated procedures only), submission of bids, evaluation, award decision, standstill, and finally completion of contract.

In addition, a number of cases decided upon by the Court of Justice of the EU (the CJEU) in the 1990s retrofitted various procurement principles that it ruled were implicit in the public procurement directives current at that time.

These include the principles of equal treatment, non-discrimination, mutual recognition of standards, transparency, and proportionality. Public sector bodies must follow these principles regardless of whether the EU procurement directives apply. The most recent versions of the procurement directives each now emphasize that "contracting entities shall treat economic operators equally and non-discriminatorily and shall act in a transparent way."[471]

Then there is the growing body of case law. The CJEU takes into account EU Treaty principles to a significant degree when considering novel cases. In the last five years, the CJEU decisions have provided the most restrictive and legalistic source of EU procurement law.

There is now quite a minefield of legislation, regulation, principles and case law that any public sector body must navigate when embarking upon a procurement. It is certainly a challenge to be agile within this kind of environment.

First, the procurement process takes an inordinate amount of time. When the Institute for Government compiled the report "System Error – Fixing the flaws in Government IT", it found that IT procurements take an average of 77 weeks, and so "most large projects are 'late' before they have even started".[472] The costs and resources involved in any public sector body embarking on such a procedure, not to mention the costs and resources incurred by potential bidders (who may walk away empty-handed), means that these procedures in themselves create a barrier to any new project. Broadly speaking, services contracts for any project worth more than €125,000 must be awarded following a public procurement. At the lower end of the project size, the cost of the public sector body conducting the procedure, or a bidder taking part in the procedure, represents a significant part of the overall cost of the project.

Secondly, there is the problem with the procedure itself. For complex service contracts, such as IT change initiatives involving software development, the competitive dialogue procedure is generally regarded as the most appropriate procedure. However, under the competitive dialogue procedure the bidders cannot submit their best and final offer until the dialogue stage has been completed. The legal test for closing dialogue is when the public sector body can "identify one or more solutions ... capable of meeting its needs".[473] In practice, this means that the contract should be ready to be signed and that supplier should be ready to start implementing the high level design the day after contract signature. This has been interpreted as meaning that every aspect of the proposed solution should be specified in sufficient detail for the supplier to be able to deliver it and – in many cases – to give a fixed price for it.

Furthermore, in a recent case it was held that if a public sector body subsequently makes any material modification to the selected solution, this may amount to the creation of a new contract which needs to be re-tendered. The decision in this case has served to increase the pressure on public sector bodies to specify in minute detail every aspect of the solution before completing the dialogue stage.[474]

Agile Procurement

An influential paper from Emergn puts the suppliers' point of view as a response to the UK Government IT Strategy that stresses agility and involvement of Small/Medium Enterprises (SMEs). It found that many procurement staff regard feedback as "bad in that it creates opportunities for change leading to variation in the work requested from the supplier." [475] The paper proposes that procurement should be involved from the very beginning of a relationship. Procurement experts must not treat technology development as a commodity service. Large project procurements often fail because of inflexible use of standard forms and contracts. This, Emergn argues, slows the agility of both suppliers and customers. They propose that cultural fit should take precedence over date and price, and that commitment to specifics should wait until the project has progressed so that both customer and supplier can commit together once enough has been researched. [476] Experts in buying and negotiation are too distant from the technology experts they argue, and those experts are conversely so intimate with the requirements that they overlook the importance of the "commercial realities of the contract". When the contract is signed, relationships between procurement, technology staff and supplier must be maintained, they say, to drive collaborative program delivery. [477]

The solution is to encourage more *hybrid managers* rather than specialist roles, such as "Procurement Manager" or "Vendor Manager". Hybrid managers will need a combination of procurement and technical skills to create an "end-to-end value chain". They conclude:

> "If an organization is looking to apply increased agility in its IT development programs, the time has come for managerial skills to be integrated in the creation of a new breed of procurement executive encompassing both sourcing and supplier management expertise." [478]

The evolutionary acquisition strategy and associated DOD-5000 lifecycle pursued over the last decade has only a weak associated procurement process. The Australian Department of Defence (AU DOD) adopted these standards for its own acquisitions, but then found that the competitive tendering and contracting process simply replicated and reinforced waterfall approaches. It was a 12-step process from contract planning through to post-project performance management. Each step could only commence when the previous step was completed. Budgets for each project were estimated at an early stage when only the broad scope was determined, being thereafter very inflexible to the discovery of the detail of the requirements.[479] Conflict often occurred between the government and the suppliers as contract managers moved in and out of roles. New contract managers often had little or no knowledge of the requirements of the project, and often worked for a different unit of the organization than the unit that managed the initial contract award.[480]

Diane Jamieson has analyzed the disconnect between procurement and the Agile process, and found that:

> "Key (Agile) ideas are not consistently embraced by procurers, viz: Anticipate and manage for change (principle 2); Continually review business needs (principle 10); Have reasonable work expectations of both customer and supplier personnel (principles 5, 8); Embrace interim deliveries (principles 1, 3, 7) Have suitable communications channels (principles 4, 6); and Maintain positive relationships with suppliers (principles 2, 4, 5, 6, 12). The next challenge is to link these principles to an appropriate procurement methodology."[481]

Jamieson proposes an agile procurement process where budgets are estimated incrementally as scope is incrementally explored. This should result in smaller variances from budgets, she argues, and improved customer supplier relationships. Each supplier would guarantee the delivery dates of iterations, and given a fixed number of people and reasonable certainty of overhead costs. A price would be set at the beginning of each iteration when the backlog for that iteration was agreed. Calibration of the team's performance in terms of *velocity* of output would take place, and the total number of iterations required would be estimable. This would give flexibility to descope any items that would not produce a net benefit for the agreed estimates.[482]

As a success story to highlight the advantages of agile procurements, Jamieson cites the on-going enhancement of the Joint Command Support System (JCSS) by ADI, an Australian software supplier. Elements of adaptive budgeting and iterative development (although ADI makes no claim to use a specific agile method) are used to keep budgets on track. The JCSS project has been delivered in seven phases at a total cost of $58 million.[483]

The ADI team maintains a *product backlog* of required enhancements. At the start of each year this is matched to a fixed budget allocated by the Australian DOD.[484] Each year, the AU DOD makes two deployments, each resulting from a series of short iterations, each typically less than a month long. The graphs of actual spend versus budget show low levels of variance against budget. Many of the deployments are made at a lower cost than budgeted, and the average annual cost has stayed comfortably within allocated budgets.[485]

An extension of this idea of incremental budgeting is the concept of *Agile Commitment Management*. Mauricio Concha defines a more sophisticated framework to complement an agile approach with the accounting concept of *commitment management*. The aim is to provide cost control and risk visibility, and a clear basis for contract collaboration between customer and supplier.[486] This is an extension to the principle of *Commitment Accounting*, where any rolling contract to purchase goods or services must be accounted for on the basis that a firm order is implied for at least as long as the contract termination notice period. Commitment Management is an approach to planning and controlling the buyer's commitment to purchase future services based on a rolling framework agreements. It uses the commitment between the buyer and the supplier to the product backlog as the basis for identifying commitments at the start of every iteration. A major benefit, Concha says, is in:[487]

> "Achieving continuous risk visibility during the project by … measuring risk in terms of qualitative metrics, as well as potential losses incurred if a business value goal is not met."

These risks are:

♦ Current Risk: as perceived at the moment of the measure. Because risks are future events that may, or may not occur. Since the scale of the impact cannot be fully known until it occurs, if it occurs at all, this is a subjective assessment using perceived probability of occurrence and perceived likely impact

♦ Risk Mitigated: The cost of putting in place countermeasures to the risks of failure

◆ Post Project Assessment of Risk Management: A comparison of the initial business risks, mitigation costs, costs of putting into action contingency plans, and the cost of risk that did occur.[488]

An Argument Against the Role of Agile in Government

Alistair Maughan has queried whether agile contracts will work for government. His argument is based on four major propositions:

◆ **Certainty of price seems to require a BDUF.** A clear specification of outputs is required up-front, he says, to know how much a specified system will cost to build before committing funds. Agile projects provide an alternative model that fixes a budget, but does not fix the specification. Maughan argues that government bodies will not accept what seem like open-ended arrangements.

◆ **Agile projects do not appear to be open or transparent.** Procurement requires a comparison of different bidders on a like-for-like basis. Traditional procurements compare BDUF specifications rather than suppliers (as noted earlier in this section). In deciding on best value for money, it uses this input as a proxy for real-world comparison of likely outcomes. Maughan argues that because agile does not give a specification of outputs up-front it cannot give a definitive up-front price.

◆ **The agile approach seems to offer insufficient means of remedy if things go wrong:**

"This is a particularly sensitive issue for government, where departments suffer public opprobrium if their project isn't a resounding success. The press, the National Audit Office, and the Public Accounts committee (PAC) will give government a kicking if they cannot make suppliers pay for the damage they caused. Agile makes it hard to apportion blame because the customer is intimately involved in the work. Since agile contracts lack clear contractual delivery obligations or remedies, how do you enforce it properly? How do you recover loss or damage if there's a problem?" [489]

♦ **Agile appears to be a poor fit to government**: Maughan argues that agile decision-making cannot work in centralized organizations such as governments:

"You can have an IT project with a watertight contract, and detailed deliverables and appropriate remedies. Or you can have an agile project. You can't have both." [490]

The Counter-Argument

Susan Atkinson responds to Alistair Maughan's argument above point by point as follows:[491]

♦ **Certainty of price does not require a BDUF.** Certainty of price for a fixed specification is the wrong area of focus, she points out.

"BDUF is one of the most damaging aspects of the traditional contract on software development projects. There is an assumption that if a supplier meets a BDUF specification, then the customer will achieve the desired business value from the resulting solution. However, there is often little connection between delivering against a BDUF specification, and delivering the desired business value to the customer. One of the biggest risks of software development is that the supplier builds the 'wrong product'."

♦ **Agile projects can be open and transparent.** Transparent and non-discriminatory criteria can be used to initiate supply of agile development services, Atkinson argues. Because public sector bodies are not achieving certainty of pricing at present, she says, they should be looking at new ways of assessing bids. Software development involves the transformation of ideas into a product. Public sector bodies should instead be looking for the supplier that is most able to understand their needs and to create a solution that delivers the most value to the public sector body by addressing those needs.

♦ **The agile approach can offer means of remedy if things go wrong:** The dynamics in an agile project are quite different from those in a traditional project. This means that the remedies may be different, but no less rigorous. The reason why so many contractual remedies are required in a traditional contract is that the customer's exposure in terms of upfront investment is enormous. She continues:

"The customer may have invested months and possibly years of resources before the supplier delivers anything of any tangible value. Clearly, if the product is suboptimal for any reason the customer needs some form of redress to recover this wasted investment. However, in an agile project the supplier delivers something of tangible value at the end of each iteration. The exposure of customer is therefore much smaller, and the need for contractual recourse is accordingly reduced."

♦ **Government can make the agile approach work:** Whilst trust is one of the core values of the agile approach, Atkinson says that this does not imply a naïve approach should be taken to commercial matters. One of the real benefits of the agile approach is that it provides a transparent development process where the customer has much greater visibility of whether the project is on track or not. Atkinson concludes:

"Maughan refers to centralized decision-making in government. However, governments are now realizing that the world is too interconnected, complex and dynamic for 'command and control' of services, and are moving away from centralized approaches."

UKBA Immigration Case Work Project

The need for flexible contracting arrangements is of paramount importance in agile project management. One model that can provide this is that of *time and materials* framework contracts. These provide a mechanism for employing specialist contractors by the hour. However, government must take care to monitor the contractors.

An example of a failure to do so occurred at the UK Borders Authority (UKBA), which has an annual spend of over £2bn. In 2009 it began to drastically reduce its workforce from 22,580 to 20,469 that year, with a further reduction of 3,500 planned for 2015.

The bulk of future expected savings, and improvements in service delivery, depended largely on a BPR exercise to transform casework procedures, which cost £1bn a year, and also on the successful delivery of the £385 million Immigration Case Work (ICW) project initiated in 2009. Both these measures were expected to allow consolidation of the 4m applications that are received every year for temporary migration, permanent migration, and asylum, to be handled at 'centers of excellence' in the UK and to reduce the number of overseas visa processing centers from 130 to 25. [492]

The UKBA planned a rollout in 14 separate deployments, and set up a contract through a framework agreement that allowed for a *time and materials* approach to the ICW project. It had some initial successes with easy to implement *lipstick on a pig* functions such as a new search function and a module to guide caseworkers through the regulations (see the FBI Sentinel project case in Part I for a similar situation in the first phase of a long project).

But by 2012, both the ICW and the parallel BPR exercise were a combined £28m over budget and the optimistic expectation of annual savings have been revised down, from £139m to £106m.[493]

Unfortunately, the project board did not monitor the situation carefully enough. They were over optimistic in assessing the project status that was perceived as *green* status in 2011, and only updated to a realistic assessment of the status as *red* just ahead of the arrival of NAO auditors in 2011. A new project executive was appointed who admitted that the release schedule was unrealistic and that the project was not going to deliver until 2016.[494] The project board had not:

◆ Challenged the IT contractors about their use of resources

- Ensured that implementation was being planned with front-line staff, who were confused about the timing of releases

- Carried out any in-depth discussion of spending in their board meetings

- Coordinated the work of different development teams that were preparing different releases of software in parallel. [495]

This case demonstrates the need for care when managing projects with external contractors. Contracting for incremental development using a *time and materials* approach can work. With care, the *burn rate* of the team can be controlled – in this case spend was only 12% higher than expected. However, there are responsibilities that come with direct control of a project, and top management need to have robust *tight* management in place to carry out those responsibilities.

Agile Contracts

with Susan Atkinson

According to the "State of Agile Survey 2011", the ability to change organizational culture is now the single largest barrier to the adoption of the agile approach, with over half the respondents citing this as their biggest problem.[496] Legal, management, and procurement functions have yet to adapt practices and values that take account of the challenges of today's environment, and have barely changed in the last thirty years. Much of the thinking underlying the traditional contract is rooted in the Industrial Revolution and its production line practices. Often, even if an organization is running an IT project internally, it will apply the same management practices as if it had outsourced it to a third party supplier. Organizational policies often create contractual relationships between departments inside a single organization that can produce the same effect as the traditional contract. Whilst there has been much discussion of the need to change the traditional contract model, these dialogues have been led principally by the agile community. [497] Unfortunately, the proposed solutions do not get to the crux of the matter. The understanding of the legal dynamics of contracts by agilists is limited, and the legal profession appears to be largely oblivious to the shortcomings in the traditional contract model. It has been surprisingly quiet in supplying alternatives reflecting the agile approach.

Various organizations have now put forward possible contract models. However, these do not fully address the problem. The DSDM was one of the first organizations to put forward a contract model. Although an interesting model, it is now more than ten years old, and does not reflect the current version of DSDM, and is not a comprehensive contract. Its 12 clauses do not address the difficult issues of measuring the progress of the supplier, ensuring that the customer is getting value for its money, and defining supplier warranties.[498]

Other attempts include the Norwegian Computer Society PS2000 contract model, and the Danish Ministry of Science, Technology and Innovation contract for short-term agile IT projects. However, both of these contract models are complex and do not offer the flexibility and dynamism required in agile projects.

Contracts are often obsessed with complexity of detail. Yet there is another aspect to complexity, largely over-looked by contracts to date, and that is dynamic complexity. Dynamic complexity exists where cause and effect are subtle, and where the effects over time of interventions are not obvious. We cannot address dynamic complexity with complex contract models. A different approach is required. A solution to the contract model requires a much greater understanding of complexity theory, chaos theory, and systems thinking. We must give greater focus to the target outcomes that an organization is trying to achieve when it embarks on an IT project. And the solution may be simpler than we think.

Conclusions

The use of waterfall procurement exacerbates the risks already inherent in waterfall approaches to managing a project. Waterfall procurement encourages waterfall project behaviors, which, conversely encourage and amplify waterfall tendencies in procurement approaches.

Fixed price contracts all too often become a game of change control management. This happens when there is a lack of trust between the Government and the supplier. If there is no *meta-game* advantage to the supplier for keeping in the customer's good books in anticipation of the next piece of work that is coming along, then the relationship can quickly deteriorate into a sophisticated version of the *prisoners' dilemma*. Both sides may take defensive, but ultimately self-destructive, standpoints.

Agile procurements and contract wordings can help move relationships in line with the Agile Manifesto. Collaboration should be favored over negotiation, and flexibility favored over pre-determined delivery. The concepts of Agile Commitment Management, Agile Procurement and Agile Contracts, promise to embed flexibility into government-supplier relationships and reduce the risks of project failure. Further research is needed to define contract models that can support these processes.

Questions

Refer to Arboblast, Vodde, and Larman's paper (see Endnote <u>499</u>, page 21). Do you agree with the following statements?

1. "The issue of change is largely inherently addressed within the overall philosophy of an agile approach because of a re-prioritizable backlog and adaptive iterative planning; no special (traditional) change-management process, board, or request mechanism is needed."

2. "The ideal termination model in an agile contract is to allow the customer to stop, without penalty, at the end of any iteration".

Chapter 21

Can we legislate for agile? The DOD experience

> *We want to work agile into our acquisition and systems engineering lifestyle.* [500]

Richard Spires
CIO, Department of Homeland Security

A major inhibitor to adoption of the agile approach in governments around the world is the regulations and 'best practice' guidance that have built up over the years. These have been centrally produced in order to improve technical development in diverse government bodies, but often they have just ended up stifling effectiveness.

This chapter looks at the regulations that apply to project management in the US Department of Defense (DOD), and how they either encourage or discourage agile adoption. It is possible for Government organizations to be agile despite some difficult and prescriptive regulations, but it is an up-hill struggle.

I start the story in 1988 with the impact of the publication of the DOS-STD-2167 standard which was widely, but mistakenly, interpreted as mandating a waterfall approach. The subsequent 2167A standard tried to clarify and stress the need for incremental delivery, but waterfall projects continued unabated even though efforts were made to sweep up all the regulations under an umbrella standard (Mil-Std-498).

Congress then got involved, and the Clinger-Cohn Act was passed in 1996 which begat the DOD-5000 series of regulations which tried to reinforce the need for evolutionary development. Unfortunately an inflexible approach to project management continued, so the National Defense Act of 2012 required the DOD to review its regulations yet again, and the result was the release of interim guidance called the "IT Box" approach, which attempts to reinforce the intent of the DOD-5000 series of guidance.

This sorry history of attempts to inculcate an agile military development approach shows that you cannot legislate for a change in attitudes. A leadership approach is needed to implement agile project management in the DOD and its suppliers, not further regulation.

Background

The US Department of Defense (DOD) is the USA's largest employer. It processes a huge amount of information. As of 2010, it had more than 170,000 people working in management and IT. It processed business data on 7.3m people either on active duty, in the National Guard, working in civilian posts or receiving benefits.[501]

Government Procurement Processes prefer BDUF

The US military standard DOD-STD-2167 was mentioned briefly in the above discussion on waterfall standards.[502] McDonald has charted the history of the rise and fall of this and other attempts to impose waterfall, top-down methods. He found that:

> "Although military procurers could not directly impose such regulations on their suppliers, they could use contractual software development standards as a way to reach into private companies and perform the same disciplining function indirectly. Many in the military certainly believed that programmers were badly in need of such discipline." [503]

The Joint Logistics Commanders (JLC) developed the DOD-STD-2167 standard as a default approach to software design for weapons systems – but flexibility was always intended, even if it was rarely achieved. The standard sets out clearly that:

> "Software development is usually an iterative process, in which an iteration of the software development cycle occurs one or more times during each of the system life cycle phases." [504]

In addition, the standard provided an appendix specifically requiring:

> "Tailoring of activities, products, and reviews required during each software development phase." [505]

The standard was approved in 1985, but sub-contractors still railed against the imposition of processes on their internal development processes. Many criticisms were leveled at the standard – especially a general misunderstanding that it forced a top-down approach and that it contained archaic requirements that were a decade out of date.

Within a year, in 1986, a replacement standard DOD-STD-2167A was drafted and, after discussion, was authorized in 1988. This revision removed all mention of the top-down approach that the earlier standard had appeared to mandate. The foreword made clear this new approach:[506]

> "This standard is not intended to specify or discourage the use of any particular software development method. The contractor should select software development methods (for example rapid prototyping) that best support the achievement of contract requirements." [507]

However, a recent report by the National Research Council found that:

> "The DOD is hampered by a culture and acquisition-related practices that favor large programs, high-level oversight, and a very deliberate, serial approach to development and testing. Programs that are expected to deliver nearly perfect solutions and that take years to develop are the norm in the DOD. ... Moreover, the DOD's process-bound, high-level oversight seems to make demands that cause developers to focus more on process than on product, and end-user participation often is too little and too late. ... The key to resolving the chronic

problems with the DOD acquisition of IT systems is for the DOD to adopt a fundamentally different process—one based on the lessons learned in the employment of agile management techniques in the commercial sector." [508]

The impact of the Clinger-Cohen Act

The Clinger-Cohen Act (CCA) formed part of the Information Technology Management Reform Act which itself was part of the 1996 National Defense Authorization Act. The CCA transferred ultimate responsibility for IT developments to the OMB and required every federal agency to develop and maintain an Information Technology Architecture.

Because of the CCA, the DOD-5000 series of instructions were issued. These are a detailed set of instructions to government defense bodies dealing with project management of systems development. Some of these instructions are intended to facilitate incremental development, and therefore can be seen as 'agile friendly'. Some of them seem to require a waterfall approach to projects, and therefore could inhibit agile adoption.

An example of an 'agile friendly' requirement is for systems to be built using a Modular Open Systems Approach (MOSA). This does not refer to what are, confusingly, commonly known as *open systems*. MOSA refers to systems that have clearly understood connections to other modules. The objective is to be able to build systems out of basic building blocks. They should have easy to understand interfaces that programmers can easily take apart and reuse in different configurations – like Lego® bricks. The MOSA approach is expected to help incremental implementation, and make upgrades easier once a system is implemented.[509]

The massive Defense Acquisition Guide (DAG) is a 900+ page long document that pulls all of the DOD-5000 series and supplementary guidance together in one place. It is reissued on a monthly basis as various items are revised. It defines two basic approaches to projects: *evolutionary acquisition strategies* and *single step strategies*. An *Acquisition Strategy* is required to justify which approach is planned for each project. The DAG states that the "DOD preference is evolutionary acquisition". This new evolutionary lifecycle was designed to specifically meet the requirements of the CCA which requires that:[510]

- Each acquisition supports core, priority functions

- Outcome-based performance measures are linked to strategic goals

- Processes are redesigned to reduce costs, improve effectiveness and maximize the use of Commercial Off the Shelf (COTS) solutions

- The right government department or private company carries out each function

- An Analysis Of Alternatives (AOA), Return on Investment (ROI) and a whole Life-Cycle Cost Estimate (LCCE) is made

- Measures and accountability for the progress of each program are established

- Each acquisition is consistent with an overall architecture called the Global Information Grid

- Each program has a compliant information assurance strategy

- All important systems must be registered with the DOD Chief Information Officer (CIO).

Problems with the DOD Evolutionary Process

However, some of DOD-5000 is not so 'agile friendly'. The need to drive delivery in regular increments driven by immovable deadlines is not reinforced by the DAG. It does not clearly articulate the *timebox* concept that scope should be cut as required to meet timescales. Projects are still required to produce a great deal of pre-planning documentation before development work can be authorized to proceed, even on incremental projects:

"(Even in) an evolutionary (project), the Acquisition Strategy should fully describe the initial increment of capability (i.e., the initial deployment capability), and how it will be funded, developed, tested, produced, and supported. The Acquisition Strategy should preview similar planning for subsequent increments, and identify the approach to integrate and/or retrofit earlier increments with later increment improvements." [511]

In 2009, the Defense Science Board (DSB) reported to Congress with an evaluation of the DOD's Information Technology (IT) developments. The report proposed a new acquisition process for IT and especially stressed the importance of continuous user participation and iterative development of technology.[512] In parallel, the Congress Panel on Defense Acquisition Reform came to similar conclusions:

"In the context of the acquisition of IT, the Panel finds that the existing requirements process is ill-suited for the rapidly evolving nature of the IT marketplace which requires an iterative dialogue on requirements. The current process is too inflexible and prone to the kinds of over-specification that has long been an issue." [513]

More attempts to control behavior by legislation ensued. Additional sections were added to the National Defense Authorization Act for fiscal year 2010 onwards. The requirements pulled towards and away from the agile approach. Section 804 required the Secretary of Defense to complete a review of the process for identification and acquisition by "an iterative approach to urgent operational needs". [514] However, Section 805 still required extensive and specific processes for planning and oversight processes for the acquisition of major automated information systems. The Secretary of State was required to ensure that EVA is used to track all IT projects. Although some have attempted to use EVA on agile projects the tracking of spend against detailed, pre-planned activities is seen as many as a barrier to agile working (see page 190).[515]

Governing Requirements using the IT Box

The Joint Oversight Requirements Council (JORC), chaired by the Chairman of the Joint Chiefs of Staff, has provided a useful impetus for moving towards more incremental development. [516] JORC gives overall priorities to new acquisitions across all military services, and in 2010, it released some guidance for business systems development projects to supplement DOD-5000 which included a technique called the *IT Box*. This defines how performance and cost ranges should be agreed and how authority for change approval should be delegated. The idea is to define clear boundaries and improve delegation to development projects. [517]

The IT Box is so called because it delineates four boundaries that control, inform, constrain, and direct a project. An Information Systems Initial Capabilities Document (IS ICD) is then produced to kick off the project with just enough design (EDUF), Rather Than Too Much. The IT Box Is Illustrated in Figure 15. It defines the governance of change control for the essential requirements for new software. It delegates detailed decisions to those responsible for development, while keeping control over strategic decisions.

The boundaries are flexible to the extent that the team responsible for development may negotiate changes as required, but remain strong enough to ensure consistency and control of projects from a strategic point of view. The four walls around the box of requirements are: [518]

♦ Governance of requirements: a statement as to how the contents and timing of each release will be agreed, tracked, and controlled – especially how the users and the team will collaborate. Of importance here is a statement as to how stakeholders from a multi-organization environment will interact and who will act as the final arbiter and decision-maker. Scrum defines a similar role of the *product owner*. DSDM defines the role of a *business sponsor* who would appoint a *business visionary* for day-to-day collaboration with the team.

♦ Operational Environment: This defines the constraints that exist for the hardware on which the computer system must run.

Emphasis is placed here on determining the *total cost of ownership* (TCO) over the whole life of the use of the system, which might be for decades. This requires the breaking out of costs into annual estimates, including a budget for the final decommissioning of the solution when it is either no longer required, or has to be replaced. Worked into these costs must be the costs and timing of the *refresh cycle* to upgrade the systems as the hardware and operating software are upgraded and replaced over time.

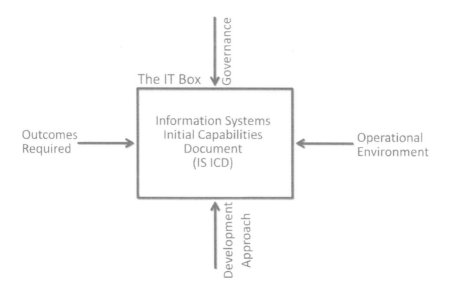

Figure 15: The DOD IT Box: a Framework for Capturing Essential IT Requirements

- ◆ Development Approach: This defines how the systems will be acquired and developed – not only must the cost of any contract with suppliers be included, but also a budget for the DOD to run the procurement and manage with suppliers.

- ◆ Outcomes Required: these define the effectiveness of the capabilities of the required system – in other words not just what will be delivered, but whether it has a positive operational impact. These outcomes are broad and shallow in definition. Broad, because the entire scope of the program must be included, not just the first phase. Shallow, because it is the minimum outcomes that must be met are focused on. This avoids the problems of either over-specifying an expensive solution, or committing to assumptions on what the technology can achieve. It is important to balance the need to avoid trying to achieve impossible outcomes with the need to explore potential opportunities to harness unrecognized technological possibilities that will emerge as development progresses.

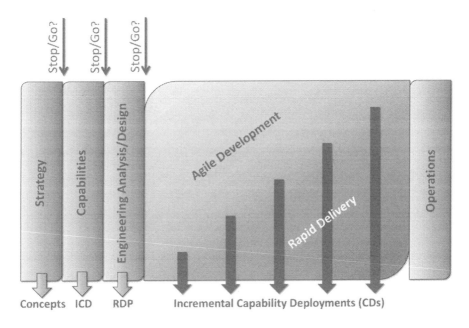

Figure 16: DOD Requirements/Acquisition Process Requirements process[519]

Careful planning is required for each Capability Drop (CD) (see Figure 16). Software is broken into small, independent modules, and extensive use is made of re-useable *widgets,* which are modules that perform simple, common operations across many applications. The project board, not the team, agrees the timing and objectives for each CD. This means that the sponsor not the team has control over the sequencing of CDs and prioritization of development as a whole. The team, however, has freedom to decide how to meet those objectives. They do not need to seek top management permission to detailed changes to over-complex requirements specifications and detailed project plans.

One criticism of the use of the IT Box is that it could lead to the treatment of software development as a separate activity ring-fenced from hardware development and implementation planning by governance processes that could remain too inflexible. Projects using an agile approach within the IT Box concept must be careful to adopt an integrated team approach, and not have separate software and hardware test teams, for example.[520]

It is a hybrid model somewhere between waterfall and agile. The initial work is segmented into three planning phases (strategy, definition of capabilities, and engineering analysis/design). Before iterative development can get underway these three *gates* must be hurdled. Once these gates are passed, the possibility of change of direction is reduced. There is the need for a sign-off by the relevant MDA of an Information Systems Initial Capabilities Document (ICD), and then the production and agreement of further planning documents Requirements Definition Packages (RDPs) before development work can get under way. The development is further decomposed into Capability Drop (CD) documents that define each phase of delivery.

A more detailed look at the proposed iterative development required is shown in Figure 17. Each CD must consist of a lengthy prototyping phase with a discrete *stop/go decision* by the MDA before build can commence. These two phases may stretch up to 2 years in length before any deployment is achieved.

Phasing of delivery into pre-planned CD documents and the separation of prototyping from build and implementation may constitute a type of iterative development. However, is it really driven by emerging understanding of the solution? Or is it the substitution of a grand waterfall with a series of smaller (but not so small) document driven waterfalls? An improvement on the single step waterfall approach, but not in line with the 12 Agile Manifesto Principles since the need to "seek out requirements, even late in development" is not encouraged. The DOD still mandates that requirements for each CD must be fully developed before each step starts. The delivery timescales are in 12 to 18 month phases, which does not equate to the principle of delivery frequently, in weeks or months rather than years. Finally, the concept of a *sustainable pace of development* is not promoted.

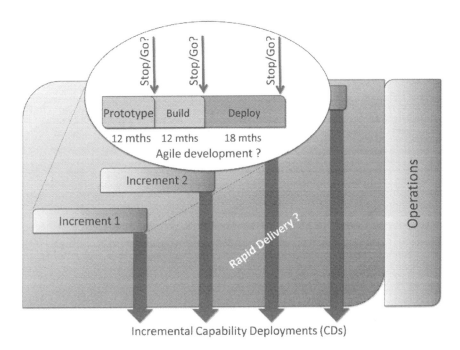

Figure 17: A criticism of the DOD BCL model is that it treats each phase of development as a mini-waterfall project

The agile approach encourages a steady and efficient output of work rather than the team starting and stopping at a series of artificial review gates. The sponsors, developers, and users should be able to maintain a constant pace indefinitely. At regular intervals, the team reflects on how to become more effective, then tunes and adjusts its behavior accordingly. Stephany Bellomo has highlighted the problems implied by the BCL:

> "This directive straddles the new and the old acquisition processes. ... Clearly, this is interim guidance that is trying to move in the direction

of new acquisition concepts, but is still holding rather tightly to the old." [521]

However, the SEI notes that although DOD-5000 does not preclude the use of agile:

"(The tactical and strategic benefits from agile are) not likely to occur without changes to the traditional DOD mindset."[522]

Table 10: Explanations of selected DOD Acronyms[523]

Acronym	Definition
BCL	Business Capability Lifecycle: An interim approach for the development of defense business systems. Created as a supplement to DOD-5000, it is an integrated approach to producing JCIDS documents, and meeting the requirements of the Investment Review Board (IRB) and the Defense Business System Management Committee (DBSMC).
CD	Capability Drop: A lower level document that specifies the characteristics of a "widget" or "app" for partial deployment of the solution.
IS ICD	Information Systems Initial Capabilities Document: the minimum requirements for a new system "based upon what is achievable with today's technology".
JROC	The Joint Requirements Oversight Council reviews and agrees all Joint Capabilities Integration and Development (JCID) documents
KPP	Key Performance Parameters.
MDAPs	Major Defense Acquisition Programs
MDAs	Milestone Decision Authorities – The bodies authorized by DOD-5000 to tailor the regulatory information requirements and acquisition process.
OSD	Office of the Secretary of Defense: The staff function that supports the Secretary of Defense. This includes the Deputy, Under and Assistant Secretaries, and Directors.

Questions

1. Section 804 is part of US public law and requires specific development techniques to be used in defense projects. Is it desirable to state in law that particular methods should be used?

2. Do you feel that the 'IT Box' could work as an enabler for agile to flourish, or as a straightjacket that could stifle agility?

3. The 'IT Box' was a response to the requirements of the JROCM 008-08 memorandum.[524] Do you think that it meets those requirements?

Chapter 22

Traditional Audit Approaches

We saw in Part I that the GAO was critical of three aspects of the agile implementation at VA. To recap: first, because of the short timescales, VA had decided not to complete conversion of all the data from the interim solution, and not all interfaces were in place. Second, the GAO was very critical of the VA's approach to testing. Third, that half of the system functionality did not match the previously documented requirements.

The VA responded to the GAO defending their agile approach. The fast implementation was a necessity, and the testing that was carried out was done closely in tandem with development to get feedback on bugs fast:

> "The testing approach is compatible with agile development, where unit, functional and end-user testing are collaboratively accomplished and all significant errors are identified and resolved prior to deployment." [525]

The VA was proud of the fact that the solution was developed very quickly and was free of any category 1 or category 2 bugs. They felt this was a vindication of the collaborative testing approach taken.

This divergence of viewpoints on what constituted the most effective approach stemmed from different perspectives. The stakeholders were collaborating closely with the development team and checking for internal consistency and real world usability. However, the auditors were checking for conformance to a superseded requirements document. They cited instances where there was an inconsistency between tests that the users had signed off, and the original documentation of requirements. It is debatable whether this really was a demonstration of ineffective testing, or a demonstration of agility in the face of changing user demands. The auditors also criticized the amount of rework that went on from one iteration to another. However, rework is to be expected when iterating. Agile developments make the need for rework obvious at an early stage, rather than continuing regardless in the hope that the designs will eventually work.[526]

We saw this process at work also in the FBI Sentinel Case Study in Part I. In that case, audit reports had taken a traditional view of what needed to be done to correct the causes of failure in the collapse of the Trilogy VCF project. The auditors recommended more discipline, more detailed oversight of costs, more planning and scheduling, and BDUF documentation of business requirements.

Conclusions

In Parts I and II there are many examples of those responsible for assurance and audit taking a waterfall ruler to measure agile performance. In the UK we have seen a traditional gated review approach continuing to be used while departments are being asked to become more agile (see page 236).

David Posner, Director of IT Management Issues at the GAO, recognizes elements of agility as a common critical success factor in a survey of seven successful IT projects worth a total of $5bn:

> All seven (projects) in one form or another attacked the development process in terms of phases or increments. This is something that has been called for over many years – it is highlighted in the IT reform plan. Incremental development was a big part of the success of these programs.[527]

As governments become more agile, it is important that assurance and audit approaches move quickly to support this new approach.

Chapter 23

Final Conclusions

Evidence from governments around the world give a resounding 'thumbs up' for the use of agile for large-scale initiatives, and not just for small projects. The team that rescued the Sentinel project by the adoption of the Scrum approach was large. The FBI spent over $78m on it the two years to 2012 with a team of over 50. Nevertheless, the savings were even larger. The agile approach delivered 88% of what the previous project team had budgeted $458m for.[528] At the Department of Veteran Affairs, the fast and effective setup of the Educational Benefits system cost $207m and was achieved in 18 months. VA declared it a "nearly flawless, stunning, and unpredicted success".[529]

What governments need now is agile leadership. The technical risks of developing solutions are the responsibility of suppliers, but the business risks of project failure belong to those in government. Use the agile approach to manage these risks and lead your projects to success!

Endnotes

1. www.gilb.com/tiki-download_file.php?fileId=431
2. Abbas 2008
3. Toynbee 2012
4. Office of the Auditor-General 2012
5. Zients 2010
6. London Evening Standard 2011
7. Gilb 1976
8. Gilb 1985
9. Kundra 2010a
10. UK Cabinet Office 2011c and UK Cabinet Office 2011b
11. van Roekel 2012
12. Kundra 2010a
13. Transport for London 2012
14. Hamer et al. 1998
15. Many books spend most of their time discussing the detail of the various 'flavors' of agile before discussing scaling them up. See for example a bottom-up discussion in Leffingwell 2007. Other books, such as Larman, Vodde 2009 and Larman, Vodde 2010 spend many pages on detailed discussions of scaling to large teams without taking into account the requirements of large organizations.
16. DSDM and Scrum: Craddock et al. 2012, and Glass 2001
17. Dinning 2009 and Bell et al. 2010
18. Courier Mail 2012
19. Williams, Hodgson 2009
20. General Dynamics UK 2010
21. General Dynamics UK 2010, p.5
22. Craddock et al. 2012, p.2
23. General Dynamics 2009
24. Henson, Prior 2009, Slide 7
25. Beck 1999
26. DSDM Consortium 2008
27. Thanks to Dot Tudor for pointing out to me that if workaround is possible, but painful, then a requirement should be considered a *Should Have* rather than a *Could Have*.
28. Cohn 2005, p.189
29. Jamieson et al. 2005, p.6
30. Henson, Prior 2009, Slide 9
31. General Dynamics UK 2010, 4-5
32. General Dynamics UK 2010, p.5
33. Madahar 2012
34. Henson, Prior 2009, Slide 13-14
35. Slabodkin 2011 and also saarelainen 2011, p.136
36. MIDS-Link 16, BOWMAN, Ground Asset Tracking System,, Variable Message Format, FAC NAV, NORTaC and NORMANS
37. 3SDL 2010
38. Henson, Prior 2009, p.7
39. US GAO 2011f, Appendix III
40. CRS 2006, p.1
41. Walters 2009, p.7

[42] VA 2012

[43] US GAO 2011f, p.15

[44] US GAO 2011f, Appendix III

[45] US GAO 2011f, p.22

[46] GAO 2011c, p.9

[47] GAO 2011c, 12 and 15

[48] GAO 2011c, p.13

[49] GAO 2011c, p.8

[50] I have read Schwaber (2011) and Beck (1999) carefully and I cannot find any specific references to interfaces, user training, planning changes to business processes or preparing smooth transition of technology solutions to Business as Usual/Operations. Interestingly Stephens and Rosenberg (2003) did not note that XP does not concern itself with these areas. Again, I must emphasize that I am not saying one method is better than another, just you must be aware that each has its own focus, and applying just one method inflexibly without looking at the others has risks.

[51] DSDM Consortium 2008, 10-11, 26, 41, 97, 143,166

[52] Association for Project Management 2006,PMI 2011 and OGC 2011

[53] Maze 2012

[54] GAO 2011c, p.7

[55] GAO 2011c, p.11

[56] Perera 2012

[57] OIG 2002a

[58] OIG 2002b, xii -x

[59] OIG 2011, p.7

[60] OIG 2006a, p.xi

[61] Israel 2012, p.76

[62] OIG 2006a, ii-iii

[63] As stated in a memorandum of understanding (MOU) signed by the FBI, DOJ, and DHS CIOs in June 2005; see OIG 2006a, p.38

[64] OIG 2006a, p.iii

[65] OIG 2006b, p.i and FBI 2006

[66] OIG 2006b, p.x

[67] OIG 2007, p.ix

[68] OIG 2007, p.i

[69] OIG 2007, p.vi

[70] IBM Center for the Business of Government 2011

[71] OIG 2008, p.ix

[72] OIG 2008, p.5

[73] FBI 2006

[74] OIG 2009, p.iii

[75] Israel 2012, p.76

[76] FBI 2006

[77] Israel 2012, p.78

[78] Israel 2012, p.75

[79] OIG 2010b, p.2

[80] OIG 2010b, p.8

[81] OIG 2010a, p.4

[82] OIG 2010a, p.5 and OIG 2010a, p.13

[83] OIG 2010a, p.21

[84] FBI 2006

[85] OIG 2011, p.1

[86] OIG 2011, p.25

[87] OIG 2011, p.24

[88] OIG 2011, p.19 and OIG 2011, p.23

[89] OIG 2011, Appendix I

[90] OIG 2011, p.17

[91] OIG 2011, Appendix II

92 MicroPact 2012

93 FBI CIO 2012b

94 FBI CIO 2012d, p.1

95 FBI CIO 2012c

96 FBI CIO 2012a

97 AU Prime Minister Kevin Rudd 2009

98 State of Queensland Department of Housing 2005b, p.1

99 State of Queensland Department of Housing 2005a, p.2

100 See UK Cabinet Office 2009 for more on PRINCE2.

101 State of Queensland 2008, p.1

102 State of Queensland 2008, p.2

103 AU CAG 2010

104 Met Office 2010

105 Shepard 2010

106 PRINCE2: OGC 2009, DSDM and Scrum: Craddock et al. 2012, and Glass 2001

107 Williams 2012a

108 Avison, Fitzgerald 2003

109 Fitzgerald 1998

110 Highsmith 2012. Three other experts also attended who brought different methodological perspectives: Alistair Cockburn, Jim Highsmith, and David Thomas. Cockburn had just written a book on the use of diagrams to describe user requirements, Highsmith a book on collaborative development, and Thomas was working on UML based notation.

111 Thomas 2007

112 Fowler 2012

113 £80 million spent by the London Stock Exchange and at least an additional £400m million by securities companies Drummond 1996.

114 Drummond 1996

115 Schwaber 2011a, p.4

116 Shewhart 1931, Dedication and Imai 1991

117 Schwaber 2004, p.3

118 Poppendieck 2003, p.8

119 Israel 2012, p.76

120 Boehm 2002, p.65

121 Vogt 2002

122 UK NAO 2011a

123 Berry 2011 and Kundra 2010a, p.13

124 RAND Corp 2008

125 RAND Corp 2008. For the purposes of explanation and brevity to the general reader I have used "DOD-5000" as shorthand for the series of "5000"guidance materials. Please see US DOD for the complete index. Don't forget to notify me if any links are broken, and I will attempt to send you the correct link within 30 days. eBook owners can turn on automatic errata correction to receive updated versions of the click-through endnotes.

126 OMB 2007, p.1 and CIO Council 2011

127 CIO Council 2011, p.4

128 Highsmith 2012

129 Boehm, Ross 1989

130 US Public Law 2002

131 Williams 2012a

132 Comparing Schwaber 2010a to Schwaber 2011b and Sutherland, Schwaber 2007. The word 'software' was used 339

times in the 2007 version, only six times in the 2010 version and zero times in the 2011 version.

[133] Aviation Week 2011

[134] UK NAO 2006b, p.8

[135] UK NAO 2006b, p.8

[136] UK NAO 2006a, p.50

[137] UK NAO 2006a, p.49

[138] Treasury 2005, p.29

[139] GAO 2003b

[140] HM Treasury and Cabinet Office 2011, Table 3.C

[141] UK Cabinet Office 2011f, p.6

[142] UK NAO 2006a, p.35

[143] US GAO 2009c, p.10

[144] US GAO 2010, p.78

[145] Weigelt 2010

[146] Kundra 2010b

[147] USD(AT&L) 2008a

[148] Boehm, Hansen 2001

[149] Boehm, Hansen 2001

[150] Note: Rather confusingly, Boehm uses the term 'architecture'. I have changed this to "approach" because LCA does not relate to a technical architecture, but to the "architecture" of the project processes.

[151] Boehm, Hansen 2001, p.7

[152] DoD 2003

[153] Hantos 2008, p.27

[154] Hantos 2008, p.29

[155] US GAO 2012, p.20

[156] Levin 2003

[157] GAO 2003a

[158] Gates 2009

[159] GAO, p.11

[160] Lorell et al. 2003, 35-36

[161] OMB 2006, 11, 34, 38, 101, Appendix 12

[162] OMB 2006, 10, 12, 71, Appendix 3

[163] US GAO 2008a

[164] OMB 2006

[165] OMB 2006, 71, Appendix 3

[166] US DOD 2003

[167] OMB 2003, p.20

[168] GAO 2005, 9 and 13

[169] US GAO 2008a, p.11

[170] US GAO 2009a, p.17

[171] Kundra 2010a, p.1

[172] Kundra 2010a, Introduction

[173] Kundra 2010a, p.14

[174] OGC 2011

[175] Berry 2011

[176] Bell et al. 2010 and Dinning 2009

[177] Treasury 2005, 29 and Boxes 4.2 and 4.7

[178] US GAO 2009b

[179] UK HM Treasury 2003

[180] UK HM Treasury 1991 and Great Britain. Her Majesty's Stationery Office 1997

[181] UK Daily Telegraph 2002

[182] UK NAO 2003

[183] Beath, Orlikowski 1994, p.370. The materials they reviewed were from the writings of James Martin, discussed further in Part III.

[184] Gomaa, Scott 1981

[185] Leland 1997

[186] Craddock et al. 2012

[187] Williams 2012a

[188] Cooper 1994

[189] Davies et al. 2009

[190] Nuseibeh 2001

[191] Boehm 2000

[192] Serbu 2011

[193] Kundra 2010a, 23-24

[194] UK HM Treasury 2003, Box 23

[195] UK HM Treasury 2003, Box 4.3

[196] UK HM Treasury 2003, Section 5.17

[197] UK HM Treasury 2003, Box 4.2

[198] UK HM Treasury 2003, Para 3.4

[199] UK HM Treasury 2003, Para 6.15

[200] Serbu 2011

[201] Fowler 1999

[202] Fowler 1999, Gamma, Eric in foreword

[203] Schwaber 2011b, p.15

[204] Dyba, Dingsøyr 2008, p.3

[205] Richards 2010

[206] Levin 2003, Enclosure II, Table 2

[207] Kessler, Sweitzer 2007, p.72

[208] Kessler, Sweitzer 2007, p.72

[209] UK HM Treasury 2003, p.81

[210] US GAO 2008b and US GAO 2011c

[211] VA Office of Inspector General 2011

[212] Williams 2012a

[213] Schwaber 2011b

[214] Schwaber 2011b

[215] Gilb, Tom communication to the author July 2012

[216] August 1991, p.34

[217] Carmel et al. 1993

[218] Beath, Orlikowski 1994, p.350

[219] Work and Pensions Committee 2010

[220] UK NAO 2012c, p.37

[221] Carmel et al. 1993, p.44

[222] Boehm, Bose 1994, p.1

[223] Boehm, Bose 1994, p.1

[224] UK NAO 2011f

[225] UK NAO 2011e

[226] US GAO 2011e, p.1

[227] US GAO 2011b

[228] US GAO 2011d, p.28

[229] US GAO 2007c

[230] ANSI 99-001-2008 and Project Management Institute 2008, 26 and 43

[231] OGC 2011, p.63

[232] OGC 2011

[233] Vijayasarathy, Turk 2008

[234] UK NAO 2011d

[235] UK ICO 2012

[236] Lilley 2010

[237] Conservative Home 2012

[238] COSO 2004

[239] East 2012

[240] TIGTA, p.8 found these problems which a concurrent report prepared by GAO appears to have missed - see GAO 2011a, p.4

[241] GAO 2008, p.1

[242] HM Treasury 2004

[243] COSO 2004

[244] IRM 2002

[245] Canada et al. 2010

[246] Canada et al. 2009

[247] UK HM Treasury 2003, p.29

[248] IRM 2002, p.6

[249] ISO 2009

[250] ISO 2009, p.7

[251] DWP Department for Work and Pensions 2011, p.69

[252] Williams et al. 2011

[253] Campaign for Change 2011

[254] Iaffan 2012 and UK DWP 2011, p.85

[255] DWP Department for Work and Pensions 2011

[256] North Carolina State College of Management 2007

[257] IRS 2007b

[258] IRS 2007a, p.39

[259] UK HMRC 2011, p.40

[260] UK HMRC 2011, p.40

[261] DWP Department for Work and Pensions 2011, p.101

[262] US GAO 2007b, p.8

[263] US GAO 2007a

[264] Adapted from APM 2011.

[265] Williams 2012a

[266] Morgan 2009, 79-81

[267] Morgan 2009, 82-82

[268] Giotis 2003

[269] Anderson 2005, p.193

[270] Deming 1986, 18-96

[271] Anderson 2005, p.194

[272] Samset et al. 2006, p.4

[273] US GAO 2009d, p.1

[274] US GAO 2009d, p.9

[275] US GAO 2009d, p.38

[276] By the confusingly named "Partnerships British Colum-bia" in Canada, and by "Partnerships UK" in Britain.

[277] US GAO 2009d, p.38

[278] Dearden et al. 2010

[279] OGC 2011, p.63

[280] Hasnain, Hall 2008

[281] Fruhling, Tarrell 2008, p.6

[282] Beck 1999, p.46 and also see Stephens, Rosenberg 2003, p.8 who, unusually, gives credit to XP for refocusing developers on the importance of frequent unit testing.

[283] Beck 1999, 100-102

[284] Williams, Kessler 2003

[285] Fruhling et al. 2008, 7-9

[286] Fruhling et al. 2008, p.9

[287] Stephens, Rosenberg 2003, p.8

[288] Fruhling, Tarrell 2008, p.34

[289] Samset et al. 2006, p.2

[290] Morris 1977 and Pease 1981

[291] Meeren et al. 2005

[292] de Gelder 2009, p.3475

[293] de Gelder 2009, p.3480

[294] de Gelder 2009, p.3478

[295] Vijayasarathy, Turk 2008

[296] Schwaber 2011a, p.8

[297] Schwaber 2011a, p.9

[298] Craddock et al. 2012, p.3

[299] Schwaber 2011a, 10-11

[300] Schwaber 2011a, p.13

[301] Schwaber 2010b

[302] Schwaber 2011a, 10-11

[303] Schwaber 2011a, p.12

[304] DSDM Consortium 2008, p.41

[305] DSDM Consortium 2008, p.23

[306] Schwaber 2010b

307 Lee-Kelley, Sankey 2008, p.52

308 Lee-Kelley, Sankey 2008, p.53

309 Lee-Kelley, Sankey 2008, p.53

310 Cooper, Kurland 2002, p.511

311 Cooper, Kurland 2002, p.528

312 Baker 2002

313 Public Law 100-690

314 CIO US DoI 2005

315 Faisal 2011

316 Faisal 2011, p.4

317 DOI1 2012

318 DOI1 2012

319 Cohn 2005, p.254

320 Gilb, Finzi 1988

321 Gilb, Brodie 2005

322 Note that in the UK a *product breakdown structure* is first created to identify the outputs required.

323 OMB 2006, p.10

324 OMB 2006, p.50

325 Alleman et al. 2003, p.1

326 Solomon 2011, p.1

327 Sulaiman 2007

328 Sulaiman 2007, p.2

329 Sulaiman 2007

330 Park 2012

331 Forrest 2012

332 UK NAO 2011b

333 Unless otherwise stated, information in this chapter was provided to me directly by team members in discussions.

334 UK NAO 2011b, p.8

335 UK NAO 2011b, p.6

336 Williams 2012b

337 Beaven 2012

338 Beaven 2012

339 London Evening Standard 2011

340 UK Government 2012

341 USDA CIO 2011b, p.3

342 USDA CIO 2011b, p.3

343 USDA CIO 2011b, p.3

344 USDA CIO 2011a, p.5

345 USDA CIO 2011a

346 Cohn 2005, p.21

347 Thomas 2011, p.8

348 Glass 2001

349 Wang et al. 2007

350 Nerur, et al 2005, p.74

351 Beath, Orlikowski 1994

352 Nerur, et al 2005, p.75

353 Nerur, et al 2005, p.76

354 Davies, Gray 2011, p.6. They call this preferred approach *loose-tight* project management, although I prefer *light-tight*, which I have used here, because lightness has more positive connotations than looseness. Also the word *loose* is very close to the word *lose* which I use elsewhere to describe *lose/lose* situations etc.

355 DSDM Consortium 2008, p.137

356 Davies, Gray 2011, p.6

357 Treasury Board of Canada Secretariat 2010

358 UK NAO 2012b, 7-8

359 UK HM Treasury 2011 and Treasury Board of Canada Secretariat 2010

360 UK NAO 2004, p.7

361 CMMI Product Team 2011, p.5

362 CMMI Product Team 2011,

p.22

363 Adapted from CMMI Product Team 2011, p.23. Note: For reasons of backward compatibility and to 'integrate' the previous SW-CMM model, the CMMI actually presents an alternative "capability model" which focuses on the state of the organization's processes relative to an individual process area, as opposed to the more widely used "maturity' representation" referenced here which characterizes the overall state of the organization's processes.

364 UK NAO 2008a, p.6

365 UK NAO 2010a, p.1

366 UK NAO 2012b, p.35

367 See: GAO-12-461, GAO-12-202, GAO-12-7, GAO-12-26, GAO-11-742, GAO-11-586, GAO-11-705R, GAO-11-475, GAO-11-297, and GAO-11-168.

368 GAO 2011b, p.1

369 US GAO 2011a

370 GAO 2011d, p.5

371 Swoyer 2005

372 Swoyer 2005

373 West, Grant 2010, p.2

374 See Alleman et al. 2003, p.3

375 Giotis 2003

376 Israel 2012, 74, 79

377 Swoyer 2005

378 UK NAO 2010c, 1, 14

379 Turner, Jain 2002, p.154. Note that they were reviewing version 1.1 of the CMMI, but their general conclusions are still valid.

380 Turner, Jain 2002

381 Turner, Jain 2002, 160-161

382 UK NAO 2012c

383 Campaign for Change 2012

384 UK NAO 2012b, p.34

385 Public Accounts Committee 2012, Q131 to Q140

386 UK NAO 2012b, p.8

387 Finkelstein 1992

388 Finkelstein 1992

389 Carnall 2007

390 The term "modular approaches" is used in Kundra's report - I have taken the liberty to translate this as "agile", but it can be argued that while agile is modular, modular is not necessarily agile; see Kundra 2010a

391 Kundra 2010a

392 Stephen et al. 2011

393 UK Cabinet Office 2012b, p.9

394 UK NAO 2011c

395 UK Cabinet Office 2012b, p.9

396 Stephen et al. 2011, 14, 30 See Figure 1 for a diagram which illustrates the lack of clarity over co-ordination of the implementation of the strategy.

397 Stephen et al. 2011, 14, 30

398 TechAmerica Foundation 2010, p.18

399 Vogt 2002, p.62

400 UK NAO 2012a

401 AU CAG 2010

402 Weigelt 2010

403 Magee et al. 2012

404 Standish Group 1995

405 AU Victorian Ombudsman 2011

406 What size constitutes a mega-project? Davies uses a rule of thumb of £1bn for construction projects. If we assume that it is the value of the intellectual effort of planning and design that relates to risk, not the cost of concrete and steel, then a size of £50m - £100m for IT projects might be indicated as being *mega-projects*. Davies et al. 2009, p.18.

407 Jamieson et al. 2005, p.4

408 Flyvbjerg et al. 2002, p.6

409 Davies et al. 2009, p.19

410 Organ 2003

411 UK Cabinet Office 18/10/2010

412 UK Cabinet Office 2011e, p.2

413 UK Cabinet Office 2011d

414 UK NAO 2011f, p.4

415 UK Cabinet Office 2011a

416 Campaign for Change 2011

417 Collins 2012

418 UK Cabinet Office 2009, p.1

419 IRS 2007a

420 PASC 2011

421 UK NAO 2010b, 6, 25

422 UK NAO 2008b, p.11

423 Comptroller and Auditor General (India) 2004

424 Flyvbjerg, Budzier 2011

425 UK Cabinet Office 2010, APM 2011, FRC 2005, and UK NAO 2010d

426 UK Cabinet Office 2012a

427 Strassmann 1997

428 Strassmann 1997, 142-144

429 Doran 1981

430 Gane, Sarson 1977

431 Longworth, Nicholls 1986

432 UK NAO 2011f, p.27

433 US GAO 2011b, Summary

434 APM 2007

435 UK Cabinet Office 2011d, p.11

436 Agile was not the first movement to use a manifesto to provoke a religious like zeal to its converts! See Martin 1983 and Martin 1989-90

437 $100m as a donation in 2005, and an additional $100m was raised in 2010 with James Martin providing half as matched funding alongside other donors such as George Soros University of Oxford 2012

438 UK - The Independent 2012

439 Martin 2012

440 To see the debate unfolding see examples such as Naur, Randell 1969

441 Benington 1987

442 See Leffingwell 2007, p.17 and also Larman 2006

443 Benington experiences were with hand machine coded programs running on IBM SAGE computers with only 65k of memory. It is easy to read too much into his paper which was limited to "programming problems that are likely to arise during Forrester's 1960-1965 period of real-time control applications".

444 Royce 1970, p.2

445 Royce 1970, p.332

446 Kimble 2008 and read about Ted's concepts here Stonebraker 1988

447 Middleton 1994

448 Middleton 1994

[449] Martin 1989-90

[450] Mercurio et al 1990

[451] In fact only 29 pages out of 788 refer to prototyping, timeboxing and iterative development Martin 1991, 216-227, 312, 172-188. This mammoth book was supported by 6 hours of video tapes emphasizing up-front analysis, planning and design before coding. See Martin 1991, p.351 and also the complex intricate diagrams used in ISP Martin 1991, Figure 21.9.

[452] Craddock et al. 2012, p.2

[453] Beath, Orlikowski 1994, p.372 and Beath, Orlikowski 1994, p.361

[454] Finlay, Mitchell 1994

[455] Martin, McClure 1985

[456] Martin, Odell 1992

[457] Coad, Yourdon 1990

[458] Rumbaugh et al. 1999

[459] Arisholm et al. 2006

[460] Boehm, Hansen 2001, 8-9 . Boehm notes that in a recent survey of 16 OOA&D books, only six listed the word "performance" in their index, and only two listed "cost."

[461] Dzidek et al. 2008, p.17

[462] Middleton 1994

[463] Beath, Orlikowski 1994

[464] Maughan 2011

[465] Although one major lot did not sell - bids for the single nationwide license would meet the reserve price of $1.3bn were not realized. The highest was for only $472m from Qualcomm FCC

[466] Milgrom 1995

[467] Bulow et al. 2009

[468] AgileManifesto.org 2001

[469] UK NAO 2011f

[470] European Commission (1985), "White Paper for the Completion of the Internal Market".

[471] Directive 2004/18/EC (2004) (the Procurement Directive) Article 2 on the coordination of procedures for the award of public works contracts, public supply contracts, and public service contracts and Directive 2004/17/EC (2004) (the Utilities Procurement Directive) Article 10 on the coordination of the procurement procedures of entities operating in the water, energy, transport, and postal services sectors.

[472] Stephen et al. 2011

[473] UK Public Contracts Regulations (2006), Section 18(24)

[474] Case C-454/06 - pressetext Nachrichtenagentur GmbH v Republik Österreich (Bund), APA-OTS Originaltext - Service GmbH and APA Austria Presse Agentur registrierte Genossenschaft mit beschränkter Haftung.

[475] Emergn 2012, p.4

[476] Emergn 2012, p.5

[477] Emergn 2012, p.6

[478] Emergn 2012, p.7

[479] Jamieson et al. 2005, p.2

[480] Jamieson et al. 2005, p.3

[481] Jamieson et al. 2005, p.5

[482] Jamieson et al. 2005, p.6

[483] Jamieson et al. 2005, p.6

[484] Jamieson et al. 2005, p.6

[485] Jamieson et al. 2005, p.7

486 Concha et al. 2007, p.149

487 Concha et al. 2007, p.150

488 Concha et al. 2007, p.151

489 Maughan 2011

490 Maughan 2011

491 In correspondence with the author elaborating on her article: Atkinson 2011

492 UK NAO 2012d, p.27

493 UK NAO 2012d, p.27

494 UK NAO 2012d, p.28

495 UK NAO 2012d, p.28

496 Version One 2012

497 Arbogast et al. 2012, p.499

498 Stephens 2006

499 Arbogast et al. 2012, p.21

500 Federal Computer Week 2012

501 DoD 2010a, p.3

502 DoD 1988, p.53

503 McDonald 2010, p.37

504 US DOD 1985, p.1

505 US DOD 1985, p.78

506 US DOD 1985, p.78

507 DoD 1988, p.3

508 NRC 2010, p.ix

509 DoD 2012, 295-296 and DoD 2012, 48-49

510 USD(AT&L) 2008b, 48, Table 8

511 DoD 2012, p.48

512 Defense Science Board 2009

513 PANEL ON DEFENSE ACQUISITION REFORM 2010, p.23

514 Congress 2009, Sec. 804

515 Congress 2009, Sec. 805 4259

516 Wills 2012, p.4

517 The Joint Capabilities Integration and Development System (JCIDS) "IT Box" Wills 2012, Command and Control Requirements Management DoD 2010b and DoD 2010a. At the time of publication this model was described as an 'interim' model yet to be incorporated into DOD 5000.02.

518 Wills 2012, 9-11

519 Wills 2012, p.17

520 Wills 2012, p.12

521 Bellomo 2011, p.4

522 Lapham 2012

523 I collated and derived these from several sources. See the following for more information: USD(AT&L) 2008b; Wills 2012; JROC 2001

524 Wills 2012, p.4

525 US GAO 2011f, p.67

526 US GAO 2011f, p.8

527 Francis Rose 2011

528 FBI CIO 2012b

529 US GAO 2011f, Appendix III

Bibliography

3SDL (2010) Case Study: Exercise Bold Quest 2010
http://www.3sdl.com/success-stories/exercise-bold-quest.aspx

Abbas, Noura (2008) Historical Roots of Agile Methods: Where did Agile Thinking Come from?
http://eprints.soton.ac.uk/266606/1/xp2008camera_ready.pdf

AgileManifesto.org (2001) Manifesto for Agile Software Development
http://agilemanifesto.org/

Alleman; Glen B.; Henderson, Michael (2003) Making Agile Development Work in a Government Contracting Environment - Measuring velocity with Earned Value
http://www.niwotridge.com/PDFs/ADC%20Final.pdf

Anderson, David J. (2005) Stretching agile to fit CMMI level 3 - the story of creating MSF for CMMI reg; process improvement at Microsoft corporation. In : Agile Conference, 2005. Proceedings, pp.193–201

APM (2007) Co-Directing Change – A guide to the governance of multi-owned projects

APM (2011) Directing Change (2nd Edition)

Arbogast, Tom; Larman, Craig; Vodde, Bas (2012) Practices for Scaling Lean and Agile Development

Arisholm, Erik; Briand, Lionel C.; Member, Senior; Hove, Siw Elisabeth; Labiche, Yvan (2006) The Impact of UML Documentation on Software Maintenance: An Experimental Evaluation. In IEEE Transactions on Software Engineering 32, p.2006

Association for Project Management (2006) APM body of knowledge. 5th ed. High Wycombe: Association for Project Management

Atkinson, Susan (2011) Agile can fix failed GovIT says lawyer. Campaign4Change
http://ukcampaign4change.com/2011/06/13/agile-can-fix-failed-govit-says-lawyer/

AU CAG (2010) Information systems governance and control, including the Queensland Health Implementation of Continuity Project

AU Prime Minister Kevin Rudd (2009) John Patterson Oration. ANU News
http://news.anu.edu.au/?p=1638

AU Victorian Ombudsman (2011) Own motion investigation into ICT-enabled projects
http://www.ombudsman.vic.gov.au/resources/documents/Investigation_into_ICT_enabled_projects_Nov_2011.pdf

August, Judy H. (1991) Joint application design. The group session approach to system design / Judy H. August. Englewood Cliffs, N.J: Yourdon Press; London : Prentice-Hall International (UK) (Yourdon Press computing series)

Aviation Week (2011) Last Raptor Rolls Off Lockheed Martin Line
http://bit.ly/M0Dpv4

Avison, David E.; Fitzgerald, Guy (2003) Where now for development methodologies? In Commun. ACM 46, pp.78-82

Baker, George (2002) Distortion and Risk in Optimal Incentive Contracts. In Journal of Human Resources, pp.728-751

Beath, Cynthia Mathis; Orlikowski, Wanda J. (1994) The Contradictory Structure of Systems Development Methodologies. In Information Systems Research 5 (4), pp.350–377
http://bit.ly/LT0q7C

Beaven, Michael C. (2012) Riding the Paradigm – where agile meets programme
http://digital.cabinetoffice.gov.uk/2012/06/20/riding-the-paradigm-where-agile-meets-programme/

Beck, Kent (1999) eXtreme programming eXplained. Embrace change / Kent Beck. Reading, MA: Addison-Wesley

Bell, Tim; Andreae, Peter; Lambert, Lynn (2010) Computer Science in New Zealand high schools. In : Proceedings of the Twelfth Australasian Conference on Computing Education - Volume 103. Darlinghurst, Australia, Australia: Australian Computer Society, Inc (ACE '10), pp.15-22
http://bit.ly/P8n2Ql

Bellomo, Stephany (2011) A Closer Look at 804. A Summary of Considerations for DoD Program Managers
http://www.sei.cmu.edu/reports/11sr015.pdf

Benington, H.D (1987) Production of large computer programs. In : Proceedings. 9th International Conference on Software Engineering, March 30-April 2, 1987, Monterey, California, USA. Washington, D.C, Baltimore, MD: IEEE Computer Society Press; ACM Order Dept., p.299
http://bit.ly/PZTUgT

Berry, John (2011) Competency Model For IT Program Management. US OPM
http://www.chcoc.gov/transmittals/TransmittalDetails.aspx?TransmittalID=4058

Boehm, Barry (2000) Requirements that Handle IKIWISI, COTS, and Rapid Change. In Computer 33, pp.99–102

Boehm, Barry (2002) Get ready for agile methods, with care. In Computer 35 (1), pp.64–69
http://ieeexplore.ieee.org/stamp/stamp.jsp?arnumber=976920

Boehm, Barry; Bose, Prasanta (1994) A Collaborative Spiral Software Process Model Based on Theory W. In : Proceedings, 3rd International Conference on the software process. Applying the software process: IEEE, pp.59-68

Boehm, Barry; Hansen, W. (2001) The Spiral Model as a Tool for Evolutionary Acquisition." CrossTalk

Boehm, Barry; Ross, R. (1989) Theory-W Software Project Management Principles and Examples. In IEEE Transactions on Software Engineering 15, pp.902–916

Bulow, Jeremy; Levin, Jonathan; Milgrom, Paul (2009) Winning Play in Spectrum Auctions. Stanford EDU
http://www.stanford.edu/~jdlevin/Papers/AWS.pdf

Campaign for Change (2011) Agile for Universal Credit – a good choice says report
http://ukcampaign4change.com/2011/10/05/agile-for-universal-credit-a-good-choice-says-report/

Campaign for Change (2012) Breaking Down Barriers
http://ukcampaign4change.com/

Canada, Government of; Treasury Board of Canada; Secretariat (2009) Policy on the Management of Projects. Canadian Treasury Board
http://www.tbs-sct.gc.ca/pol/doc-eng.aspx?id=18229&section=text

Canada, Government of; Treasury Board of Canada; Secretariat (2010) Framework for the Management of Risk. CA TBC
http://www.tbs-sct.gc.ca/pol/doc-eng.aspx?id=19422&section=text

Carmel, Erran; Whitaker, Randall D.; George, Joey F. (1993) PD and joint application design: a transatlantic comparison. In Commun. ACM 36, pp.40-48

Carnall, C. A. (2007) Managing change in organizations. 5th ed. Harlow: Financial Times Prentice Hall

CIO Council (2011) Case Study: SSA Program Manager Development Practices. Developing a cadre of highly skilled, trained, and qualified program managers to support program and project success. US SSA
http://bit.ly/Mw61L4

CIO US DoI (2005) Memo dated October 2, 2005. OVERVIEW OF E-GOVERNMENT ACT IMPLEMENTATION. US DoI
http://www.doi.gov/ocio/egov/upload/FY2005-E-Gov-Annual-Report-DOI.pdf

CMMI Product Team (2011) CMMI® for Development, Version 1.3 CMMI-DEV, V1.3
http://www.sei.cmu.edu/reports/10tr033.pdf

Coad, Peter; Yourdon, Edward (1990) Object-oriented analysis. Englewood Cliffs, N.J. ; London: Yourdon Press (Yourdon Press computing series)

Cohn, Mike (2005) Agile estimating and planning. Upper Saddle River, N.J: Prentice Hall PTR; London : Pearson Education [distributor] (Robert C. Martin series)

Collins, Tony (2012) Gateway reviews. Campaign for Change
http://ukcampaign4change.com/category/gateway-reviews/

Comptroller and Auditor General (India) (2004) Audit Report - LSGIs for the year ended 31 March 2004 - CHAPTER I
http://www.cag.gov.in/html/LB/Kr/LB_05_CHAPTER_I.pdf

Concha, Mauricio; Visconti, Marcello; Astudillo, Hernán (2007) Agile commitments. In : Proceedings of the 8th international conference on Agile processes in software engineering and extreme programming. Berlin, Heidelberg: Springer-Verlag (XP'07), pp.149-152
http://bit.ly/NuWXt8

Congress (2009) National Defense Authorization Act for Fiscal Year 2010, 10 U.S.C., Pub. L. 111-84. Section 801
http://www.gpo.gov/fdsys/pkg/PLAW-111publ383/pdf/PLAW-111publ383.pdf

Conservative Home (2012) Not exactly clear support for Lansley from Cameron at PMQs
http://bit.ly/LqxC52

Cooper, Cecily D.; Kurland, Nancy B. (2002) Telecommuting (4)
http://bit.ly/MrPspG

Cooper, R. G. (1994) Third Generation New Product Processes. In Journal of Product Innovation Management 11, pp.3–14
http://processprotocol.com/pdf/pdt98.pdf

COSO (2004) Enterprise risk management. Integrated framework : Executive Summary Framework : September 2004. New York: Committee of Sponsoring Organizations of the Treadway Commission

Courier Mail (2012) Nine workers caught in Queensland Health payroll rip-off
http://www.couriermail.com.au/news/nine-workers-caught-in-queensland-health-payroll-rip-off/story-e6freon6-1226423118609

Craddock, Andrew; Richards, Keith; Tudor, Dorothy; Roberts, Barbara; Godwin, Julia (2012) The DSDM Agile Project Framework for Scrum v1.1. DSDM Consortium
http://bit.ly/M0CLxA

CRS (2006) Theft of Veterans' Personal Information, and DVA's Information Technology Reorganization: Issues for Congress
http://www.policyarchive.org/handle/10207/bitstreams/4376.pdf

Davies, Andrew; Dodgson, Mark; Gann, David (2009) From iconic design to lost luggage: Innovation at Heathrow Terminal 5. Copenhagen Business School: DRUID

Davies, Andrew; Gray, Ian (2011) Learning Legacy. Lessons learned from the London 2012 Olympic and Paralympic Games construction programme. London Olympic Delivery Authority
http://bit.ly/PWRLRS

Dearden, Andy; RIZVI, Haider; GUPTA, Subodh (2010) Roles and Responsibilities in agile ICT for Development
http://www.bcs.org/upload/pdf/ewic_ihci10_paper3.pdf

Defense Science Board (2009) DoD Policies and Procedures for the Acquisition of IT
http://www.acq.osd.mil/dsb/reports/ADA498375.pdf

Deming, W. Edwards (1986) Out of the crisis. Quality, productivity and competitive position / W. Edwards Deming. Cambridge: Cambridge University Press

Dinning, N. (2009) Technological Context Knowledge and skills. Exploring specific knowledge and skills to support programmes in technology. Materials for consultation to support Ministry decision making.
http://bit.ly/NpSPM4

DoD (1988) DOD-STD-2167A Military Standard: Defense System Software Development. In : [[United States Department of Defense]]

DoD (2003) NSSAP 03-01 Guidance for Space System Acquisition Process. DoD
http://bit.ly/NuTv1B

DoD (2010a) A New Approach for Delivering IT Capabilities in the Department of Defense. DoD
http://bit.ly/M0CAlX

DoD (2010b) Chairman of the Joint Chief of Staff Manual - Joint Command and Control (C2) Capability Needs/Requirements Management Procedures
http://www.dtic.mil/cjcs_directives/cdata/unlimit/m326501.pdf

DoD (2012) Defense Acquisition Guidebook

DOI1 (2012) Exhibit 300: Capital Asset Summary
http://www.itdashboard.gov/investment/exhibit300/pdf/010-000000319

Doran, George T. (1981) There's a S.M.A.R.T. way to write managements's goals and objectives. In Management Review 70 (11), p.35
http://bit.ly/NuWDKW

Drummond, Helga (1996) Escalation in decision-making. The tragedy of Taurus. Oxford [England] ;, New York: Oxford University Press

DSDM Consortium (2008) DSDM Atern The Handbook

DWP Department for Work and Pensions (2011) Department for Work and Pensions Annual Report and Accounts 2010-2011
http://www.dwp.gov.uk/docs/dwp-annual-report-and-accounts-2010-2011.pdf

Dyba, Tore; Dingsøyr, Torgeir (2008) Empirical studies of agile software development: A systematic review. In Inf. Softw. Technol 50, pp.833-859
http://dl.acm.org/citation.cfm?id=1379905.1379989

Dzidek, Wojciech J.; Arisholm, Erik; Briand, Lionel C. (2008) A Realistic Empirical Evaluation of the Costs and Benefits of UML in Software Maintenance. In IEEE Trans. Softw. Eng 34, pp.407-432
http://dl.acm.org/citation.cfm?id=1383055.1383295

East, Robyn (2012) IRS CADE2 Investment Dashboard
http://www.itdashboard.gov/investment?buscid=506

Emergn (2012) Sourcing for Agile
http://www.emergn.com/wp-content/uploads/2012/05/TP-Sourcing-for-Agile.pdf

Faisal, Ahmed (2011) Accelerating Deployment of a Law Enforcement Reporting System at DOI through TechStat. DoI Law Enforcement Reporting Investment. DoI
http://bit.ly/NuWCXd

FBI (2006) FBI Announces Award of Sentinel Contract
http://www.fbi.gov/news/pressrel/press-releases/fbi-announces-award-of-sentinel-contract

FBI CIO (2012a) Exhibit 300 - Jun 26, 2012
http://www.itdashboard.gov/investment/exhibit300/pdf/011-000003211

FBI CIO (2012b) Federal IT Dashboard. as at 1st June 2012
http://www.itdashboard.gov/investment?buscid=441

FBI CIO (2012c) Investment Dashboard
http://www.itdashboard.gov/investment?buscid=441

FBI CIO (2012d) Sentinel: Exhibit 300: Capital Asset Summary
http://www.itdashboard.gov/investment/exhibit300/pdf/011-000003211

FCC: FCC Auctions: Factsheet: Auction 73
http://wireless.fcc.gov/auctions/default.htm?job=auction_factsheet&id=73

Federal Computer Week (2012) Agile development gaining in popularity at DHS
http://fcw.com/articles/2012/05/15/dhs-agile.aspx

Finkelstein, Anthony (1992) A software process immaturity model. In SIGSOFT
Softw. Eng. Notes 17, pp.22-23

Finlay, Paul N.; Mitchell, Andrew C. (1994) Perceptions of the Benefits From the
Introduction of CASE: An Empirical Study. In MIS Quarterly 18 (4), pp.353–370
http://bit.ly/OvlriV

Fitzgerald, B. (1998). In Fitzgerald,B. (1998) 'An Empirical Investigation into the
Adoption of Systems Development Methodologies', Information & Management,
34(6), p.317-328

Flyvbjerg, Bent; Bruzelius, Nils; Rothengatter, Werner (2002) Megaprojects and
risk. An anatomy of ambition / Bent Flyvbjerg, Nils Bruzelius and Werner
Rothengatter. Cambridge: Cambridge University Press

Flyvbjerg, Bent; Budzier, Alexander (2011) Why Your IT Project May Be Riskier
Than You Think. In Harvard Business Review 89 (9), pp.23–25
http://bit.ly/OHnhyj

Forrest, David (2012) A victory for Agile. US HHS - HealthData
http://www.healthdata.gov/blog/victory-agile

Fowler, Martin (1999) Refactoring. Improving the design of existing code / Martin Fowler. Reading, MA: Addison-Wesley (The Addison-Wesley object technology
series)

Fowler, Martin (2012) Writing The Agile Manifesto
http://martinfowler.com/articles/agileStory.html

Francis Rose (2011) GAO highlights 9 critical success factors for IT projects - FederalNewsRadio.com. Interview with Director US GAO David Posner

FRC, U. K. (2005) Revised Turnbull Guidance
http://www.frc.org.uk/documents/pagemanager/frc/Revised%20Turnbull%20Guidance%20October%202005.pdf

Fruhling, Ann L.; McDonald, Patrick; Dunbar, Christopher (2008) A Case Study: Introducing eXtreme Programming in a US Government System Development Project
http://bit.ly/P8mav3

Fruhling, Ann L.; Tarrell, Alvin E. (2008) Best Practices for Implementing Agile Methods. A Guide for Department of Defense Software Developers. IBM Centre for the Business of Government (E-Government/Technology series)
http://faculty.ist.unomaha.edu/fruhling/FruhlingReport.pdf

Gane, C.; Sarson, T. (1977) Structured Systems Analysis. Tools and Techniques. N Y: Improved Systems Technologies

GAO: GAO-12-5SP, Summary of GAO s Performance and Financial Information Fiscal Year 2011

GAO (2003a) GAO-03-1073 Defense Acquisitions: Improvements Needed in Space Systems Acquisition Management Policy
http://www.gao.gov/assets/240/239753.pdf

GAO (2003b) GAO-03-645T Best Practices: Better Acquisition Outcomes Are Possible If DOD Can... GAO
http://www.gao.gov/new.items/d03645t.pdf

GAO (2005) GAO-05-276 Information Technology: OMB Can Make More Effective Use of Its Investment Reviews
http://www.gao.gov/new.items/d05276.pdf

GAO (2008) GAO-08-904T Risk Management: Strengthening the Use of Risk Management Principles in Homeland Security
http://www.gao.gov/new.items/d08904t.pdf

GAO (2011a) GAO-12-26 Business Systems Modernization: Internal Revenue Service's Fiscal Year 2011 Expenditure Plan. US GAO
http://www.gao.gov/assets/590/585642.pdf

GAO (2011b) GAO-12-7 Information Technology: Critical Factors Underlying Successful Major Acquisitions
http://www.gao.gov/assets/590/585842.pdf

GAO (2011c) Veterans' Education Benefits: Enhanced Guidance and Collaboration Could Improve Administration of the Post-9/11 GI Bill Program. GAO-11-356R
http://www.gao.gov/assets/100/97478.pdf

GAO (2011d) GAO-12-26 Business Systems Modernization: Internal Revenue Service's Fiscal Year 2011 Expenditure Plan
http://www.gao.gov/assets/590/585642.pdf

Gates, Robert M. (2009) Defense Budget Recommendation Statement - Secretary of Defense
http://www.globalsecurity.org/military/library/news/2009/04/dod-speech-090406.htm

Gelder, B. de (2009) Why bodies? PNAS (1535)
http://bit.ly/M0BLcP

General Dynamics (2009) General Dynamics UK team completes Foundation Review...
http://bit.ly/NVjShD

General Dynamics UK (2010) Application of DSDM in a Complex Project Environment. Helping clear the 'fog of war'. DSDM Cons.
http://bit.ly/O0zMWz

Gilb, Tom (1976) Software metrics. Lund: Studentlitteratur

Gilb, Tom (1985) Evolutionary Delivery versus the "waterfall model. In SIGSOFT Softw. Eng. Notes 10 (3), pp.49-61

Gilb, Tom; Brodie, Lindsey (2005) Competitive engineering. A handbook for systems engineering, requirements engineering, and software engineering using Planguage / Tom Gilb ; editor, Lindsey Brodie. Oxford: Elsevier Butterworth Heinemann

Gilb, Tom; Finzi, Susannah (1988) Principles of software engineering management. Wokingham: Addison-Wesley

Giotis, Theofanis (2003) UK Government Gateway Project and Microsoft MSF

Glass, R.L (2001) Extreme programming: the good, the bad, and the bottom line. In IEEE Software 18 (6), pp.112–111
http://ieeexplore.ieee.org/stamp/stamp.jsp?arnumber=965816

Gomaa, Hassan; Scott, Douglas B. H (1981) Prototyping as a tool in the specification of user requirements. In : Proceedings of the 5th international conference on Software engineering. Piscataway, NJ, USA: IEEE Press (ICSE '81), pp.333-342
http://bit.ly/Mb00r6

Great Britain. Her Majesty's Stationery Office (1997) Appraisal and evaluation in central government. Treasury guidance. 2nd ed

Hamer, David H.; Sullivan, Geoff; Weierud, Frode (1998) Enigma variations: an extended family of machines. In Cryptologia 22, pp.211-229
http://dl.acm.org/citation.cfm?id=295513.295518

Hantos, Peter (2008) Defense Acquisition Performance Assessment - The Life-Cycle Perspective of Selected Recommendations. Space and Missile Systems Center
http://www.dtic.mil/cgi-bin/GetTRDoc?AD=ADA484646

Hasnain, Eisha; Hall, Tracy (2008) Investigating the Role of Trust in Agile Methods Using a Light Weight Systematic Literature Review. Edited by P.Abrahamsson. XP 2008
http://scholar.googleusercontent.com/scholar?q=cache:ozCMtX6kRg8J:scholar.google.com/&hl=en&as_sdt=0,5

Henson, Stuart; Prior, Jon (2009) UK MOD CIDS Technology Demonstrator Programme. UK MoD. International Data Links Symposium 2009 (IDLS2009)
http://bit.ly/NrckBd

Highsmith, Jim (2012) History: The Agile Manifesto
http://www.agilemanifesto.org/history.html

HM Treasury (2004) THE ORANGE BOOK 2004.pdf. UK HM Treasury
http://www.hm-treasury.gov.uk/d/orange_book.pdf

HM Treasury and Cabinet Office (2011) Major project approvals and assurance guidance
http://www.cabinetoffice.gov.uk/sites/default/files/resources/major-project-approvals-assurance-guidance.pdf

IBM Center for the Business of Government (2011) Chad L. Fulgham
http://www.businessofgovernment.org/bio/chad-l-fulgham

Imai, M. (1991) Kaizen. (ky'zen). The key to Japan's competitive success: Compañía Editorial Continental
http://books.google.de/books?id=XsAkgTGo5ncC

IRM, AIRMIC ALARM (2002) A Risk Management Standard. IRM
http://www.theirm.org/publications/documents/
Risk_Management_Standard_030820.pdf

IRS (2007a) IT Modernization Vision & Strategy

IRS (2007b) IRS Risk Management Insights
http://poole.ncsu.edu/erm/documents/Hesspresentation04.27.07.pdf

ISO (2009) ISO 31000 Risk management - principles and guidelines. 1st ed.: 2009-11-15. Geneva

Israel, Jerome (2012) Why the FBI Can't Build a Case Management System. In Computer, pp.73–80
http://bit.ly/LSYVXe

Jamieson, Diane; Vinsen, Kevin; Callender, Guy (Eds.) (2005) Agile Procurement: New Acquisition Approach to Agile Software Development. Washington, DC, USA: IEEE Computer Society (EUROMICRO '05)

JROC (2001) CHARTER OF THE JOINT REQUIREMENTS OVERSIGHT COUNCIL. CJCSI 5123.01A
http://www.dtic.mil/doctrine/jel/cjcsd/cjcsi/5123_01a.pdf

Kessler, Carl; Sweitzer, John (2007) Outside-in software development: a practical approach to building successful stakeholder-based products. First: IBM Press

Kimble, Chris (2008) SDM - Session 5, Semi-Formal Methods
http://www.chris-kimble.com/Courses/sdm/Session_5.html

Kundra, Vivek (2010a) 25 point implementation plan to reform federal information technology management. Washington [D.C.]: The White House
http://bit.ly/OviNJU

Kundra, Vivek (2010b) Memorandum - Immediate Review of Information Technology Projects
http://www.whitehouse.gov/sites/default/files/omb/memoranda/2010/m10-31.pdf

laffan, michael (2012) Automated Service Delivery Suspended
http://www.pcs.org.uk/en/department_for_work_and_pensions_group/dwp-news.cfm/id/80DF8049-858A-42EB-9F2182688938019E

Lapham, Mary Ann (2012) DoD Agile Adoption. Necessary Considerations, Concerns, and Changes. In CrossTalk, Software Engineering Institute at Carnegie Mellon University January/February 2012, 1/10/2012
http://bit.ly/P8laXZ

Larman, Craig (2006) Agile and iterative development. A manager's guide. 8th ed. Boston [u.a.]: Addison-Wesley

Larman, Craig; Vodde, Bas (2009) Scaling lean & agile development. Thinking and organizational tools for large-scale Scrum / Craig Larman, Bas Vodde. Boston, Mass. ; London: Addison-Wesley

Larman, Craig; Vodde, Bas (2010) Practices for scaling lean & agile development. Large, multisite, and offshore product development with large-scale Scrum / Craig Larman, Bas Vodde. Upper Saddle River, NJ: Addison-Wesley

Lee-Kelley, Liz; Sankey, Tim (2008) Global virtual teams for value creation and project success (1)
http://bit.ly/NsYIJt

Leffingwell, Dean (2007) Scaling software agility. Best practices for large enterprises / Dean Leffingwell. London: Addison-Wesley (The Agile software development series)
http://bit.ly/OHlY2n

Leland, Nicolai (Ed.) (1997) Skunk Works Lessons Learned. AGARD Conference Proceedings: Strategic Management of the Cost Problem of Future Weapon Systems. Drammen, Norway, 22-25 September 1997

Levin, Robert (2003) GAO-04-71R Space Acquisitions: Committing Prematurely to the Transformational Satellite Program... US GAO
http://1.usa.gov/PWOMsE

Lilley, Roy (Ed.) (2010) Health Bill Transition Risk Register. NC-15-Oct-10-Dept-Bd-Version-v1.1.xlsx
http://bit.ly/OvfP8j

London Evening Standard (2011) Francis Maude insists that the days of "archaic" Whitehall benefits are numbered
http://bit.ly/O0wzGC

Longworth, G.; Nicholls, Derek (1986) SSADM manual. Version 3 / Gordon Longworth and Derek Nicholls. Manchester: NCC Publications

Lorell, Mark A.; Lowell, Julia; Younossi, Obaid (2003) Evolutionary acquisition - Implementation challenges for defense space programs. Santa Monica, CA: Rand Corporation
http://www.gao.gov/new.items/d0471r.pdf

Madahar, Bob (2012) Open to ideas (Defence Management Journal, 49)
http://www.defencemanagement.com/article.asp?id=399&content_name=ICT&article=12608

Magee, Ian; Gash, Tom; Stephen, Justine (2012) System upgrade? The first year of the Government's ICT strategy. UK IfG

Martin, James (1983) Information Systems Manifesto

Martin, James (1989-90) Information engineering. Englewood Cliffs, N.J: Prentice Hall (James Martin books on information systems)

Martin, James (1991) Rapid application development. New York: Macmillan

Martin, James (2012) About James Martin - Books Written
http://www.jamesmartin.com/about/books_written.cfm

Martin, James; McClure, Carma L. (1985) Action diagrams. Clearly structured program design / James Martin, Carma McClure. Englewood Cliffs, NJ: Prentice-Hall

Martin, James; Odell, James J. (1992) Object-oriented analysis and design

Maughan, Alistair (2011) Agile will fail GovIT, says corporate lawyer - Public Sector IT
http://www.computerweekly.com/blogs/public-sector/2011/04/agile-will-fail-govit-says-cor.html

Maze, Rick (2012) In 4 years, 745,000 have used Post 9/11 GI Bill. Air Force Times
http://www.airforcetimes.com/news/2012/06/military-in-4-years-745000-people-have-used-gi-bill-071612w/

McDonald, C. (2010) From Art Form to Engineering Discipline? A History of US Military Software Development Standards, 1974-1998. In IEEE Annals of the History of Computing 32 (4), pp.32–47

Meeren, Hanneke K. M.; van Heijnsbergen, Corné C. R. J.; Gelder, Beatrice de (2005) Rapid perceptual integration of facial expression and emotional body language. PNAS
http://www.pnas.org/content/102/45/16518.full.pdf

Mercurio et al (1990) AD/Cycle strategy and architecture. In IBM Systems Journal 29 (2), p.172

Met Office (2010) Just Enough Project Management

MicroPact (2012) Inside the FBI – Getting Agile with Sentinel
http://www.micropact.com/blog/detail/inside-the-fbi-getting-agile-with-sentinel

Middleton, Peter (1994) Euromethod: The lessons from SSADM. In Walter Baets (Ed.) Proceedings of the Second European Conference on Information Systems, ECIS 1994, Nijenrode University, The Netherlands, 1994: Nijenrode University Press, pp.359–368
http://bit.ly/NuTVVK

Milgrom, Paul (1995) Auction Theory for Privatization: Cambridge University Press

Morgan, Dave (2009) Covert Agile: Development at the Speed of ... Government. In : Agile Conference, 2009. AGILE '09, pp.79–83

Morris, Desmond (1977) Manwatching. A field guide to human behaviour / Desmond Morris. London: Cape

Naur, P.; Randell, B. (1969) Conference sponsored by NATO Science Committee, Garmisch, 7-11 Oct. 1968. Brüssel: Scientific Affairs Division, NATO
http://bit.ly/LSXFTS

Nerur, Sridhar; et al (2005) Challenges of migrating to agile methodologies (5)
http://bit.ly/LjBO1R

North Carolina State College of Management (2007) The Opera Enterprise Risk Initiative
http://www.poole.ncsu.edu/erm/index.php/articles/entry/chris-hess-roundtable/

NRC (2010) Achieving effective acquisition of information technology in the Department of Defense. Washington: National Academies Press

Nuseibeh, B. (2001) Weaving together requirements and architectures. In IEEE Computer 34 (3), pp.115–119 citeulike-article-id:776563

Office of the Auditor-General (2012) Realising benefits from six public sector technology projects
http://www.oag.govt.nz/2012/realising-benefits/docs/realising-benefits.pdf

OGC (2009) Managing and Directing Successful Projects with PRINCE2
http://www.best-management-practice.com/gempdf/
PRINCE2_2009_Overview_Brochure_June2009.pdf

OGC (2011) Managing successful programmes. 2011st ed. [London]: Stationery Office

OIG (2002a) An Investigation of the Belated Production of Documents in the Oklahoma City Bombing Case. March 19, 2002
http://www.justice.gov/oig/special/0203/report.pdf

OIG (2002b) FBI's MANAGEMENT OF INFORMATION TECHNOLOGY INVESTMENTS
http://www.justice.gov/oig/reports/FBI/a0309/final.pdf

OIG (2006a) Sentinel Audit I: The FBI's Pre-Acquisition Planning for and Controls Over the Sentinel Case Management System. March 2006, Report 06-14
http://www.justice.gov/oig/reports/FBI/a0614/final.pdf

OIG (2006b) Sentinel Audit II: Status of the Federal Bureau of Investigation's Case Management System. December 2006, Report 07-03
http://www.justice.gov/oig/reports/FBI/a0703/final.pdf

OIG (2007) Sentinel Audit III: Status of the Federal Bureau of Investigation's Case Management System, Audit Report 07-40. August 2007, Report 07-40
http://www.justice.gov/oig/reports/FBI/a0740/final.pdf

OIG (2008) Sentinel Audit IV: Status of the Federal Bureau of Investigation's Case Management System. December 2008, Report 09-05
http://www.justice.gov/oig/reports/FBI/a0905/final.pdf

OIG (2009) Sentinel Audit V: Status of the Federal Bureau of Investigation's Case Management System. November 2009, Report 10-03 Redacted
http://www.justice.gov/oig/reports/FBI/a1003_redacted.pdf

OIG (2010a) Sentinel Audit VII: Status of the FBI's Implementation of the Sentinel Project. October 2010, Report 11-01

OIG (2010b) Sentinel Audit VI: Status of the FBI's Implementation of the Sentinel Project. March 2010, Report 10-22
http://www.justice.gov/oig/reports/FBI/a1022.pdf

OIG (2011) Sentinel Audit VIII: Status of the FBI's Implementation of the Sentinel Project. December 2011, Report 12-08. US OIG
http://www.justice.gov/oig/reports/2011/a1208.pdf

OMB (2003) Implementing the President's Management Agenda for E-Government
http://www.cio.gov/documents/2003egov_strat.pdf

OMB (2006) CAPITAL PROGRAMMING GUIDE (PART 7). OMB
http://www.whitehouse.gov/sites/default/files/omb/circulars/a11/current_year/part7.pdf

OMB (2007) The Federal Acquisition Certification for Program and Project Managers. The White House
http://1.usa.gov/MaY02f

Organ, Joe (2003) eGov monitor Feature: Government IT in the 1980s: The CCTA, Privatisation and Project Failures. eGov Monitor
http://www.egovmonitor.com/features/jorgan04.html

PANEL ON DEFENSE ACQUISITION REFORM (2010) Findings And Recommendations. HOUSE ARMED SERVICES COMMITTEE
http://bit.ly/NIyJfB

Park, Todd (2012) Welcome to the new HealthData.gov. US HHS - HealthData
http://www.healthdata.gov/blog/welcome-new-healthdatagov

PASC (2011) Public Administration Select Committee PASC Good Governance: the Effective Use of IT
http://www.publications.parliament.uk/pa/cm201011/cmselect/cmpubadm/uc715-v/uc71501.htm

Pease, Allan (1981) Body language. How to read others' thoughts by their gestures / Allan Pease. London: Sheldon (Overcoming common problems)

Perera, David (2012) Jack Israel on FBI Sentinel. Fierce Government
http://bit.ly/MwWqEI

PMI (2011) The Standard for Program Management, Second Edition: Project Management Institute: Amazon.com: Kindle Store
http://www.amazon.com/Standard-Program-Management-Edition-ebook/dp/B004MME6H0/ref=sr_1_2?ie=UTF8&qid=1341853914&sr=8-2&keywords=pmi+program+management

Poppendieck, Mary (2003) Lean Software Development: An Agile Toolkit. Addison Wesley
http://bit.ly/PWOtOq

Project Management Institute (2008) A guide to the project management body of knowledge. (PMBOK guide). 4th ed. Newton Square, Pa: Project Management Institute

Public Accounts Committee (2012) Oral evidence taken before the Public Accounts Committee - The Introduction of the Work Programme - HC 1802-i. Interview with Robert Devereux. UK HOUSE OF COMMONS

RAND Corp (2008) The Defense Acquisition Workforce: An Analysis of Personnel Trends Relevant to Policy, 1993-2006. With assistance of Gates, Susan M, Keating, Edward G, Jewell, Adria D et al. RAND Corporation
http://bit.ly/NpQdOi

Richards, Keith (2010) Agile Project Management: Integrating DSDM Atern into an existing PRINCE2 environment. UK TSO

Royce, Winston W. (1970) Managing the Development of Large Software Systems. In : Proceedings, IEEE WESCON, pp.1-9
http://www.cs.umd.edu/class/spring2003/cmsc838p/Process/waterfall.pdf

Rumbaugh, James; Jacobson, Ivar; Booch, Grady (1999) The unified modeling language reference manual. Reading, Mass. ; Harlow: Addison-Wesley (The Addison-Wesley object technology series)

saarelainen, tapio (2011) Enhancing Situational Awareness by Means of Combat-ID to Minimize Fratricide and Collateral Damage in the Theater. ICDT 2011 : The Sixth International Conference on Digital Telecommunications

Samset, Knut; Berg, Peder; Klakegg, Ole Jonny (2006) Front end Governance of Major Public Projects
http://bit.ly/NIxQDR

Schwaber, Ken (2004) Agile project management with Scrum. Redmond, Wash: Microsoft Press

Schwaber, Ken (2010a) Scrum Basics
http://www.agileleantraining.com/download/Scrum-Guide-1.pdf

Schwaber, Ken (2010b) Telling It Like It Is - July 27 2010. Wordpress
http://kenschwaber.wordpress.com/2010/07/

Schwaber, Ken (2011a) The Scrum Guide
http://www.scrum.org/storage/scrumguides/Scrum_Guide.pdf

Schwaber, Ken (2011b) The Scrum Guide
http://www.scrum.org/storage/scrumguides/Scrum%20Guide%20-%202011.pdf

Serbu, Jared (2011) CIOs cite struggles with agile development. FederalNewsRadio.com
http://www.federalnewsradio.com/?nid=697&sid=2399940

Shepard, Alan (2010) Just Enough Project Management. UK Met Office. UK Met Office

Shewhart, W.A (1931) Economic control of quality of manufactured product: American Society for Quality Control
http://books.google.de/books?id=EoynRAl0Po4C

Slabodkin, Greg (2011) New combat ID tool would give pilots on-demand capability
http://defensesystems.com/articles/2011/02/28/c4isr-1-blue-force-tracking-sidebar.aspx

Solomon, Paul (2011) Analyzing and Measuring Information Quality - Improving the Quality of Earned Value Management Information
http://journal.thedacs.com/issue/58/195

Standish Group (1995) Unfinished Voyages
http://www.standishgroup.com/sample_research/unfinished_voyages_1.php

State of Queensland (2008) Summary - Mid-term Review of the Responding to Homelessness initiative
http://bit.ly/Mw1Oqw

State of Queensland Department of Housing (2005a) Paving the Way. Housing people in need in the Smart State
http://www.communities.qld.gov.au/resources/housing/about-us/info-paper.pdf

State of Queensland Department of Housing (2005b) Responses to Homelessness
http://www.communities.qld.gov.au/resources/housing/about-us/homelessness.pdf

Stephen, Justine; Page, James; Myers, Jerrett; Brown, Adrian; Watson, David; Magee, Ian (2011) System Error. Fixing the flaws in government IT. Institute for Government. UK
http://bit.ly/PWNjCC

Stephens, Matt; Rosenberg, Doug (2003) Extreme programming refactored. The case against XP / D. Rosenberg, M. Stephens. Berkeley, Calif: Apress; Berlin : Springer

Stephens, Richard (2006) Commentary on the draft DSDM Contract
http://www.dsdm.org/wp-content/uploads/2011/06/Contract-Commentary.pdf

Stonebraker, Michael (1988) Readings in database systems. San Mateo, CA: Morgan Kaufmann Publishers

Strassmann, Paul A. (1997) The squandered computer. Evaluating the business alignment of information technologies / Paul A. Strassmann. New Canaan, Conn: Information Economics Press

Sulaiman, Tamara (2007) AgileEVM - Earned Value Management The Agile Way
http://bit.ly/Svnjgu

Sutherland, Jeff; Schwaber, Ken (2007) The Scrum Papers
http://www.crisp.se/scrum/books/ScrumPapers20070424.pdf

Swoyer, Stephen (2005) Agile Programming and the CMMI: Irreconcilable Differences? ADT
http://bit.ly/Q1DqDK

TechAmerica Foundation (2010) Government Technology Opportunity in the 21st Century (GTO-21)
http://www.techamerica.org/Docs/gwd4r5.pdf

Thomas, David (2007) PragDave: Some Agile History
http://pragdave.pragprog.com/pragdave/2007/02/some_agile_hist.html

Thomas, Elizabeth Scanlon (2011) Breaking the addiction to process. An introduction to Agile project management. Ely: IT Governance Pub

TIGTA: The Customer Account Data Engine 2 Program Management Office Implemented Systems Development Guidelines; However, Process Improvements Are Needed to Address Inconsistencies

Toynbee, Polly (2012) After G4S, who still thinks that outsourcing works? The Guardian
http://www.guardian.co.uk/commentisfree/2012/jul/16/who-thinks-outsourcing-works?newsfeed=true

Transport for London (2012) Congestion Charge Scheme - CChargeLondon.co.uk - Information, Payment, Technology, Effect on Traffic, Businesses & Environment
http://www.cchargelondon.co.uk/history.html

Treasury Board of Canada Secretariat (2010) A Guide to Project Gating for IT-Enabled Projects
http://www.tbs-sct.gc.ca/itp-pti/pog-spg/irp-gpgitep/irp-gpgitep-eng.pdf

Treasury, H. M. (2005) Managing Public Money
http://www.hm-treasury.gov.uk/d/mpm_whole.pdf

Turner, Richard; Jain, Apurva (2002) Agile Meets CMMI: Culture Clash or Common Cause? In : Extreme Programming and Agile Methods — XP/Agile Universe 2002, pp.153–165 citeulike-article-id:6527920

UK - The Independent (2012) The $100m man: Why philanthropist James Martin gave away his fortune. In UK - The Independent Profiles - People, 2012
http://ind.pn/NVnQXx

UK Cabinet Office (2009) PRINCE2 - Glossary of Terms v1.0

UK Cabinet Office (2010) Management of risk. Guidance for practitioners. 3rd ed. London: TSO

UK Cabinet Office (18/10/2010) "No stone unturned" - Francis Maude unveils millions in efficiency savings
http://www.cabinetoffice.gov.uk/news/no-stone-unturned-francis-maude-unveils-millions-efficiency-savings

UK Cabinet Office (2011a) Best Management Practice (BMP) Portfolio
http://www.cabinetoffice.gov.uk/resource-library/best-management-practice-bmp-portfolio

UK Cabinet Office (2011b) Government ICT Strategy
http://www.cabinetoffice.gov.uk/sites/default/files/resources/uk-government-government-ict-strategy_0.pdf

UK Cabinet Office (2011c) Government ICT Strategy

UK Cabinet Office (2011d) Managing Change – Maximising Value for Money in Major Projects
http://www.publicserviceevents.co.uk/ppt/MC11_SteveMitchell.pdf

UK Cabinet Office (2011e) Overview of the Major Projects Authority
http://www.cabinetoffice.gov.uk/sites/default/files/resources/mpa-overview_0.pdf

UK Cabinet Office (2011f) Starting Gate: MPA Guidance for Departments https://update.cabinetoffice.gov.uk/sites/default/files/resources/MPA%20Starting%20Gate%20guidance%20for%20Depts%20September%202011.pdf

UK Cabinet Office (2012a) Major Projects Authority - Assurance Toolkit
http://www.cabinetoffice.gov.uk/resource-library/major-projects-authority-assurance-toolkit

UK Cabinet Office (2012b) One Year On: Implementing the Government ICT Strategy

UK DWP (2011) Jobcentre Plus Annual Report and Accounts 2010-11 HC 1165
http://www.official-documents.gov.uk/document/hc1012/hc11/1165/1165.pdf

UK Government (2012) The Civil Service Reform Plan
http://www.civilservice.gov.uk/wp-content/uploads/2012/06/CSRP-web.pdf

UK HM Treasury (1991) Economic appraisal in central government (The Green Book). A technical guide for government departments
http://bit.ly/OvbTEI

UK HM Treasury (2003) The Green Book. Appraisal and evaluation in central government. [New ed.]. London: TSO

UK HM Treasury (2011) Major project approvals and assurance guidance
http://www.hm-treasury.gov.uk/d/major_projects_approvals_assurance_guidance.PDF

UK HMRC (2011) Annual Report and Resource Accounts 2010-11
http://www.hmrc.gov.uk/about/annual-report-accounts-1011.pdf

UK ICO (2012) Reponse to FOIA Request 678713. UK Information Commissioner's Office
http://bit.ly/Nt5Eq3

UK NAO (2003) Recommendations Database
http://www.nao.org.uk/recommendation/report.asp?repId=423

UK NAO (2004) National Audit Office Report (HC 877, 2003-2004) Improving IT procurement: The impact of the Office of Government Commerce s initiatives on departments and suppliers in the delivery of major IT-enabled projects (Full Report)

UK NAO (2006a) National Audit Office report (HC 33-I 2006-07) Delivering successful IT-enabled business change

UK NAO (2006b) National Audit Office Report: Getting the best from public sector office accommodation

UK NAO (2008a) Department for Work and Pensions: IT Programmes

UK NAO (2008b) NAO Report (HC 930 2007-08) HM Revenue & Customs transformation programme
http://www.cag.gov.in/html/LB/Kr/LB_05_CHAPTER_I.pdf

UK NAO (2010a) Minimising the cost of administrative errors in the benefit system - National Audit Office
http://www.nao.org.uk/publications/1011/errors_in_the_benefits_system.aspx

UK NAO (2010b) NAO report (HC 21 2010-2011) Department for Work and Pensions: Support to incapacity benefits claimants through Pathways to Work (full report)

UK NAO (2010c) NAO VFM rept (HC 452 2009-10) Reorganising central government

UK NAO (2010d) The Statement on Internal Control: A guide for audit committees

UK NAO (2011a) A snapshot of the Government's ICT profession in 2011
http://www.nao.org.uk/publications/1012/government_ict_profession.aspx

UK NAO (2011b) Digital Britain One. Shared infrastructure and services for government online : cross government : report. London: Stationery Office

UK NAO (2011c) Implementing the Government ICT Strategy: six-month review of progress. NAO Report (HC 1594 2010-2012)

UK NAO (2011d) NAO Report (HC 708 2010-2011) National Health Service Landscape Review

UK NAO (2011e) The expansion of online filing of tax returns HC 1457, Session 2010-2012
http://www.official-documents.gov.uk/document/hc1012/hc14/1457/1457.pdf

UK NAO (2011f) The failure of the FiReControl project
http://www.nao.org.uk/publications/1012/failure_of_firecontrol.aspx

UK NAO (2012a) Efficiency and reform in government corporate functions through shared service centres. NAO Report (HC 1790 2010-2012)

UK NAO (2012b) NAO Report (HC 1701 2010-2012) The introduction of the Work Programme

UK NAO (2012c) National Audit Office Report (HC 1793 2010-2012) Child Maintenance and Enforcement Commission: Cost Reduction (full report)

UK NAO (2012d) National Audit Office Report (HC 467 2012-2013) The UK Border Agency and Border Force

UK Daily Telegraph (2002) What price a PFI project?, 2002
http://www.telegraph.co.uk/finance/2765424/What-price-a-PFI-project.html

University of Oxford (2012) Futurist pledges $50m in matched funding
http://www.ox.ac.uk/media/news_stories/2009/090412.html

US DOD: DoD 5000 Series https://acc.dau.mil/CommunityBrowser.aspx?id=18532

US DOD (1985) DOD-STD-2167, Military Standard: Defense System Software development [superseding DOD-STD-1679A (Navy) and MIL-STD-1644B (TD)]. In : [[United States Department of Defense]]
http://www.everyspec.com/DoD/DoD-STD/DOD-STD-2167_278/

US DOD (2003) The Program Managers' Guide to the Integrated Baseline Review Process
http://bit.ly/MaWOMr

US GAO (2007a) GAO-07-36 National Nuclear Security Administration: Additional Actions Needed to Improve Management of the Nation's Nuclear Programs. US GAO
http://1.usa.gov/MwViAP

US GAO (2007b) GAO-07-518 Department of Energy: Consistent Application of Requirements Needed to Improve Project Management. US GAO
http://www.gao.gov/new.items/d07518.pdf

US GAO (2007c) GAO-07-736 2010 Census: Census Bureau Has Improved the Local Update of Census Addresses Program, but Challenges Remain
http://www.gao.gov/new.items/d07736.pdf

US GAO (2008a) GAO-08-1051T Information Technology: OMB and Agencies Need to Improve Planning, Management, and Oversight of Projects Totaling Billions of Dollars
http://www.gao.gov/assets/130/120968.pdf

US GAO (2008b) GAO-09-45 Tax Administration: IRS Needs to Strengthen Its Approach for Evaluating the SRFMI Data-Sharing Pilot Program
http://www.gao.gov/assets/290/283133.pdf

US GAO (2009a) GAO-09-1002T Homeland Security: Despite Progress, DHS Continues to Be Challenged ... GAO
http://www.gao.gov/assets/130/123290.pdf

US GAO (2009b) GAO-09-431T Defense Acquisitions: DOD Must Balance Its Needs with Available Resources and Follow an Incremental Approach to Acquiring Weapon Systems
http://www.gao.gov/new.items/d09431t.pdf

US GAO (2009c) GAO-09-543T Defense Acquisitions: Measuring the Value of DOD's Weapon Programs Requires Starting with Realistic Baselines
http://www.gao.gov/assets/130/122182.pdf

US GAO (2009d) Public transportation - Federal project approval process remains a barrier... [Washington, D.C.]: GAO

US GAO (2010) GAO-10-227SP NASA: Assessments of Selected Large-Scale Projects
http://www.gao.gov/new.items/d10227sp.pdf

US GAO (2011a) Decision SGT, Inc.
http://www.gao.gov/assets/600/590586.pdf

US GAO (2011b) GAO-11-297 FEMA: Action Needed to Improve Administration of the National Flood Insurance Program
http://www.gao.gov/assets/320/319467.pdf

US GAO (2011c) GAO-11-383 Catastrophic Planning: States Participating in FEMA's Pilot Program Made Progress, but Better Guidance Could Enhance Future Pilot Programs
http://www.gao.gov/new.items/d11383.pdf

US GAO (2011d) GAO-11-873 Quadrennial Homeland Security Review: Enhanced Stakeholder Consultation and Use of Risk Information Could Strengthen Future Reviews
http://www.gao.gov/assets/590/585314.pdf

US GAO (2011e) GAO-12-7 Information Technology: Critical Factors Underlying Successful Major Acquisitions
http://www.gao.gov/new.items/d127.pdf

US GAO (2011f) Veterans Affairs Can Further Improve Its Development Process for Its New Education Benefits System. GAO-11-115. GAO
http://www.gao.gov/new.items/d11115.pdf

US GAO (2012) GAO-12-563T, DOD Faces Challenges in Fully Realizing Benefits of Satellite Acquisition Improvements
http://www.gao.gov/assets/590/589487.pdf

US Public Law (2002) BOB STUMP NATIONAL DEFENSE AUTHORIZATION ACT FOR FISCAL YEAR 2003. PUBLIC LAW 107–314—DEC. 2, 2002

USD(AT&L) (2008a) DoD Directive 5000.01, May 12, 2003; Certified Current as of November 20, 2007 -- POSTED JANUARY 24, 2008
http://www.dtic.mil/whs/directives/corres/pdf/500001p.pdf

USD(AT&L) (2008b) DoD Instruction 5000.02. Operation of the Defense Acquisition System
http://www.dtic.mil/whs/directives/corres/pdf/500002p.pdf

USDA CIO (2011a) Cloud Email
http://www.cio.gov/documents/USDA_CloudEMail_Final.pdf

USDA CIO (2011b) Consolidating 21 email systems into an enterprise system using Cloud Services
http://www.cio.gov/documents/USDA_CloudEMail_Final.pdf

VA (2012) GI Bill Publications
http://www.gibill.va.gov/resources/student%5Fhandouts/

VA Office of Inspector General (2011) Audit of the Project Management Accountability System Implementation. Rpt #10-03162-262
http://www.va.gov/oig/52/reports/2011/VAOIG-10-03162-262.pdf

van Roekel, Steven (2012) Maximizing our Return on IT. The White House
http://www.whitehouse.gov/blog/2012/02/14/maximizing-our-return-it

Version One (2012) State of Agile Survey 2011
http://www.versionone.com/pdf/
2011_State_of_Agile_Development_Survey_Results.pdf

Vijayasarathy, Leo R.; Turk, Dan (2008) Agile Software Development: A Survey of Early Adopters. In Journal of Information Technology Management

Vogt, Christian (2002) Intractable ERP: a comprehensive analysis of failed enterprise-resource-planning projects. In SIGSOFT Softw. Eng. Notes 27, pp.62-68

Walters, Jonathan (2009) Transforming Information Technology at the DVA. IBM Centre for the Business of Government
http://www.isaca.org/Knowledge-Center/cobit/Documents/WaltersVAReport-June09.pdf

Wang; Xiaofeng; O'Conchuir; Eoin; Vidgen; Richard (2007) A Paradoxical Perspective on Contradictions in Agile Software Development
http://aran.library.nuigalway.ie/xmlui/handle/10379/1582

Weigelt, Matthew (2010) Federal CIO pursues relentless efficiency via TechStat meetings. Washington Technology
http://bit.ly/NpP0qc

West, Dave; Grant, Tom (2010) Agile Development: Mainstream Adoption Has Changed Agility. Forrester Research
http://www.forrester.com/Agile+Development+Mainstream+Adoption+Has+Changed+Agility/fulltext/-/E-RES56100

Williams, Bridget; Holmes, Chris; Hunt, Josh (2011) Developing an online service: Customer research into Automated Service Delivery. DWP
http://research.dwp.gov.uk/asd/asd5/rports2011-2012/rrep734.pdf

Williams, Laurie (2012a) What agile teams think of agile principles. In Commun. ACM 55 (4), pp.71-76

Williams, Laurie; Kessler, Robert R. (2003) Pair programming illuminated. Boston, Mass.; London: Addison-Wesley

Williams, Neil (2012b) INSIDE GOVERNMENT – a few highlights. UK GDS
http://digital.cabinetoffice.gov.uk/2012/02/28/inside-government-a-few-high-lights/

Wills, Patrick (2012) The IT Box - A Primer. Defense Systems Management College

Work and Pensions Committee (2010) The CMEC and the Child Support Agency's Operational Improvement Plan. Report, together with formal minutes, oral and written evidence. UK House of Commons
http://bit.ly/MaWuNs

Zients, Jeff (2010) OMB plans 25-point IT reform - FederalNewsRadio.com. Federal News Radio
http://www.federalnewsradio.com/?nid=697&sid=2194228

Index

Upcoming eBooks...

Check out those footnotes in a single click with the eBook companion

eBook editions:
- **Part I**
- **Part II**
- **Part III**

Maitland
& Strong

Printed in Great Britain
by Amazon.co.uk, Ltd.,
Marston Gate.